Praise for *Imagined Truths*

"Richard Lemm applies a poet's line-by-line discipline, eye for detail, and ear for language to every sentence in this exceptionally vivid, affecting memoir. And since the questions American war resisters posed in the 1960s are, alas, even more relevant today, *Imagined Truths* is as important politically and historically as it is emotionally and stylistically."
STEVEN HEIGHTON, author of *Reaching Mithymna* and *The Waking Comes Late*

"*Imagined Truths* is a tumultuous adventure of a memoir, powerfully evoking life in America during a time of radical change. This is a poignant story of a father who died young, a mother who spent years in an asylum, and their son, who made his way in Canada after dodging the draft. In this rollicking, haunting, and compelling book, *Imagined Truths* speaks of the stories that shape us into the people we become."
ANNE SIMPSON, author of *Speechless* and *Strange Attractor*

"Who could ever have imagined such a truthful book? From its family history, tracing the sturdy Lemms from Germany to the earliest logging outfits out West beside the Pacific. From the horrors of a mother confined for a generation to a lunatic asylum. From a young man's active sports life that became an active political career and then, bang, the decision to become a draft-dodger, leaving the US for Canada. Then, equally truthfully, a whole series of other careers, as a bookseller, as a poet, and as a Canadian literary scholar and teacher, who ends up in PEI. An amazing life has produced an amazing book . . . even including "Henderson's Goal." After you read this book, the words "American" and "Canadian" will be even more meaningful to you."
DOUGLAS GIBSON, publisher, editor and author

Imagined Truths

Myths from a Draft-Dodging Poet

RICHARD LEMM

TIDEWATER
PRESS

Published by Tidewater Press
New Westminster, BC, Canada

tidewaterpress.ca
978-1-990160-06-6 (print)
978-1-990160-07-3 (ebook)

LIBRARY AND ARCHIVES CANADA CATALOGUING IN PUBLICATION

Title: Imagined truths : myths from a draft-dodging poet / Richard Lemm.
Names: Lemm, Richard, author.
Identifiers: Canadiana (print) 20210268875 | Canadiana (ebook) 20210269065 | ISBN 9781990160066 (softcover) | ISBN 9781990160073 (HTML)
Subjects: LCSH: Lemm, Richard. | CSH: Poets, Canadian (English)—20th century—Biography. | LCSH: Americans—Canada—Biography. | LCSH: Vietnam War, 1961-1975—Draft resisters—United States—Biography. | LCSH: Vietnam War, 1961-1975—Draft resisters—Canada—Biography. | LCSH: Counterculture—United States—History—20th century. | LCGFT: Autobiographies.
Classification: LCC PS8573.E547 Z46 2021 | DDC C811/.54—dc23

Printed in Canada

For Lee Ellen and my long-time pals
Lance Foreman, Don Gayton, and Jef Jaisun (in memoriam)

Contents

Introduction

"Your father, after the war, was a whiz at the pinball machines," my grandmother said, with a delight in his skill that jarred with her subsequent condemnation of his prodigal habit. "Wasting his mustering-out pay on those contraptions."

This contradiction left me harboring with equal care two images of my father, two judgments. This was an early initiation into the power of ambiguities embodied in the people who matter most to us—the ambivalence that is endemic, even essential, in the construction of our memories and our memory's reconstruction of their identities.

I was still in my mother Gloria's womb when she and my father, Harvey, parted ways. I was told about this separation early on by my maternal grandmother, Aileen. No doubt she felt she had to provide me with a history to explain why I was being raised by her and her second husband, Harry, why my mother was shut away in the loony bin, otherwise known as Northern State Hospital in Sedro-Woolley, and why I should not reverently mourn the loss of my father, a war hero, for sure, but sullied, pitiable, fallen from grace.

There was my father, an ace at pinball machines. A man of flashy skill in the eyes of a boy dazzled by men who could make those pinball bells ring and clang and lights blink and glow. Then there was my profligate father, blowing the money he'd earned as a soldier, money he'd risked his life for, money that should have helped me and my mother. What were the facts, what was the truth? What had been altered by imagination, which often alters the facts for the sake of conveying the truth in more fascinating, successful, and profound ways? And what was, unreliably, fanciful?

I keep in mind Coleridge's distinction, in *Biographia Literaria*, between Imagination and Fancy. Fancy is casual and superficial, compared with imagination. "Always the ape," he wrote, fancy is "too often the adulterator and counterfeiter of memory." Imagination is "vital" and transformative. I had read the Classics Illustrated comic version of *The Rime of the Ancient Mariner* and, long before studying Coleridge in university, was enthralled by the revelatory power of imagination. Yet one person's imagination is another's fancy.

As Canadian poet Earle Birney famously wrote in "The Bear on the Delhi Road," "It is not easy to free / myth from reality." Liberating reality from myth can be equally challenging. As with a culture's history—an inevitable blend of fabricated myth and empirical fact—one's personal history is often a conflation of fact and lore.

Memory is not only selective, it's highly imaginative. And revisionist. Or an amazing liar, fabulist, con artist, spin doctor. A haunter and a healer. At the personal as well as societal levels, history is what we choose to remember about the past in order to make sense of and justify our lives. More precisely, history is what we both consciously and unconsciously choose, the two processes woven together in a mnemonic double helix. Our memories contain what we consider to be evidence about the past.

As an inveterate storyteller from an early age, I had drawn on that imaginative memory to tell tales about my family and ancestors from elementary school onward. I know now, and was somewhat aware then, that I liberally mixed fact and lore into the brew of my family mythology to intoxicate my listeners.

When, in my last year of high school, I became intensely interested in reading about history, American and otherwise, my keenness did not extend to my family's past. If history was worth-while, it was to be found in the bestselling masterwork *The Rise and Fall of the Third Reich*, in Tolstoy and Dickens, in James Michener's *Hawaii*, and other gripping historical novels. I cared deeply about what I was discovering of the externalized past—of American and British history and literature, ancient Greece and China, African-Americans, the Russian Revolution, early cinema, the evolution of blues and jazz—that kind of past. But I was in flight from my personal past, from the ancestors who were more present and influ-ential within my psyche, my identity, than Aristotle, Sappho, Lao Tzu, Emma Goldman, and Duke Ellington. I had no interest in reading about the history of German-Americans and how it might relate to my paternal ancestry, let alone the local history of Grays Harbor County on the Washington coast where my great-grand-mother was matriarch of a logging camp and my grandmother and mother were born.

There was also a complacency, an emotional and intellectual lazi-ness, in the way I consciously dealt with my past: content to recycle and embellish my treasure trove of remembered and imagined tales without the kind of investigation that might validate, while correct-ing, the mythology. In recent years, I have taught life writing classes and workshops on the art and craft of memoir, biography, and the personal essay. I urge my students to learn everything they can about their family, their ancestry. I strongly suggest that they save all doc-umentation and significant artifacts, even if the stuff appears to have little or no value now, for they will likely be grateful in later years. I am preaching what I did not practice.

It's a truism that many people become more interested in their ancestral past as they age and confront their mortality, finding meaning and solace in placing their lives within an enduring legacy. My interest, especially in my Dutch-German ancestry, might also have been fueled by residing for years in Canada's ethnic "mosaic," as opposed to the American "melting pot." I was permanently settled in Atlantic Canada, where the ancestors-and-heritage game is played more avidly—where people commonly ask, "Who's your father?" and "Who's your mother?"—than in my first Canadian home of British Columbia. And perhaps my sense of self and lineage needed to balance the abundant awareness of my maternal heritage and mythology with that of my father's line of descent. After all, I had grown up surrounded by my mother's people in Seattle and on the Washington coast, and on my father's side I had only Grandma Rosie Lemm, an occasional and largely mysterious presence.

If fact had been altered by imagination during my youth, now imagined truths were being revised by archival facts, and I was reimagining my family myths. This process had lagged decades behind my research into American history, my deconstruction and re-envisioning of national and cultural mythology. In the 1990s, a half-century after my birth, I began to research and learn more about my paternal family history, and the two processes melded together.

Over the years I've heard and read assertions that America periodically needs an external enemy to further the economic and political goals of various factions, to underpin its foundational myths, and to shape transformations of its identity. I'm tempted to see this too: a nation fostered by violent conquest and expansion, by genocide and slavery, still intermittently needing an enemy and war or threat of war, not only for geopolitical advantage and domestic political gain, but also to sustain its self-image and citizens' investment in the ongoing project of American exceptionalism.

But America, as with any society, also needs internal enemies. Two decades after 9/11, there is a welcome diminution or hiatus of that need for an external adversary, with the exception of hostility to "illegal" immigrants from Latin America. However, the conjuring and demonization of internal enemies is as intense as when I came politically of age in the 1960s. And arguably more severe and dangerous. In the 1960s, I was among the "left-wing" and "anti-war" people viewed as internal enemies by many Americans. During the Vietnam War, draft dodgers and deserters who moved to Canada were seen as traitors by some of their ex-fellow citizens. But that faded away. Almost entirely. At my 2016 high school reunion in Seattle, a classmate objected to my presence in a group photo: "I served in the army, Rich, and I don't like what you did." Flabbergasted, I almost left, but was bolstered by friends, including Vietnam vets.

In any family and any society, imagined truths come into conflict. Our personal and cultural histories are a continuous negotiation of clashing myths, as we engage in an unending act of conscious manipulation of fact and imagination. Of myth-making. History is the story an individual or nation tells itself, in an ongoing process of reinvention, and that story is one of imagined truths.

1

The All-American Boy

My paternal grandmother lived in a modestly elegant apartment in the Central District of Seattle until she died when I was eleven, and I visited her with my maternal grandparents once every two or three months, for an hour or two on Sunday afternoons. The operative word for and truth of that experience, I now believe, is "reserve": the restraint on both sides, bred of the tension of tragic circumstance and loss, which they intimately had in common but, for whatever reasons, could not openly, actively share. For Grandma Rosie the loss was her only child, my father, a Canadian citizen ironically slain on a Seattle highway after he had survived the slaughter overseas in an American uniform. Grandma Aileen had largely lost a daughter, who had also made it through those war years, only to be divorced soon after while pregnant soon after, and who then had her ex-husband perish with his fiancée. One child buried beneath a white cross in the military section of Washelli Cemetery. One child entombed indefinitely in Northern State Mental Hospital with a "nervous breakdown." My parents were never mentioned during those visits with Rosie Lemm.

There was abundant emphasis on good etiquette and courtesy among my maternal relatives—that valorization of proper manners among people of rural and working-class backgrounds, not to mention the reverse snobbery of those people in the presence of higher-class pretension and rudeness. But their good manners were softened, worn lightly. There was starch in the air at Grandma

Lemm's. I wasn't daunted, for she was kindly, warm, uncritical, and unthreatening—indeed, she seemed quite fond of and pleased with me. Yet we weren't relaxed. The past was too stiff a curtain between us.

One of my prized possessions, however, was a gift from Rosie during fourth grade when I joined the elementary school band: a Buffet Evette clarinet. Buffet has been a renowned French manufacturer of woodwind instruments since the mid-nineteenth century, most celebrated for its clarinets, the primary choice of professionals. As I assembled my gift, wide-eyed at the beauty of the exotic grenadilla wood, Grandpa Harry said, "This is no ordinary clarinet. It's top of the line. Your Grandma Lemm paid a lot of money for it." He added, in his I-had-to-work-hard-at-your-age-for-every-bean-on-my-plate voice, "You'd better show your appreciation and practice every day." I didn't need encouragement or scolding then, for I loved band practice until sports began to crowd out other activities— Scouts, drama, and music—in ninth and tenth grade. I quit the band to play football, and the clarinet languished in a closet. I loved playing sports, but I also knew, as the saying goes, that people don't attend football games to watch the marching bands. There's a photo of me on one knee in front of unwrapped gifts under our Christmas tree. Future veteran of gridiron wars, I'm holding my new football helmet. The all-American boy.

I was in third grade when I was given my first dictionary, a Merriam-Webster Collegiate edition. My grandparents, ever thrifty, likely saw this as a long-term investment, rather than believing I was exceptionally precocious.

One day, I found myself staring at the dictionary's front cover and was startled by the thought that Great-Grandma Webster had composed the dictionary. I immediately descended the stairs and presented my discovery to Grandma, daughter of the putative lexicographer.

"Great-Grandma wrote the dictionary, didn't she?"

"Of course not. Why would you think that?"

"Well, her last name's Webster," I said confidently, pleased with my impressive logic.

"Do you have any idea how many Websters there are?" Grandma said, unhelpfully, and turned her attention back to her Mickey Spillane novel. "And her first name's Lillian, not Merriam. You know that. What's wrong with your brain today? You're not two years old."

"Maybe Great-Grandma was related to Merriam Webster?" I ventured, feeling my discovery sinking into quicksand.

"His name was Noah Webster, way back in the nineteenth century, and no, they weren't related. No idea who Merriam was."

Grandma was not the kind of person to look something up, though she was quick to tell me to go search for the answers. We owned the *World Book Encyclopedia*, and it's possible but not likely that I came back to Grandma bursting with the information that George and Charles Merriam were Massachusetts publishers who bought the rights to Noah Webster's dictionary after he died. My misconception did reveal the lofty esteem in which I held Great-Grandma, a respect and reverence shared universally by her huge clan, including my grandmother and Lillian's other four living children. Why couldn't Great-Grandma have written the dictionary, I wanted to ask Grandma, she's done so much else? Wasn't she descended from a great astronomer? Instead, I went back to my room, chastened, looking sadly at the dictionary, which had briefly been an intimate heirloom, not just an important book: a talisman instead of a tool.

"Your great-grandmother's maiden name was Kepler," Grandma had told me one day. "That's German," she said, her lips shaping a crescent moon of pride. There were good Germans in Grandma's books, and there were the Huns, Jerrys, Nazi monsters, and temporarily deranged masses goose-stepping to their Führer's murderous mania. "Lilian's descended from the famous astronomer, Johannes Kepler." I had no idea why he was famous, but I knew the name and was vaguely aware this was a person worth being descended from.

And astronomy was cool because it was connected with space travel and science fiction, meteors and Martians. I'd been given a model Palomar Observatory telescope the previous Christmas, and had been peering at moon craters, hoping to spot signs of life. Grandma had taken me to see *Project Moonbase* at the Embassy Theatre, which inspired daydreams of leading America's first mission to the moon. It seemed natural that—ahead of the film's time—the president and a fellow lunar-naut were female. I wasted no time name-dropping my ancestor at school, to the blank or annoyed indifference of most friends and the admiration of a few easily impressed. Typically, Grandma offered no follow-up to this revelation. And once again, my famous curiosity did not extend to my ancestors.

I was a normal and exceedingly active boy, something that my mother, when she returned home from Sedro-Woolley, was extremely proud of: her son the Boy Scout with merit badges paraded on his sash; football player and track star in his varsity letterman's jacket; winner of his high school's Memorial Day Writing Contest with an essay on his father's and grandfather's World War II heroism; and on top of that an honours student and devout altar boy.

None of those activities required me to consider larger issues of society. Even my benevolent scoutmaster, Mr. Goldman, eschewed patriotic displays apart from the obligatory pledge of allegiance. My favorite and best subjects in junior high, along with music and drama, were math and biology, not socials and English, which I entirely forgot. Except for a sweetly earnest English teacher-in-training who bafflingly loaned me her old leather-bound copy of Goethe's *Faust*, saying, "You may not understand it, but I believe you'll enjoy it," which turned out to be memorably true. At home, my grandfather paid scrupulous attention to the news on radio and TV and in the daily papers. Sporadically, he launched comments into the air, balloons, not grenades, with his opinions inside drifting through the rooms or stuck to the ceiling. Or occasionally popping when they were racist and I objected. My grandmother was always a study in casual disinterest, while I was largely oblivious until his focus and comments settled on sports.

My emerging social awareness in high school was, at first, focused on American race relations, from illuminating conversations with my African-American friend Tom Gayton and his parents, Leonard and Emma, to arguments with my garden-variety bigoted grandfather. The Anglo-Catholic priest, Father Kappas, at St. Clement's Episcopal Church where I was an altar boy, was a racial justice beacon, converting the nearly all-white parish he inherited into a multiracial congregation reflecting our "mixed" neighborhood, as we then called it.

My junior year, however, was my preppy phase. I served as junior class and varsity athletes' club treasurer, was devoted to football and track, and continued to shine brightly in math and biology while flickering dimly in English and history. I was preoccupied with my first romantic liaison, with a classy girl one year older and several rungs higher on the socioeconomic ladder. And there was my spiritual ardor en route to a non-celibate priesthood. Amidst strapping on my football helmet, unclasping Gwendolyn's bra, stealing money from my grandfather's wallet to pay for our dates at fancy restaurants, and donning altar-boy vestments, there was only one forewarning of the political eruptions in my brain the next year.

One day during the Cuban Missile Crisis in 1962, when I was

watching TV coverage of the confrontation, the anchor reported that Russia's leader, Nikita Khrushchev, had countered America's demand to remove Russian missiles from Cuba by pointing out that American missiles were stationed in Turkey and aimed at Russia only ninety miles from the USSR border, the same distance as Cuba from Florida. The anchor reported matter-of-factly the official American response: the presence of US missiles in Turkey was irrelevant, an invalid comparison.

When I heard that news anchor report on President Kennedy's brisk dismissal of Khrushchev's gripe, I stood in front of the TV with a lucid skepticism, and remember thinking, We have missiles only ninety miles from Russia? Wow. That sure seems like a valid comparison and complaint.

The precise hour of the final confrontation, I was in biology class. The principal was keeping everyone apprised of the worsening situation with announcements on the intercom while we were dissecting frogs. That would have been my last act on earth, not something sublime such as praying to Jesus or catching a touchdown pass or fondling genitals with Gwendolyn. Every few minutes, our instrument-wielding hands would freeze in mid-air as the principal informed us how much closer on their collision course the American and Russian ships were. We'd briefly worry, contemplate our mortality, then return to our work and chatter.

"Here's the latest report," the principal said. I saw Jody halt, carrying a full gallon jar of formaldehyde from the back room. "The ships are less than a mile apart. Our ships have ordered the Russians to stop. If the Russians don't, ours will fire across their bow. This is, in naval law, an act of war."

Jody dropped the jar of formaldehyde, the fumes hit the air, and all hell broke loose. Most students fled the room, but some were in their chairs or slumped on the floor, rubbing their eyes and gagging or gasping for air. (I am usually superb in a crisis—I faint afterward.) I saw Mr. McGrath soaking paper towels in the sink and putting them to his nose and mouth. I did the same, opened windows, and helped stricken students escape the classroom. Invaluable lesson: if a nuclear holocaust is imminent, put down the jar gently.

Once the missiles were removed from Cuba in the fall of 1962, my concentration re-focused on panties, jockstraps, and altar-boy cassocks. The crisis caused, however, the first crack in my patriotic foundation, a crevice which would soon and dramatically widen, allowing critical knowledge and re-envisioning to pour through. That fracture, I later saw, had earlier origins—the various rebellions, for instance, of the 1950s from Elvis and James Dean to the Beat writers—going back to the Enlightenment-infused critical reasoning of the Founding Fathers. But the missile crisis provoked my first conscious awareness of a metamorphosis in my nationalism and allegiance to America.

The celestial calm before the secular storm, during a summer pilgrimage with Father Kappas, was at Saint Gregory's Abbey, an Anglican Benedictine monastery in a rural setting outside Three Rivers, Michigan. Father Kappas was an oblate of the order, having taken the vows of chastity and obedience, but not poverty. Our priest was revisiting the early sites of his vocation, and Tom and I were brought along to help with the driving, provide youthful companionship, and, most of all, inspire our gestational calling to the priesthood.

I'd imagined the monks would be quite otherworldly, fully absorbed in divine contemplation and sacred ritual. Their daily lives involved a good deal of those, and we joined in their orisons and rites. But Tom and I also found ourselves working with them in the woods, hauling out trees they'd felled. Their modest logging operation helped fund the monastery, as did their small dairy. We were impressed by their muscular robustness and by the sheer joy they found in manual labor. I also reveled in evening discussions; not only about theology and other religious subjects, but about philosophy and history. We were also surprised by the monks' vibrant sense of humor and effusive laughter. These were men who worshipped with the utmost solemnity and veneration, and in the evenings debated the merits of Kierkegaard and Camus, Mozart and Bach.

For several days, I swam and floated in intermingling currents of euphoria, serenity, reverence, gaiety, and intellectual exhilaration. I felt both peacefully content and vividly alive. I also knew it was not a life for me: too regimented, too confined, not to mention the absence of women and vow of celibacy. Yet I wanted to find, absorb, and contribute to other milieus where I felt such sublime tranquility, harmony, plenitude, and vitality. And I wanted to find them in the natural world and human communities.

From the sublime atmosphere of the abbey, we descended into the earthy air of Chicago. While Father Kappas visited a clerical chum, Tom and I were hosted by an old friend of Tom's father who had become a prosperous medical doctor and lived with his family in an upper-middle-class Black neighborhood. One evening, he took Tom and me to the elegant London House, one of the premier jazz clubs in North America. The maestros on stage that night were the Oscar Peterson Trio with Ray Brown on bass and Ed Thigpen on drums. The Trio were London House regulars. The doctor was a distinguished patron, and his esteem ushered his underage charges through the door without question. The doctor ordered drinks, and my lifelong love affair with dry martinis began.

The best table in the house was reserved for the doctor: right beside the piano on the low stage with an unimpeded view of Peterson's face, hands, and keyboard. Ray Brown to the left, Thigpen and his drum kit behind. This was my first live concert other than the Seattle Symphony. When Peterson's fingers began moving on the keys, articulating the melody, then launching into improvisation, with Brown and Thigpen laying down rhythms and beats and Brown also exploring the melody and chord progressions, I was transported into a newly discovered magical realm, by a wizardry I had barely, if ever, imagined. I was transfigured by that magic, especially by Peterson's inspired melodic inventiveness, technical brilliance, emotional versatility and force, effervescent energy, intimate rapport with his audience, and upbeat sensibility even when his blues-based music invoked sadness rather than rejoicing.

I realized that evening, with crystal clarity and diamond certainty, that I wanted to be an artist too. The desire to be a priest vanished as if struck by a Flash Gordon blaster, leaving a small mound of dust. All those holy feelings I'd had in St. Clement's Church, and the desire to merge those sacred sensations with God's divinity and the blessed radiance of saints, suddenly transmuted into a luminous secular ecstasy: the rapture of artistic creation, of wondrous works of art, of artist and audience melding. I was transmuted from priest aspirant to wishful artist.

After returning home I never again attended St. Clement's church. Whenever I saw Father Kappas in the neighborhood, I avoided him. I did not doubt my transformation, but I felt too embarrassed and guilty about letting him down. Therefore, I did worse: I abandoned him. Tom, who became Tomás, a poet and civil rights lawyer in California, remained close with Father Kappas and called on him in his San Francisco retirement. One of my deepest regrets is that I did not visit Father Kappas to explain myself, to attempt an ongoing communion of mind and spirit, and to express my gratitude.

In my senior year, my preppy feathers molting and bohemian

plumage sprouting, I replaced Father Kappas with other mentors for my new calling as an artist. Two superb English teachers were catalysts for my slide away from math and science into the arts. Eva Doupé was elegantly dignified, aesthetically passionate, and intellectually demanding. She introduced us both to Melville's dark vision in *Moby Dick* and Walt Whitman's resplendent journey in *Leaves of Grass*, to Holden Caulfield's youthful rebellion in *The Catcher in the Rye* and Robert Frost's mature wisdom. James Brittain was old school in his conservative suits, earnest formality, and gently rigorous insistence on both thinking unconventionally and grasping traditional literary forms. He had us free-write to electronic music and scan Shakespeare's sonnets.

Another inspiring elder was Brennan King, who had become Franklin High's head baseball coach in the 1950s and head football coach in my senior year. His athletes grace the Halls of Fame for several major sports leagues. Coach King had that knack of making me love every grueling and glorious moment on the field. His pat on the helmet and "Love ya baby" were equal to an A+ from Brittain and Doupé. His frequent refrain, "Run it again," when a play hadn't met his expectations became a lifelong fiat.

Friends, too, were instrumental, nurturing my social and political as well as artistic awareness. A loose-knit, iconoclastic group formed and expanded throughout my senior year. Salient people, for me, included Don Gayton (no relation to Tom), who was headed into science but loved literature. He introduced me to Dostoyevsky, Kafka, Brecht. He later joined the Peace Corps, trained as an agronomist, migrated to Canada as a draft dodger, and became a notable scientist, ecologist, and nature essayist. Jef Jaisun, future blues musician and co-editor of the legendary underground paper *Berkeley Barb*, steered me to H.L. Mencken and left-wing journalists. Poki Namkung, future medical doctor and public health officer in

California, invited me into the aesthetic realm of her father, Johsel Namkung, a Korean-born musician who became, with the utmost artistry, the Pacific Northwest's foremost nature photographer. Bill Corr Jr., quiet and enigmatic, whose father would become another mentor and home a portal into the realms of progressive ideas and reformist and revolutionary history.

Then there was my new girlfriend, Darlene, aspiring writer and visual artist, a straight-A student who had fallen out with her rigidly conformist and uptight middle-class parents. They opposed her embrace of "beatnik" values and rebellious behavior, including dating an African-American football player. Her father's racist and violent response to this relationship sent her fleeing to a room in the YWCA and a part-time clerical job at the telephone company.

Shortly after graduation, I decided to move out of my home. I was now working full-time at Church Supply Corporation, a downtown store that provided the Episcopal, Lutheran, and Greek Orthodox churches in Washington State with vestments, bibles, candles, and other ecclesiastical necessities. The job had been arranged by Father Kappas as a generous act of kindness and, perhaps, as a lifeline for my faith. I had money for a 1955 Chev and rented a room for $25 a month in a Central District house owned by Bill Corr Sr., my friend's self-taught intellectual and socialist father. My roommates were Bill's oldest son, John, a poet and former English teacher, Jim Bucknell, a Robinson Crusoe understudy earning money as a carpenter for his back-to-the-land home in the San Juan Islands, and Jef Jaisun with his sixteen guitars, mandolins, and banjos.

That first year after graduation, I eagerly entered circles of people quite knowledgeable about the Vietnam War, America's foreign policy and military roles, other wars and nations, modern ideologies, the Cold War, and the draft. I began learning about peace movements and war resistance, and about conscientious objection, which I had thought was only for Jehovah's Witnesses and Quakers. It gradually dawned on me that I was a conscientious objector to war and that this realization, this identity, would eventually clash with the reality that "Uncle Sam Wants You," as the enlistment posters declared from World War I onward. I felt that I had leaped like Buck Rogers through space and arrived in a new galaxy with scintillating stars, and at the heart of this galaxy was the Corrs' house, presided over by Bill and his wife, Cecilia.

During the Depression, Bill had no university option and, an Irish American in New York City, went to work as a longshoreman and union organizer on the docks. He'd been shot in the back by a goon and hounded by anti-communist Feds. His intellectual hunger and political vision had him devouring Marx, Engels, and Lenin, the novels of Maxim Gorky, and countless other books and journals that filled the walls of the Corrs' living room and spilled over into stacks on tables and floor. Bill supported his family as a carpenter and independent contractor, building and remodeling homes for people who valued both his craftsmanship and social values. He charged according to his customers' ability to pay.

There were frequent large gatherings in the living room, and small ones in the kitchen nook, attended by a cross-section of Seattle's older left-wing intelligentsia and left-leaning artistic community. The Corrs' four sons sometimes joined with friends, such as me, bringing the Dylan and Ferlinghetti generation together with the Shostakovich and Pasternak.

Joining that circle were Bob and Nancy Grimm, new close friends of Bill Sr., who had moved from Michigan to Seattle for medical residencies, Bob in neurology and Nancy in child psychiatry. They described themselves as liberals and held Bill in the highest regard. Over the next few years, after they settled in Portland, Oregon, I was welcomed and absorbed into their lives, friendships, and home filled with books, music, and visual arts; science and medicine; wilderness treks and nature conservation; liberal political journals and causes; gourmet cooking and a feast of intellectual, playful, and often soulful conversation. Eventually, I would embrace them as my chosen parents.

Another Corr connection and influence on my conscientious objection was Waldo Chase. Born in Seattle in 1895, he lived in the log cabin he'd built near the village of Union on Hood Canal on the eastern side of Washington's mountainous Olympic Peninsula. This area was part of the Skokomish Tribe's homeland. Union was the site of an artists' colony from 1924 to 1952. Waldo had spent a good part of World War II in an Oregon conscientious objector work camp, one celebrated for its many artists doing alternate service there. Waldo was one of those artists, and he and his brother Corwin, also an artist, were especially influenced by Chinese and Japanese art, and the Pacific Northwest became their subject.

The single bookshelf that ran atop the log walls of his cabin outlined the intellectual and spiritual history of Waldo Chase. The story began with the works of Marx, Lenin, and Engels, which yielded to the collected works of Freud, which gave way to the complete editions of Jung, which bowed, finally, to the writings of the India-born philosopher Krishnamurti. I respectfully considered his advocacy of Krishnamurti's distilled and serene wisdom, but concluded it was too simplistic and placid for me. I had registered as a philosophy major at the University of Washington, determined to plunge into the churning cross-currents of Western thought.

In September 1964, I joined the other 23,000 students on the vast UW campus. I felt utterly lost. Alienated. Shrunk to microscopic unimportance. In the Corrs' living room and breakfast nook, I felt that I belonged, if occasionally daunted and often listening in silent awe, yearning to earn my right to speak with learned and cultured authority. On campus, among neophyte peers, I felt helplessly insecure and inadequate. I sat glumly through Anthropology lectures with seven hundred students and frosh English with sixty. Walking onto campus, my brain and body felt as if they were being dragged underwater by a squid tentacle. One day mid-way through the academic year, circumnavigating campus for over an hour, unable to steer my car or brain into a parking lot, I realized I would never return, that I was dropping out. As soon as I drove away, my brain and body burst through the surface and I again fully belonged to the vivid world around me.

The day I veered away from campus, a newborn dropout, feeling the immense relief of the afterbirth sliding from my brain, I also had a long moment of panic combined with elation about my draft status. Mine was II-S, the classification of student deferment. We were obliged by law to notify the Selective Service System of any developments that might change our status, and this would alter mine to I-A, "available immediately for military service." These were pre-lottery days, so I would inevitably be summoned sooner or later for my physical, which I would pass. This was the source of panic. The elation was from knowing I would no longer hide behind a student deferment and must step to the plate as an applicant for conscientious objection.

In the following weeks, and for years after, I told people that I had two equal motivations for dropping out: first, giving up my student deferment and, second, feeling alienated by a giant university with huge, impersonal classes. I'm sure that I put greater weight, at times, on my moral rejection of a student deferment. This was dishonest, and I knew it. Over time, in Canada, with the draft and Vietnam receding into history, I owned up to the primary reason for failing to return to campus: the lonely misery of feeling minuscule and unworthy. The crushing of my intellectual aspirations under the weight of a colossal campus and student body. Many years later, classified by the Myers–Briggs personality inventory as a borderline introvert, I could see that the "megaversity," as we called such behemoths then, wasn't entirely to blame.

I dutifully informed Selective Service, with pride and trepidation, that I had quit university. I also needed a new job, since I had been dismissed from Church Supply Corporation for my refusal to shave off my new beard. Responding to an ad on the university's employment bulletin board, I was interviewed for a part-time position as sixth-grade recreation supervisor and teaching assistant by Dr. Eleanor Siegl, headmistress of The Little School of Seattle in the large University Unitarian Church, a spiritual home for many academic and other professional families of liberal persuasion.

Eleanor was the school's founder and a leading education innovator in Seattle. I was scrutinized by a regal person I might easily have been intimidated by, but wasn't because of her kindly manner. The job ad called for someone with a university degree and relevant experience, not a first-year dropout who'd been a biology lab assistant and Sunday school teacher. My references were Bill Corr Sr., and the Grimms. Little did I know that Eleanor and her husband Henry, the Seattle Symphony's renowned concertmaster and first violinist, were good and admiring friends with the Corrs and Grimms. Whatever they told Eleanor persuaded her to overlook my dearth of credentials. Eleanor was a pacifist, perhaps another factor in my hiring, and pacifism was part of the school's philosophy.

My job at The Little School also placed me under the wing of Rev. Peter Raible, a Unitarian minister who had marched with civil rights activists in Selma, Alabama in 1965, and whose sermons were passionate contemplations on religious traditions and historical figures, social justice and individual conscience.

As a guest in the cultured elegance of Peter's and his wife Dee Dee's home, I reveled in their magnificent library and rooms full of art. He officiated at my first wedding, to Darlene, in their luxuriant backyard. Obituaries do not mention Peter's and Dee Dee's *joie de vivre* and his joyous laughter, which inspired me as much as Peter's passionate commitment to social justice. He was very supportive of my conscientious objection and helped me prepare my file. The rules for Conscientious Objector status did not allow for an atheist position. An applicant had to express a belief in a supreme being. Who better to talk with than a Unitarian? A Unitarian prayer begins, according to one joke, with "To Whom It May Concern."

My deity-friendly agnosticism was an advantage in crafting my statement for the draft board. Bare bones agnosticism was as unacceptable as atheism. This was modern America, with a belief in God—sincere or lip-service—firmly embedded in mainstream political culture, in spite of the widely assumed separation of church and state. The phrase "under God" was added to the Pledge of Allegiance in 1954. I needed to be a CO under God in the mid-1960s. My CO application, when submitted, totaled sixty-plus pages, including photographs of me at anti-war demonstrations and letters from Rev. Raible and others testifying to my non-violence and omitting mention of my gridiron intensity.

En route to California in mid-1966 to begin our studies at San Francisco State College, Darlene and I spent a few weeks with the Grimms in Oregon, wilderness hiking and hanging out in their Portland home. One evening, discussing my CO application and its probably thumbs-down outcome, Bob said, "Of course you can't go to prison and have no choice but go to Canada." Darlene did not demur. She was disillusioned about America's militarism and neo-imperialism, and even more about its racism. She wasn't an activist ready to fling herself into the struggle, but she seemed quite open to self-exile as a form of protest. Until that evening, I hadn't considered fleeing to Canada, even with the myth of my Canadian father dear to my heart. Whenever fear of prison upwelled, I stopped it with a plug of faint hope that I might be allowed alternate civilian service. But the fear kept blowing out the stopper. Bob's words planted a Canuck flagpole firmly in my brain's ready ground. In my head was the refrain from Dylan's "Maggie's Farm," how he would refuse to work on her farm anymore. I marveled, in fact, at how readily twenty years of American mythic socialization moved out of the way to allow my psyche to look longingly north. But there had been many people and forces, for several years, shouldering my nationalistic upbringing aside.

In Seattle and then San Francisco, I sometimes dreaded going to my mailbox. I would warily lift out the mail as if it contained a letter bomb. And then the relief. Nothing from Uncle Sam. But one day the explosive device arrived. Return address: Selective Service System. Inside, an order to appear for my physical. Which I readily passed. I then awaited the draft board's verdict on my CO application, which was not long coming, and, as expected, negative. I filed an appeal, the first of several appeal stages, this one to the draft board itself.

In the late spring of 1967, living in San Francisco, I was notified by letter that, as expected, my appeal for conscientious objector status had been rejected by the Washington State appeal board. My last recourse was the Presidential appeal board, a committee of five retired generals. Aristocrats, I imagined, had better odds of avoiding the guillotine during the French Revolution. But I was told that this course of action could delay matters for a year or more. Thus, I appealed to President Lyndon Baines Johnson's retired brass.

Not long afterward, I received a startling letter from Lance

Foreman, high-school football teammate and Boys' Club president, avid reader, independent thinker, and aspiring seafarer who planned to sail the ocean in wooden boats. He was a role model who embodied the Golden Rule: an unassuming rebel with the cause of selflessly helping others. Certain he would be proud of me, I had written him two years earlier about my decision to be a conscientious objector. The only word I remember from his inflamed reply is "unpatriotic." While he had not been gung-ho pro-war and was making no effort to enlist, Lance was a conventional patriot about serving America, when Uncle Sam called, in uniform.

Lance's astonishing letter was written from Vanderhoof, British Columbia, where he was a brand-new immigrant to Canada. "What the hell are you still doing down there? Get your butt up to Canada," he wrote. He had secured a job, invaluable for one's immigration application, with a Catholic school under the aegis of St. Joseph's Frontier Apostolate. For room and board and twenty-five dollars per month, he worked as handyman, recreation supervisor, and, as needed, boys' PE coach. He was confident he could convince the school to hire both me and Darlene as his assistants, room and board only, without the handsome salary. That would be our job tickets to Canada. He then had choice words, music to my ears, about the error of American ways in Vietnam and the damage the war was doing to our country.

I contacted the Canadian consulate in San Francisco and requested immigration applications. Meanwhile, Lance, good to his word, persuaded the school to send us official job offers, for room and board. I would assist Lance with his duties, and Darlene would assist the classroom teachers.

There followed moments of bleak panic then the effort to suppress worry as we awaited replies. I had no backup plan. Most of the time, I relied on that miracle worker, repression.

When the reply from Ottawa arrived, the size and thickness of the envelopes released a tsunami of endorphins. We danced around the living room of our San Francisco apartment, Darlene seemingly happy, I ecstatic both with release from dread and with acceptance into a tantalizingly mysterious future. We still had to be interviewed by immigration officers at the border. I was not home free. But I was damn close. "Many a slip between the spoon and the lip," preached my grandmother. Don't jinx it by taking it for granted. I wouldn't. We would rise to the occasion at the border, worthy supplicants.

Fretfulness returned when Lance wrote to say that St. Joseph's had withdrawn its job offers. We could still come as volunteer workers, sharing the large cabin where Lance and a Catholic lay brother lived. Darlene and I gambled that Canadian immigration had already checked out the job offers and wouldn't do so again when we arrived at the border. Even if they found out, we reasoned, they might still admit us. After all, Canada was willing to accept two people with one semester of university and relatively few job skills. I had no choice but to dwell in fingers-crossed hope. We would work at our campus jobs for the summer and save money, take full advantage of San Francisco during evenings and weekends, and emigrate in September.

At the end of August, we quit our jobs and packed basic necessities in Lance's borrowed Beetle, leaving most of our possessions in the care of an apartment roommate, Oregon native Dee Knight, another former all-American patriot and football player being radicalized by the war. He would ship our belongings north once we were settled. I don't recall how the car migrated from Lance in the BC interior to San Francisco. I do see us pulling away from our Ocean Avenue apartment, and I know that we stopped off in Seattle for a few awkward, subdued hours with my mother and grandfather, but I cannot visualize that farewell visit, and my next image is of parking the Beetle beside Waldo Chase's log cabin near Hood's Canal.

Much to our honored surprise, Bill Corr's sons had persuaded Waldo to host a moving-to-Canada party. By nightfall, a couple dozen Seattle friends were there, with sleeping bags, gallon wine jugs and tequila, and musical instruments. A campfire was roaring. Waldo had given his blessing for the city to be on his doorstep, and music blared from someone's phonograph—Dylan, Joplin, The Beatles, Miles Davis, Aretha Franklin. Then the guitars, harmonicas, and flutes came out, and my old tenor sax that I'd given to Bill Jr. The band was honking, voices wailing, non-musicians dancing around the fire, jugs and joints making the rounds. Other songs we sang that night were emblematic of transformative experiences from my high school senior year to that eve of departure from America: "We Shall Overcome," "Oh Freedom," Woody Guthrie's "This Land Is Your Land," Sam Cooke's "Change Gonna Come," "Hit the Road, Jack," and "With a Little Help from My Friends."

Around midnight, I was feeling blue. Not because I was leaving these friends, my home, my native land. But because Darlene, several sheets to the wind, was dancing flirtatiously with male friends. And oblivious of me. When she flirted, it wasn't coquettishly, but with soulful intensity. I could no longer share in the revelry. I left the fire and Waldo's property and walked for a long while along the darkened road, surrounded by trustworthy friends the cedars, firs, hemlocks, and pines. Still feeling cavernously sorry for myself when I returned, I saw that almost everyone had hit the sack in the big cabin or under the night sky. Darlene and a male friend were sitting cross-legged, facing each other, faces illuminated by the dwindling fire's intimate glow. I stood on the opposite side of the fire, but they took no notice. I went to the car for my sleeping bag and foam pad, spread them by the fire across from my ardent partner and her soulmate *du noir*, and escaped with merciful swiftness into the dreamworld.

Shortly after dawn I awoke, the fire barely smoldering, the dew and chill on my face and hair, and Jim Bucknell squatting beside me. I looked up into his glum face.

"She's gone," he said.

"Where?"

"Back to San Francisco."

As if a deep part of me had expected this and kept it from my consciousness, I sat up, worried about something more shocking than Darlene deserting me.

"Where's the car?"

"She took it."

"What the fuck?" I scrambled out of my bag. "That's Lance's car. He trusted us. He's waiting for it up north. She has no fucking right."

But the theft of the car did divert my mind from her abandonment of me to her betrayal of Lance's generosity and trust. Bewilderment, grief, and battered self-esteem would come soon enough. I had more immediate concerns.

"What about my gear?"

"She left your backpack. She said everything you'll want is inside."

Bucknell drove me back to Seattle in his Army Jeep, top down, wind blasting some of the emotional grime from my head. As we drove by the sprawling Fort Lewis military base where my father had trained en route to Europe and the war, I thought of the irony: Harvey Lemm newly married and, in photos with my mother, looking cheerfully in love, and heading eagerly off to war, obviously unaware of the heartache and separation awaiting them shortly after the war's end, not to mention his sudden death. His son, looking gloomy, heartbroken, running away from the military and war in an old Army vehicle, with morbid flashes of fatality.

Bucknell dropped me off at the University District house where my blues musician and construction worker friend Grady lived, with a spare bedroom in which I could crash. I now had another last night in America. But this one was my twenty-first birthday, and Grady and other friends, quickly rounded up, were determined to take me to the Blue Moon Tavern.

A local rite of passage on one's twenty-first birthday—when one could drink legally in Washington State—was to down twenty-one glasses of beer at the legendary Blue Moon Tavern in the U District. Its doors opened in 1934, four months after Prohibition ended, and for a half-century the Blue Moon thrived as both a genuine blue-collar tavern and a counterculture hangout. The famous Seattle poet Theodore Roethke was a regular, and visitors included Dylan Thomas, Allen Ginsberg, and Ken Kesey, three of my heroes. Ensconced with Grady and friends in a booth, I soon surpassed my former record of a half-dozen glasses of beer, and after a dozen I'd forgotten all about Lance's car and the former love of my life. My companions teased me about my trailblazing to the men's room, and when Grady shouted "twenty-one" to the crowded tavern, my reeling brain rose and bobbed on a cheering wave and then floated out the door, supported by Grady's strong arms.

Back at Grady's, a party was in full swing, the newest Stones album blasting, and an attractive woman leaned against me and handed me a joint. I inhaled, felt a needy, lustful stir, passed out, and woke up the next morning alone in my sleeping bag in that extra bedroom.

I did spend another night in America, at my childhood home. My insistence on sleeping in my mummy bag in the backyard flummoxed my mother and saddened my grandfather. I knew it was hurtful, but I couldn't bear to languish inside, shipwrecked in my old bed with the flotsam of memories. Earlier in the day, the booze and weed and party mood had worn off, and my forlorn desolation had led my hangdog self on a leash back home for one night's refuge and restoration. I needed to share a last supper with Harry and Gloria at our table, albeit a doleful and taciturn communion. Then sleep on the grass and earth under the beloved pear tree beneath the stars.

I'm ever amazed by the fragmentary nature of memory—as much by the Grand Canyon chasms as the promontories of remembrance. There is a blank between the image of Mom and Grandpa in the front doorway, staring with expressionless faces as I waved one last time from the sidewalk, and the arrival of my Greyhound bus at Canadian Customs. I informed the driver what I was doing, disembarked and, backpack slung on my shoulders, entered the office, immigration papers in hand.

Those papers informed me in no uncertain terms that Customs and Immigration officers had the ultimate authority to permit or deny me entry to Canada as a Landed Immigrant. I was desperately hopeful enough to believe that the vetting of my application in Ottawa was reasonable assurance that I would be admitted. I was apprehensive enough to know that human capriciousness, combined with the human brain's tendency to make favorable or fatal judgments about people in mere seconds, might spell my doom. The officers' moods, upbeat or sour, could matter more than the papers in my hand.

I stood across the counter from two officers, one middle-aged and paunchy, with slicked-back gray hair and a rumpled uniform, one young, tall, and lean, clothes neatly pressed. They examined my papers in silence, with non-committal expressions.

"Empty your backpack," the older man ordered.

I had chosen to wear my new button-fly Levi's and a plaid Pendleton wool shirt. Since I'd leaned heavily in my application narrative on my maternal logging heritage, I hoped my appearance showed solid west coast lumberjack stock. I unpacked my worn pair of Levi's, other Pendleton shirts, Jockeys and wool socks, foul-weather anorak. Then my camping gear: mess kit, Bowie knife and hatchet, compass, and mountain climbing boots. My tent and down bag were strapped to the bottom of the pack frame.

"You're a mountain climber?" the young officer said with a smile and obvious approval.

"Yes," I said, deciding not to state honestly that I was a back-packer, afraid of the danger of technical climbing, and that my top-of-the-line climbing boots were for my football-injured ankles. I was ahead of the game and didn't want to lose ground.

I now revealed another dimension of my identity: an Archive Records box set of Bach's *St. Matthew's Passion*, Miles Davis' *Kind of Blue*, *The Collected Poems of Dylan Thomas*, and *The Collected Poems and Plays of T.S. Eliot*. A couple days later, unpacking at the draft dodgers' crash pad, some guys were impressed by my albums and books. Not the immigration officers.

Next to emerge was my brand-new NFL regulation leather football.

"You play football?" asked the older man gruffly.

"Yeah. High school varsity."

"What position?" His face had "test question" written all over it.

"Slotback and defensive back."

"Kinda small aren't you?"

"I'm fast," I said, as modestly casual as possible, "and good hands. And punch above my weight." I almost added "shifty" and "slippery," but decided those were ill-advised descriptors for an immigration interview.

He smiled, briefly, holding the ball and staring at the logo. "Don't like the NFL. CFL's better."

I risked asking what "CFL" meant.

"Canadian Football League," he said very slowly, as if teaching me my first words in his country's language. And then gave me a terse explanation of the differences in the Canadian game, including something strangely called the "rouge."

I listened with keen politeness, heeding Bob Grimm's advice to answer concisely, and avoid my tendency to elaborate excessively, with tangents. I'd scored another touchdown but the game wasn't over. Still, I was feeling a major rush of endorphins. Both officers were tangibly in good moods now. Poetry and long-hair music aside, I was an all-right guy.

There remained my Webster's New International Unabridged Dictionary, Second Edition, 1934, purchased from the famous Moe's Books in Berkeley. This would be my go-to dictionary for decades, and has a place of honor in my university office. It weighs more than four large laptops. When I hoisted it from my pack and placed it on the counter, the officers' eyes were wide with amazement. Rather than being an oddball item I'd have to explain, it earned me another look of admiration. Not the lexical virtues, but its sheer bulk and weight.

"You carried this all the way from Frisco?" said the younger man.

"Sure," I said nonchalantly. "Couldn't leave this behind." I felt it was safe to grin.

They disappeared into a back room. After repacking, I slowly paced the waiting area, trying not to be prematurely excited and damping down flickers of fear, including the thought that they were phoning the school up north.

They returned beaming with the happiness of people entitled and heartily willing to bestow a great blessing upon a fellow human.

Eager to inspire and observe ecstasy. No doubt they knew I was a draft dodger, and were thrilled to grant salvation in Canadian heaven. I had been waiting during the interview for them to ask if I was a draft dodger, and to ask me to explain why they should admit someone who refused to fight for his native land. What would I do if called upon to defend Canada against an invading army? On the bus ride north, I had rehearsed my answers. They did not ask me. Not one word about why I was leaving the United States. About what I'd do if the Marines stormed ashore on the beaches of Vancouver or the Russians parachuted into Toronto. I remember them, with profound gratitude, as good-hearted souls. Had they rejected me, I would remember them otherwise. I recall them glowing with a pleasure I would later see, and still do, in many Canadian faces upon hearing that I, an American, had chosen to become a Canadian.

"Welcome to Canada," the older man said, extending his hand.

I signed a few forms and the young man handed me the all-important Landed Immigrant card. It was hardly impressive: the size of a business card. But it was the equivalent of manna from paradise, a golden lotus, the ultimate get-out-of-jail-free card. And my "Ticket to Ride." The Beatles tune was in my head as I said goodbye to my first fellow Canadians and left the building.

I was startled to see the Greyhound bus still there, its disgruntled driver standing nearby.

"You waited for me. Wow, thank you," I said, too cheerfully for his liking.

"Had to. Requirement."

"I've just immigrated to Canada," I said ebulliently.

"Good for you. We're an hour behind schedule."

Welcome to Canada. *Bienvenue.*

2

The Wild West

When I crossed the border as a new immigrant, I thought of Canada as a country founded by the French and British. I was only remotely aware of the land's Indigenous peoples, for instance, through the Grimms' interest in Pacific Northwest Indigenous art. My near-oblivion resembled my earliest awareness of the American frontier, from the first European colonies to the Oregon Trail and West Coast, as an empty and promised land there for the taking. Not entirely empty, however, since there were, as Thomas Jefferson wrote in the Declaration of Independence, "merciless Indian Savages" who needed to be eradicated or removed. The continent, I later learned, was vastly populated by hundreds of Indigenous societies. The West was neither savage nor wild, but inhabited by human communities for thousands of years.

The potency of Oregon Trail mythology for countless Americans, and especially a young boy in the 1950s, cannot be over-estimated. The westward migration slowed during and after the Civil War but continued into the 1890s, and I knew that Great-Grandma Lillian was part of that epic event. As a boy, I knew precious little of the multifarious history—the hardships and deaths, the oppression of Indigenous peoples, the profiteering and scams, the clashes of religious sects, the economic and social foundations of America's future being erected westward with a combination of private enterprise and government investment, of admirable enterprises and avaricious schemes. But I believed Great-Grandma rode one of those wagons west. I believed she was a pioneer, since everyone in the family called her that, and even the local newspaper described her as such when we celebrated her ninetieth birthday. And this belief helped define my own identity.

My memory is richly stained with a few details and stories about Lillian, and Grandma Aileen's gift-of-the-gab tongue is, I am sure, the primary source. I had woven these elements into my ancestral mythology, unfurling the tapestries many times for friends, students, and literary audiences . . . over beer, during lectures, in print.

Here, then, is the myth, originating in my early childhood, strengthened by several familial sources, nurtured by books and movies and TV shows about pioneers and the American West, and embroidered lovingly over the years by yours truly. I cannot with any confidence identify what was actually told to me by Aileen, or by my mother or uncle or other relatives when I was a child, and what my imaginative memory altered and festooned over the years.

According to this acquired and embellished myth, Lillian came from a prosperous, respectable family in Boston. Grandma Aileen led me to think of Lillian's family as hoity-toity, not the uppermost crust, but sufficiently established in Boston society. Referring to them, Grandma's tone of voice and facial expression had a mixture of derision and awe—sneering at those East Coast city folk while basking in their glow—an ambivalence bred from her upbringing in the newly settled West, which vibrated with the tensions of "civilized" people cultivating their transplanted culture and grafting it to a "wilderness" or "backwoods" or "frontier" environment.

Great-Grandma Webster (née Kepler or Keplor) was born in 1860, which has left me with one of those refrains of personal-historical astonishment we all have in our heads: "Good lord, my great-grandmother, whom I knew well until her death when I was thirteen, was born a year before the Civil War began!" I take excessive delight in this, pitying my students who brag about their grandparents seeing Led Zeppelin.

The next crucial event in my great-grandmother legend is that Lilian "ran away" from her Boston family in the mid-1880s, taking the train to St. Louis. I was left to imagine why, my understanding shaped by tales of well-off children fleeing oppressive families and homes or simply giving their adventurous or rebellious natures free rein. Lillian as a female Huck Finn. Except that, in the myth, she seems to have eloped with her anonymous first husband. So there may have been, I long imagined, the element of parental disapproval of a romantic attachment. Had she married beneath her status, or a ne'er-do-well, or a Wild Bill Hickok wannabee?

Perhaps so, since "Mother dumped her first husband in St. Louis," Grandma said with an admiring smile. She said that he was "something of a loser, from what I gathered, no gumption or dash. Couldn't keep up with Mother and bored her silly. So she hooked up with Daddy Baker, your great-grandpa, and came west with him." By covered wagon on the Oregon Trail. How else? I don't know how this strand of the legend was woven in, whether from something Grandma said, or from the narratives of the Old West which were ubiquitous in the 1950s as a mythologizing underpinning and counterpoint to America's rapid transformation into a society of suburbs and freeways, mega-cities, malls, and office workers. Whichever, there entered into my ancestral lore and storytelling a great-grandmother who adventured heroically west on the Oregon Trail.

When my fifth-grade class painted a gigantic mural of western American history, I worked on the Oregon Trail section with covered wagons and told everyone that the woman on the buckboard of one wagon was my great-grandma. Although Aileen never actually said that Lillian traveled in a covered wagon or on the Trail, she did nothing to dissuade my belief and stories.

The Lillian myth blossoms in Grays Harbor County in western Washington, with Great-Grandma and her husband settling in the rural area of Melbourne, near the town of Montesano, first settled in 1852, which is eleven miles from Aberdeen, a place with a rich history long before Kurt Cobain of Nirvana grew up there. My childhood memory placed her arrival there in 1886, along with the belief that the house she lived in the rest of her life, and where I spent summer weeks with her, was built by Lillian and her husband in the mid-1880s. Their rustic home must have been relatively isolated in those early years, for Great-Grandma's nearest neighbor in the 1950s was her son Archie and his family, a quarter-mile up the road.

In my childhood imagination, their pioneer status and isolation were inspired by my grandmother's claim that "They were the first logging operation on the Washington coast." And by photos: her twin brothers, Winfield and Walter, ten feet up a mammoth cedar tree, standing on a plank notched into the trunk and posing with a two-man bucksaw; a thin, bushy-mustached man sitting on the seat of a wagon, behind a horse, reins in hand, whom Aileen called "your great-grandpa." The family, men and women, posing in front of their cedar sawmill.

Countless times, when asked about my ancestors, my origins, I have proudly said, "I come from a logging family on my mother's side. In fact, my family started the first logging show on the Washington coast." These claims have supplied me with bush cred on so many occasions, from Tasmania to Vancouver Island to rural New Brunswick. I wasn't prevaricating. I remember hearing about the logging camp from Aileen's lips as vividly as I can see her stuffing pears and peaches into canning jars while she told stories.

In 1970, exploring my new homeland during summer rambles, I was hitchhiking in British Columbia from the Nisga'a Nation to Terrace. I was picked up by a gentleman in his late fifties or early sixties named Budge Crick, foreman of the Nass River logging drive. He asked where I was from, and I said Seattle, and that my mother's family was from western Washington, the Montesano–Hoquiam area, and that theirs was the first logging operation in that area.

"No it wasn't," he said pleasantly, but firmly.

"Huh?" I managed to utter, surprised and perplexed to be contradicted on a central point of family legend by some man six hundred miles north of the American border. "How do you know that?"

"Because my family was the first."

"What?" Now I was flabbergasted, at this coincidence as much as at his challenge to my ancestral myths.

He backed up his claim with detailed knowledge of our families' mutual stomping grounds. "There were timber feuds back in those early days," he said. "Was one of your relatives ever shot in a feud?"

Indeed, part of the legend was that one of Great-Grandma's twins, either Winfield and Walter, was winged in the arm in a timber feud. I remember, or imagine I did, seeing a photo of him with his arm in a sling. So I told Budge Crick, "Why, yes."

He grinned. "That might've been one of my family."

In the fall of 1974, I moved from Vancouver to Hope, BC, a mountain town one hundred miles due east of Vancouver, where the mighty Fraser River bends westward. I had decided earlier that year to make a serious effort to become a writer. To do that I needed to leave behind the distractions of the city, and so I found a cottage outside Hope on Kawkawa Lake.

Around the cottage, up the mountain slopes above Hope and along the old flood plain of the Fraser River, there were ancient stumps of grand old cedars, covered with lichen and fungus, stages for winter wrens and their two hundred songs.

Then I went down to Seattle to visit family and friends. I was staying with Uncle Curt, my mother's only sibling, and Aunt Fern. Curt announced, out of the blue, that my great-aunt Jeanette had died. Curt and Fern had gone to Aberdeen for the funeral. I was, momentarily, upset. "Why didn't you tell me?" I asked.

"We didn't think you were interested."

"Of course I was, and would have gone to the funeral." For five years as a draft dodger, I was unable to return to the United States. Now I could, and I'd missed out on paying my respects to Aunt Jeanette and meeting up again with extended family.

"There was a trunk full of old photographs," Curt said, "and there are duplicates you can have." That afternoon, we sat at the kitchen counter, looking at photos.

"I'd forgotten that I was born in Canada. Our family had cut down all the big cedar trees in our neck of the woods," he said, chuckling, "so they packed up their belongings, including their logging gear and the cedar mill, and moved up to Canada. To Flood, BC, in fact, which is near Hope."

Lo and behold, there was my family on wagons with their possessions, traveling up the dirt and corduroy highway from Seattle to British Columbia. And there was my family in front of their cedar mill in Flood, BC, now on Hope's outskirts.

"Our family cut down all those big trees in Flood and Hope too," Curt said, grinning. "After a couple of years, we came back south to Washington."

Because of that afternoon at my uncle's kitchen counter, those photos, and the brute knowledge that my family had cut down those trees, not some faceless entity known as "logging" or abstraction such as "ecological destruction," my poetry began to change dramatically, from didactic and polemic to narrative. The poem was sitting outside my cottage windows and in my Aunt Jeanette's trunk. I was proud of my heritage, so I would have to embrace those cedar stumps with the complex perspective and ambivalent feelings much more relevant to our motives and actions as humans, and to the consequences of our actions, than simplistic, poeticized environmental screeds.

Whether Budge's family were the first loggers or not, mine weren't; the first sawmill in Grays Harbor County was up and running in 1880 and shipped its first lumber the following year. But there's a far more serious problem with the Washington-coast-pioneer-logger part of my myth.

Lillian was, in fact, born in Renovo, Pennsylvania, on August 2, 1860. Far from running away from home, she migrated west with her parents to Red Bluff (then in Shasta County), California. There is a pioneer aspect to this journey. Lillian's obituary in Aberdeen's newspaper *The Daily World* (January 20, 1960) states that "The family made the trip on the first transcontinental train, which was made up of freight cars and two passenger coaches." According to the obituary, this was in 1872. However, the American transcontinental railroad was officially opened on May 10, 1869, linking eastern and western lines. Was the obituary incorrect about the date? Or, composed in 1960, was this assertion based on family lore too far removed from historical fact? In those early years, would the same string of freight and passenger cars have remained connected all the way from Pennsylvania to the western terminus in Almeda, California? The daunting task of historians, biographers, and genealogists is to distinguish between confirmable events and appealing but unverifiable lore. As a poet, I have placed Great-Grandma as a passenger in that first transcontinental train. As a scholar, I must add the qualifier "may have been."

My discovery of her westward migration by train ironically dovetailed with what I had learned as an adult about the history of settlement in the American West. On the one hand, there was the myth—the "pioneer mystique" as Joan Didion called it in *Where I Was From*—of rugged, individualistic pioneers. While there is abundant evidence of rugged pioneers and assiduous individual effort in that history, the dominant myth—heavily politicized and commercialized into the fabric of American identity, heritage, and ideology—excludes the equally vital role of government support. Westward settlement was enabled by substantial government grants of land, cash, and other benefits, and government regulations favoring private enterprise and influential capitalists. Lillian did not struggle across the West in a covered wagon, a heroic individualist right out of a western starring Ronald Reagan. She rode in relative comfort on a government-subsidized train.

When I became an adult, Grandma Aileen's and my origin myth influenced my increasingly complex, ambivalent, and bittersweet understanding of the development of post-conquest America and the larger ecological implications of human settlement and exploitation. Grandma cooking flapjacks and roast venison for the men chopping and sawing down the great cedar trees and Douglas firs. Me proud of being from a family that wiped out old-growth forests and lamenting that fact.

During 1965, Darlene and I were among the hoards of bohemian vagabonds traversing the continent, latter-day explorers discovering America for ourselves. We stopped in St. Louis to visit a Seattle friend's uncle, a musician with the St. Louis Symphony. He took us west to a small informal commune on the historic Mutreaux Farm in the Femme Osage Valley between the towns of Defiance and Augusta. Sunday was open house for visitors from the city. Darlene and I stayed on a few days, fell in love with the setting, made a favorable impression, and returned after our travels eastward to spend several months there.

Our dwelling was an ancient farmhouse, which, local legend had it, was quarters for slaves owned by a Daniel Boone son. Daniel had spent most of the last twenty years of his long life in the Femme Osage region, much of that living with his son Nathan near Defiance. We imagined that the numerous initials, words, and symbols carved on the walls were the work of slaves. As well, the Lewis and Clark Expedition, mounted in the town of Washington twenty miles from Defiance, was rumored to have passed along the trail—now a dirt farm road—a hundred yards from the farmhouse. Thus, I was immersed in two of the most prominent mythic realities of my American youth, surrounded by the elderly Boone's landscape, and envisioning myself walking in Lewis and Clark's footsteps as I passed under persimmon and sycamore trees on my way to the farm's large pond and its raft.

In light of my emergent political views, Boone—the archetypal model for subsequent American frontier heroes—was still mostly an admirable and inspiring figure, while Lewis and Clark were towering examples of the best of America, notwithstanding that they pioneered the way for imperialistic conquests and atrocities and tragedies for Indigenous peoples following in their benevolent wake. Then there was Mark Twain, the Missouri author, whose two famous novels I had first discovered in Great-Grandma's library of venerable, cloth-bound classics, and which I'd read to her by kerosene lamplight. I re-read the adventures of Tom Sawyer and Huck Finn on the pond's raft, further steeping myself in the mythic West/Midwest. A few years later, I would "discover" history, and my awareness of figures such as Boone, and understanding of how myths develop and alter according to each era's needs, would grow well beyond those glowing sentiments in Femme Osage Valley. But at the time, it was venerable fiction and myth I wanted.

Myth was also supplied by my belief, then, that Great-Grandma Lillian had passed through St. Louis before embarking in a prairie schooner on the Oregon Trail. Perhaps she even trekked through the Femme Osage Valley. I paid homage to her as I toted pails of water from a creek and chopped firewood for our dwelling with no running water or electricity.

Lillian Webster died in January 1960, almost a century after her birth. Six months later, John F. Kennedy accepted the Democratic presidential nomination with an acceptance speech that introduced his campaign slogan and what became the byword for his presidency and brief era: the New Frontier. The best political slogans tap deeply into foundational myths and JFK's was a winner with its twin taproots of frontier mythology and the ongoing reinvention of American identity. Great-Grandma was the embodiment of the frontier, the wild and tamed west, the settlement era, enduring into my lifetime and the modern age. American poet Ezra Pound had declared in 1928, "Make It New," an obscure scholarly phrase adopted in the 1950s as a motto for modernity. In the late 1950s, there was a grand total of twenty-eight frontier western series on the new medium of television. Along with Kennedy and countless other Americans, I was making a new frontier myth, reinventing the wild west and America itself: as I read James Fennimore Cooper's *Leatherstocking Tales* to Great-Grandma by lamplight in her home, and sat on my Seattle porch with my very own pioneer—watching hydroplane races on Lake Washington and the Navy's Blue Angels fly space-age stunts over the water—Lillian Webster personified and embraced it all.

3

The Nuclear Family

In the late-1950s, my grandparents bought a color television with excellent reception, and domestic comedies—*Leave It to Beaver, The Adventures of Ozzie and Harriet, Father Knows Best*—encouraged me to believe that the nuclear family was an eternal reality, to which my immediate family was a tragic though resilient exception. One generation back, Great-Grandma Webster both embodied and complicated the nuclear family myth in her fabled role as dominant matriarch.

The Lillian Webster of my youthful imagination partly belongs in the same inventive camp as Disney's version of Davy Crockett, except that there may be more factuality in the romanticized Crockett than in my great-grandma of childhood legend. Enter historical fact, provided by Bonnie Johannes, a local historian and genealogist in Grays Harbor County, Washington, where Lillian arrived in 1910 and spent the last fifty years of her life.

In 1883 in California, she married Ambrose Baker, with whom she brought forth seven children, my grandmother Aileen being the youngest. A 1900 US Federal Census lists Lillian with seven children and the marital status of "divorced." Her 1916 marriage certificate to George Webster (who died one year later!) lists her last name as Baker but indicates that this was her third marriage. Either this was an error, or she had a husband before Ambrose or between Ambrose and George, but reclaimed the name Baker. Learning of these marriages and divorce, I couldn't resist thinking sardonically about

those who exploit the idealized fantasy of the "traditional family."
I thought of Stephanie Coontz's *Marriage: A History*, which shows
that the nuclear family prevailed for a brief time only—the later
1940s through early 1960s—and primarily in North America and
Western Europe. As evidence, here was a woman in 1900, divorced,
with seven children—all of whom turned out splendidly—who was
the materfamilias of a logging camp. A half-century later, Lucille
Ball in *I Love Lucy*—one of my and Grandma's favorite shows—was
transgressively discontent with her homemaker role and constantly
sought, unsuccessfully, fulfillment outside the housewife corral. She
needed to sit at the feet of Lillian.

I was well aware that Grandma Aileen had divorced her war-hero
husband in 1943 and married their best friend, Harry. Then came
my mother's marital breakup. This cascade of divorces flowed
against the gravity of the nuclear family paradigm.

"Your parents divorced before you were born," Uncle Curt
volunteered.

"When my mother was still pregnant?"

"I think that's how it goes," he chuckled.

Another revelation. Another explosion in the nuclear family myth
factory. Whatever led to their separation no doubt caused dismay,
bewilderment, frustration, and resentment, which I no doubt sensed
while still in the womb. Followed by heartbreak and whatever anger
and remorse after their separation. Then the afterbirth of divorce.
When I was an infant.

After their separation, my pregnant mother moved back in with
her mother and Aileen's new husband. I was born into a non-nuclear
family and household, and there I stayed, unofficially adopted, after
my mother's "nervous breakdown" and confinement in a mental
hospital two years later.

"Gloria had waited so long for your father to come home from the war," Curt said. "All that worry, you know. And then he was home, and they were together. And what happened?"

My parents' love affair and marriage, a post-war casualty.

What about the car crash, I asked, my father's death?

My grandmother had told me that Harvey and his ex-army buddies had been out drinking. The car, a stylish two-toned coupé, was my father's but a drunken pal was driving. They hit pedestrians, according to Grandma, and then smashed into a bridge buttress. Everyone died except the driver.

Uncle Curt didn't know anything about a drunk driver, but he did know something my grandmother hadn't told me.

"There was a woman in the car. Your father's fiancée."

"His what?"

"They were on their way to get married."

"You're kidding." I was thunderstruck.

"He'd been seeing a woman, and they were engaged, and they were on their way to their wedding. She was killed too. And some friends."

"Why didn't Aileen tell me? Why did she lie to me?"

"You were young and she probably didn't want to tell you something that would disturb you, or she felt you wouldn't be old enough to understand. There might have been too much embarrassment."

My uncle couldn't remember anything about my father's fiancée. But years later, while taking my mother for our ritual drive through the old neighborhood and along Lake Washington, she suddenly told me about her. My mother was like that, off in the distance for a good while, then blurting a memory out of the blue.

"Your father was going to marry this beautiful Frenchwoman. From France. She owned a restaurant on Aurora Avenue. She was a good businesswoman."

"She was French and owned her own restaurant?" I was most

intrigued and pelted my mother with questions: How did he meet her? How did she come to own a restaurant? Did you know her?

"Oh, I can't remember that, sonny boy."

Thanks to Uncle Curt, I had another person in my history of loss. Her role was small, but it haunted me: a woman from France who had almost been my stepmother. Who had died young because she fell in love with my father. Did she have a child, too, who would dwell on her identity and fate decades later? Here was another woman, a businesswoman, no one in that era would write a sitcom about.

Grandma Aileen, too, in her youth, belonged more in a Zane Grey western novel, I thought, than on *I Married Joan* or *The Honeymooners*.

"I grew up cooking for hungry lumberjacks," she told me. "Nobody sassed back to Mother, none of us kids, none of the lumberjacks. She was the real boss of that camp. Daddy was soft-spoken, mild-mannered. The men respected him. But they revered Mother.

"It was a great place to grow up. We worked damn hard, but we felt like we always accomplished something."

I have no photographs of Lillian or her daughters from those settler years. But I hear Aileen's voice, a favorite saying: "A man works from sun to sun, but a woman's work is never done." The men were the ones in those old photographs of pioneer history: there's one of Lillian's twins, Winfred and Walter, a deer slung over one's shoulder, the other posing with his rifle. But not one photo of women standing at the cookstove or over the washtub, toting pails of water, cleaning diapers and nightsoil commodes, milking cows and churning butter, peeling apples and gutting chickens. Yet I didn't need them, for I had Grandma regaling me with the nonstop, strenuous devotion, the domestic skill and artistry, and the practical intelligence of Great-Grandma and her girls. I didn't, in fact, hear much from her about the men's work. But I didn't need to, for the culture around me amply portrayed and celebrated masculine settler labors, talents, and tools. What the culture seldom showed was the work of women, and that's where Aileen came in. And I could experience some of this work directly, in my chores with our vegetable garden and during harvest and preserving time—all that spading, planting, weeding, picking, peeling, slicing, blanching, and filling and sealing of jars.

Great-Grandma herself didn't talk about those times, the toil and skill. She was the living quintessence, and her descendants were more than happy and proud to talk about her past. Even more, Lillian was not the kind of person who needed to blow her own horn or to wax nostalgic or self-satisfied about her achievements. I see her in my mind's eye and look at her photographs, and the words that come to mind are "self-possession," "deep contentment," and "completion." There is a majestic quality about her that is devoid of vanity, a sense of superiority, or imperiousness.

Also, I could instinctively grasp her benevolently potent influence in the personalities of her five living children, all of whom bore themselves with unassuming dignity, integrity, and grace, and who manifested warmth and kindness, intelligence, and benign strength of character. There was gentlemanly Great Uncle Irwin, with his unpretentious elegance and graciousness. Sweetly affable Great Aunt Miriam. Loving-hearted and generous Aunt Jeanette, who lived in Aberdeen a short drive from Great-Grandma. My own grandmother Aileen. And Great Uncle Archie, a jack-of-all-trades handyman, who lived with his family just up the road from Lillian, the one child who remained deeply rural all his life. Visiting her other children, Lillian was immersed in their middle-class, urban world. At Uncle Archie's, even though the house was comfortably middle-class, she was in a more traditional environment. Archie repaired TVs, but his family still dined on rabbit stew.

Grandma's childhood stories were her origin myth, which became part of mine, rooting my maternal family and me deep in the Pacific Northwest landscape and within American settlement history. It was evidence of personal virtue, but not of upwardly mobile class status. It was proof of her formation as a person—and as a female—of strong physical and mental fiber. From an early age, she knew about hard work, and how the work had to be done well. "You don't feed a bunch of hungry lumberjacks a crappy breakfast or supper," she'd say, steeping me in the American work ethic. "From an early age I was working. We were all working. My brothers out with the men, the saws and axes, horses and wagons, sleds and mills. My sisters and me with your Great-Grandma, non-stop in the house, yard, barn, firewood, hens and rabbits, hauling water from the well and rain barrels, cooking and laundry, tending the sick, you name it. And no vacuum cleaners back then, no automatic washers, frozen dinners, and thermostats."

Grandma didn't romanticize or glorify the work, the way so many triumphant settler accounts did, nor did she portray it as back-breaking and soul-destroying, in the manner of realistic accounts of settler hardship, suffering, and failure. Rather, there was a matter-of-fact and sunny pride in and gratitude for the work itself and how it shaped her and her siblings. I wish she had told me— or that I remembered—more about the rigors, mishaps, tensions, frustrations, times of worry, thwarted dreams. Was everyone in her family as congenial with each other as she made them sound, as they were in my young presence? What about injuries in dangerous and strenuous kinds of work? Laundry, as well as logging, could ruin backs and hands. What about the near-escapes and miraculous deliveries from harm and disaster?

Two framed pen-and-ink drawings hung on our dining room wall. Your grandmother did those, Grandpa said, she was a fine artist. But

Aileen had stopped drawing years before and brushed aside my curiosity with a wistful smile. One work, a dusky summer landscape, has faded almost entirely in my memory. The other is vivid. A silvery full moon, shimmering through the thinnest gauze of clouds, illuminates a sparse late autumn landscape. Two leafless trees, slender trunks, calligraphy of branches laced upon a pewter sky. A foregrounded meadow or pasture like burnished slate streaked with quartzite.

That moonscape took over, in her last few years, during more and more evenings, when she and Grandpa drank too much and turned hurtful and hateful, while I worried and wept upstairs and tried to transport myself into the worlds of pirates and cowboys, knights and space travelers. I knew there was glowing gladness waiting for me in the mornings, a cheerful pleasure with existence. In the turbulent recriminations of the evenings, however, my faith in that serenity, my trust in her daylight contentment with her life, could be sorely challenged and, on the worst nights, seemingly shattered. Sharp-edged fragments of slate.

I would lie on the bathroom's faded green linoleum floor in my pajamas, listening and looking through the grate through which heat would rise from the fireplace. I could see part of the sofa—Grandma's place, and sometimes both of theirs when affection or loneliness brought them together to read, watch TV, sip bourbon as more than married cohabitants.

During their fights, the heat of their voices rose through the grate, enveloping my face, inflaming my mind. When their arguments were intense, I imagined a volcano—Mount Rainier erupting—lava and sparks spewing upwards, clouds of ashes.

Other times their words became stones, flung at each other, ricocheting upwards, pinging and clanging off the grate. The fierceness of their voices, the rancor. With early adolescent fervor, and with the inspirational mentoring of Father Kappas, I had religion as a shield against the sparks and stones. But I was much less adept at wielding that shield than I was a baseball bat or football.

I was mostly aware that their unleashed resentment and anguish was directed at each other, not me. I was the innocent, helpless bystander. But it was not much comfort as they hurled nasty accusations and cruel denunciations, as they tore each other apart.

Twice, after especially vicious rows, in the morning Grandma showed me bruises on her arms. "Look what your grandfather did."

But I had seen, through the grate, what Grandpa had done. Sometimes they would stand directly below me, shouting in each other's face. I saw Grandma swing her hand at Grandpa's head, and he grab and hold her arm. She swung her other hand, and he seized that arm too. They struggled like that for a few moments, and then she relented, he released her arms, and they retreated silently to the moroseness of her sofa and his living room armchair. I never saw or heard any other physical violence or evidence thereof. After those two incidents, Grandma never accused Grandpa again.

I know that I was mesmerized by the drama. That fascination with houses burning down, ships sinking, planes plummeting to earth. The dreadful event, the excitement of it all. I'm also sure I was more than just a masochistic voyeur. I was keeping vigil—both praying that they would stop and with a child's magic power striving to restrain their dark forces. My magic wasn't strong enough to banish the diabolical forces, but it was potent enough to prevent the demons that possessed them from battering through the walls that protected us and me—destroying their marriage, our home, their guardianship of me, the happiness and pleasures I enjoyed when they weren't driven by fiends. I was defending our version of the nuclear family.

I had another station of vigil when my magic power to restrain them wasn't working. I would painstakingly descend the stairs, knowing every creak each step would make, moving when their yelling was loudest. This took time, as their accusations and insults crescendoed and waned, with periods of seething silence while they nursed their wounds in their couch and armchair caves. When they emerged again to hiss and growl and snarl, I'd proceed until I reached the turn in the stairs, where I could risk peeking around and see Grandpa's chair and the near end of Grandma's sofa. Here, I could be Merlin sending forth my wizard's gaze from my promontory.

One evening the fighting seemed more intense than ever. At the turn of the stairs, I clenched my eyes shut and envisioned their fiery words setting the house ablaze. I didn't dare peek around, for I knew they were standing between their caves, right where they could see me.

"I've had it up to here with you."

"I've had enough to last a lifetime."

"I can't stomach another day of this."

"I'd rather die than put up with another day of this."

My body and face were tensed, as always, my breathing quickened and tight, with the effort of keeping their madness inside the boundaries. This wasn't the madness of my mother, I knew, something she could hardly help, but the insanity of people who were normal with shopkeepers and customers and neighbors and even each other in the daylight and early evenings and on those nights when the bourbon sloshed them down a jovial or placidly nostalgic spillway. Now, the bourbon was a vitriolic flash flood rushing them toward disaster.

"I want a divorce."

"You can have a divorce anytime you want, just say the word."

"I'm saying it now."

"Fine and dandy by me."

I have blocked out who said what. It doesn't matter. The fatal words had been spoken. The boundary transgressed. The dyke had burst and the little Dutch boy was underwater.

My magic power was useless. Mount Rainier exploded.

I stepped through my protective barrier and hurried downstairs. I was oblivious to the stunned looks on their faces.

"Please don't divorce," I blurted. "You can't divorce, you do love each other, I know you do, you have to stay together and . . ." I went on for several more moments until my strength and voice faltered and I stood frozen in desperate expectation of reassurance.

They were now turned facing me, side by side, arms almost touching. Their faces steeled by an unfamiliar anger.

"You're the reason we're fighting," one of them said, and again I don't remember who.

"We wouldn't be fighting if we didn't have you on our hands," the other said.

"We didn't ask to raise you, we had no choice."

"So don't come downstairs where you have no business, telling us what to do."

A trapdoor opened in my mind and I fell through, their voices receding as I plunged down a long dark tunnel. No crash landing, just a dull thud on the dungeon floor. Their voices somehow close by, through the cell's iron door. I had been reading Alexander Dumas and Robert Louis Stevenson, but now the tribulations of the Count of Monte Cristo and David Balfour in *Kidnapped* were not thrilling, but terrifying.

"You keep your nose out of grownups' affairs. Do you understand?"

"Go back to your bed and don't let us ever catch you eaves-dropping again."

Released from the dungeon, I retreated feebly upstairs. Very small, fragile as Grandma's most delicate Christmas tree ornaments or Grandpa's crystal wine glasses. The fear of divorce wrecking my world was partly eased, I suspect, by their warnings, which implied that I wouldn't be cast out to the sidewalk in the morning. But the fear was mostly pushed aside by the mind-boggling blame thrust at me.

That blame was so out-of-the-blue, so contrary to all the muck they'd thrown at each other in all their fights, that even amidst my dread and hurt, as I curled into a tight ball beneath my bed covers, I sensed that they'd turned on me only because I'd surprised and embarrassed them. And while the way they stood side by side confronting me was alarming, it was strangely comforting, their unity, a sign that they weren't about to separate and leave me twice orphaned.

The next morning, after what I felt was a suitable silence, I looked at Grandma—my go-to person when the matter was emotionally delicate—and asked, "Are you and Grandpa getting a divorce?"

She glanced briefly at me, a blend of bemusement and guilty grin, and laughed. "Of course not. What put that silly idea in your head?"

"Last night . . . you and Grandpa said . . . "

"Little pitchers have big ears. Your grandpa and I say lots of things we don't mean when we're fighting. It's all over and forgotten the next morning. Nothing like a good night's sleep to put stuff behind. Now skedaddle to school."

And I did seem to forget. Shoved it deep into a brain closet. I never heard them threaten divorce again. I didn't worry that I was an unwelcome obligation. The abundant evidence that I was loved and wanted, combined with my glass-is-half-full neuro-transmitters, kept me buoyantly above water through those years of drunken fights. But I think of others who endured alcohol-and-bitterness-fueled brawls between parents or guardians who were brutal or withheld their love or whose regrets otherwise poisoned their parenting—and whose emotional and neurochemical resources couldn't keep them above water.

It was with gratitude for their love and care—not fear of disapproval and abandonment—that I often brought her bouquets of pansies, dandelions, daffodils, clover blossoms, Grandma invariably receiving them with dazzled gratitude, invariably hugging me. That I often stood beside his armchair telling him about my baseball, track, and football triumphs, Grandpa always listening with a muted but undeniable pride in his boy.

There were copious Grandma hugs, which compensated for Grandpa's male reserve. And gentle touches and caresses. I cherished every one of them, the way plants absorb sunshine, stored them in my cells and roots. I can still feel them sustaining me through chill seasons, flowing into spring's renascence and bountiful summer. Had she always been that physically affectionate? Was it partly from being the youngest of seven siblings, everyone's baby sister? Was it also restitution for sending her daughter away, for taking her daughter's son? And I rarely saw any physical affection between her and Grandpa. As with all people who love to hug and touch, she needed that contact as much as I did. Her body was wholly responsive to her heart, which she often pressed me to. The message was: If you love someone, don't just tell them, show them.

Grandma showed me skills and smarts I would need—gardening, cooking, and baking, doing laundry, ironing, cleaning house, decorating, sewing—skills that I've used far more often as an adult than the ones Grandpa taught. Yet none of these skills were as important as the gift of her love flowing forth in all that touching.

Every now and then a switch would flip on the circuit connecting her hand to her heart. Instead of a nurturing current, a nasty surge of voltage swung her hand at my face. A vicious slap, triggered by some trivial remark I'd made. It never happened when I'd said or done something worthy of a firm or stern reprimand. She gave me "a good talking to," or restriction of privileges, or temporary denial of some promised treat, for significant indiscretions or disobedience. The slaps seemed to come out of nowhere.

These outbursts were uncommon enough not to compromise my trust in her. But they left their mark. There was a demon inside her that lashed out, and the wiring to its origins was too hidden for me to discern or understand. If my loving Grandma had such a demon, others could too, such as ever-genial Uncle Curt, my kindly scoutmaster, my benevolent priest. I could, too. Was that my demon surfacing when I made sarcastic remarks to my grandparents or friends, when I pouted at home spitefully? Blessedly, I never grew to fear Grandma, to steel myself against that sudden blow. I would quickly open myself again to her almost-omnipresent love. Yet I knew that demon was there, coiled, like a rattlesnake in a TV western.

It helped that every time she slapped me, she was instantly overcome with remorse, clutching me to her, tearful, kissing my cheeks, brow, scalp. Saying, "I'm sorry, I didn't mean it, I don't know what came over me, your Grandma had a bad moment, that's all." The way she showered me with love and physical affection almost made those slaps worth it. Almost.

When we think, now, of "the art of cooking," we're not likely to picture celebrity chefs lifting canning jars out of scalding water. In our age of freezers, and apart from jams and pickles and relishes, canning no longer has a vital place in our culture. Still, the art of cooking includes canning; Grandma was a master, and I was her apprentice.

On those late August and early September days, we sliced and diced, blanched and peeled and cored. Sterilized jars and lids. On Sundays I'd return from serving mass and the handling of holy objects—bells, thurible and frankincense, water and wine cruets—and attend to Grandma's sacred utensils: paring knives, bowls, measuring spoons and cups, canning pot and rack. The reverent lowering of the jar-filled rack into the boiling water, the worshipful removal of the jars and placement on cooling racks, the miracle of lids popping, and the Doubting (but necessary) Thomas tapping of the lids with a knife blade to ensure the seal.

After we labeled each jar with its year, its vintage, I was entrusted with the ceremony of carrying jars, with utmost care, like Father Kappas bringing the chalice with consecrated wine to the altar rail, down the basement stairs to the canning cupboard. I never tired, throughout the year, of opening the cupboard doors and gazing at those magic jars, of carrying that succulent bounty upstairs for the taste of summers past.

Folding laundry, another ritual I loved, took place in the "back room" next to the kitchen. One day I was there helping Grandma. In the pile of clean clothes, I found a small beige foam pad, held it in the palm of my hand, and asked about it.

"It's for my brassiere," she said. "I had a breast cut off."

An electrical current went through my groin, which happened sometimes when I read about blades slicing through people.

"Why?"

"It happens to some women. This part of her body gets sick and has to be removed."

"Oh." The voltage increased.

"Here, I'll show you."

She unbuttoned and removed her blouse, unhooked her bra, and I saw the puckered, scarred skin where a breast used to be. She did this so calmly, as if she was showing me how to stuff a turkey or iron her skirts, that the current shut off and I gazed tranquilly, feeling an eerie reverence and honored that she was sharing this with me. She knew almost everything about my body, had tended me through the most intimate of moments, and I'd known almost nothing about hers, but now she had offered me this mystery, this knowledge. I did not know, however, the emotional price she might have once paid for this composure.

The flip side of Grandma's tranquility about this alteration of her womanhood was her love of dressing to the nines when we went downtown to shop and dine. I was always thrilled to be her "little man" on her arm as she elegantly strolled the aisles of the upscale Frederick & Nelson Department Store and purchased lipstick and perfume at the more affordable Bon Marché cosmetics counter. She was garbed in her finest for our Christmas Day visits to Curt and Fern's. Our last such visit occurred when I was thirteen.

Before that, at home, we'd opened our presents while Grandpa and Grandpa tipped themselves aslant with bourbon and then capsized amidst their annual tempest tantrums over spending too much on each other's main present. I'd escaped to the much merrier house, one block away, of the Gaytons, descendants of an esteemed Seattle African-American family, a sanctuary that was becoming my second home.

By the time I returned to don my best clothes, they'd sobered up sufficiently: Grandpa taciturn but pleasant, Grandma's jolliness restored in anticipation of a Christmas visit with her son and other grandchildren.

My uncle and aunt were living with their young son and daughter in a newer suburban home. Curt had been promoted to a supervisor's role on the assembly line at Boeing, with a higher income, and they were now solidly middle-class, with upmarket furniture and—to my eyes and feet—deluxe wall-to-wall carpet. Surely they'd be starring in a domestic comedy soon. I was sitting between Grandma and Grandpa on the handsome sofa. Curt had whipped up a batch of Tom and Jerrys—egg nog with rum and spices in mugs—no booze in mine. Grandma, mug in hand, inspired anew by Christmas spirits, began singing along with the carols on the record. Curt was wearing his kindly, indulgent smile for his tipsy mother, and Fern's expression reminded me of the cartoon strip *Grin and Bear It*.

Then Grandma rose to her feet, sashayed on her high heels to the center of the living room, crooning with Bing or Dinah about sleigh rides or boughs of holly. Curt was barely smiling, while Fern's disgruntled eyes were following the arc of Grandma's swinging arms and the half-full mug at the end of one pendulum. I was teetering between delight at my glamorous, musical grandmother, and apprehension over the expressions on my aunt and uncle's faces. Between my potential to be embarrassed by Grandma and my readiness to be dazzled by her.

One of Grandma's heels caught in the carpet, she stumbled, and the egg nog splashed on the symbol of upward mobility as Grandma tottered downward and Grandpa rose lightning quick to catch her.

"Mother, please sit down," Curt said, also rising and, I'm sure, about to smooth things over in his usual way. Fern stood up, too, rigid and silent.

Grandma handed her mug to Curt, retreated with Grandpa to the sofa, and sat down, chastened, deflated.

"You're nothing but a common drunk, Aileen," Fern said.

There was a long moment as we, the riffraff on the sofa, the reprobates, sat stunned, staring at our upright betters, my beloved and trusted aunt and uncle. I especially looked to my uncle, this benevolent man who was raised by the woman raising me, but he was soundless, not coming to Grandma's defense, his expression woven with a woof of sadness and warp of disgust.

Breaking the spell, Grandpa took my mug and placed it deliberately along with his on a side table, sprang to his feet, yanked me to mine, and gently helped Grandma to hers, saying,

"We're leaving now, and we're never coming back."

Curt and Fern said nothing, stationed like guards at the Buckingham Palace of their living room.

As I left with my hand firmly gripped in Grandpa's, I felt a hollowed-out sorrow, knowing that his indignation and pride would prevent us from returning. But I equally felt a proud solidarity with my grandparents. My nascent class sensibility was activated and strengthened. I couldn't have known the tensions that might have simmered for years between my grandma and her daughter-in-law, finally erupting over a stained carpet. What I did know is that my grandmother had been cruelly insulted, that my grandfather had forcefully stood up for her, and that I was foursquare beside them, a knight of their antiquated, scuffed, and gouged round table.

My uncle and aunt would pass through this class-ascendant period in their lives and emerge as relaxed, generous, unpretentious hosts in a cozy, modest home on the shore of a small lake north of Seattle, unperturbed by grandchildren spilling Christmas drinks on the aging carpet. But Grandma and Grandpa were long gone by then.

My mother is not in that Christmas picture, still a years-long resident of Northern State Mental Hospital. But she is present, along with her older brother Curt, in the late 1930s yearbooks of Garfield High School, rival to my Franklin High. An urban girl, Gloria did not chop firewood and cook for lumberjacks like her mother, but she achieved something else that delighted, amazed, and impressed me: she became an excellent athlete, playing softball, basketball, and tennis. I have students who think that girls and women didn't play varsity sports before the 1970s. If they time-traveled back to Seattle in my era, they'd be right. Franklin High had thirteen varsity sports for boys, and only one for girls, swimming, for which they had to ride the bus downtown to the YWCA. Girls used the ancient, dingy, basement gym, while boys had a huge, new facility. Playing basketball, girls could dribble only twice and then pass the ball, always passing and shooting with two hands. My mother remembered having the same rules as boys back in the 1930s. As for softball, "Your mother," she told me, "could really hit the ball. And I was fast, I could catch anything in the outfield." The Garfield yearbooks from that era feature girls' varsity teams in a half-dozen sports.

So there, on Garfield's baseball diamond, my future football coach was whacking awe-inspiring home runs that attracted scouts for the Negro League, and my mother was driving in runs and robbing hitters. What on earth had happened to female sports after the war and until the 1970s, to the construction of girls' and women's identity in relation to athletics and, in the bigger picture, their physical abilities? Many women, including my mother driving a delivery cart at the Boeing aircraft plant, were laid off from their wartime jobs when the soldiers returned home—sent back to their domestic roles. Yet millions more women entered the American workforce, in what some economists have argued was one of the most important factors in America's economic boom and global preeminence. Male clerks, for instance, were replaced by female secretaries. Was the suppression of girls' and women's varsity athletics, and the revival of the Victorian rationale that females were too delicate and weak, a rearguard action and soothing fiction—along with the Betty Crocker ideal of the housewife and those nuclear family sitcoms—for the male psyche and the nation's gendered identity as roles were transforming? Betty Friedan's threshold critique *The Feminine Mystique* was not far in the future, and, beyond that, legislatively mandated equal funding for women's varsity sports in American universities. But for a couple of postwar decades, females would be confined to the antiquated basement gym in my high school, shooting basketballs with two hands.

Gloria was not only athletic. She was as beautiful in her high school yearbook photos as she was in the studio wedding portrait I had in my childhood bedroom next to my father's photographs in his army uniforms. And there was the snapshot I carried in my childhood wallets. I once embarrassed myself with that snapshot. I was in eighth grade and feeling inadequate around certain male friends who clearly had girlfriends, or at least boasted they did. I had one graciously unrequited crush on a girl named Jackie, seated next to me in the row of first clarinets in the band. Apart from that, not one date or kiss or anything remotely romantic in nearly two years of junior high school. Some of my friends flashed girls' photos, and a few of those girls, claimed the boys, were in other schools, other towns, met through church or clubs or family connections. I had a solution.

My mother's brunette hair cascaded luxuriantly over her shoulders. Later, as an adult, I heard friends exclaim that my mother had a Thirties' movie star's face, lips, and complexion. One morning at school, I told a couple of buddies that I had a girlfriend named Colleen, at another school, and showed them my mother's photo. I had concocted a plausible story about our involvement. One of my buddies believed me, the other was openly dubious. I blanked out the warning signal from the skeptic, and let my ego surf the wave of the other friend's admiration. But I must have felt some need for caution, for I didn't share my fantasy with anyone else until lunch, and then I picked a popular girl in my math class who was considered very trustworthy and kind. I showed her the photo and had barely begun my spiel when she stopped me.

"That's not your girlfriend," she said in a firm but not judgmental voice. "That's an old photo. I think it's your mother. I won't tell anyone. But you better not do this anymore."

She apparently kept her word, and my two buddies, in the camaraderie of adolescent longing and angst, quietly ignored my indiscretion. I put my mother's photo away in a drawer.

A Freudian psychiatrist might have been chuffed to have me on the couch. Or might have understood that there was no sexual dynamic there, only a brief melding of the normal adolescent need for peer approval and my yearning, not yet quenched in eighth grade, to have my mother in my life: not the debilitated mother with dowdy dresses and gray permed hair and smeared too-red lipstick in a mental hospital, but the smart, athletic, lovely, and radiantly joyful Gloria of my grandmother's and uncle's stories, and of the photographs. The Gloria who was still there when my father came back from the war, when she became pregnant with me. After I secured a copy of their marriage license, with their address in the Central District of Seattle, I stood in front of a modest stucco and wooden bungalow. Imagining them, happy at first, dancing behind the living room curtains. I keep this image firmly in my mind alongside their wedding photo propped on a bookshelf beside my desk and another photo of my athletic parents on a beach, Harvey on his back with his knees bent and arms raised, Gloria in a handstand with their fingers and smiles interlocked.

As I turned fourteen in early September and school resumed, I was largely oblivious to Grandma's gradually declining health. More accurately, I grew accustomed to the changes in our routine. I had to do more of the house cleaning. Grandma cooked less, and we relied more on canned, packaged, and frozen food. I can see Grandpa at the stove—stirring canned pork and beans with sliced wieners; frying steaks and chops, bologna and Spam—while I peeled and sliced potatoes, made Jell-O, and opened the Campbell soup cans. Sometimes, in spurts of thoughtful love, I made chicken soup or beef stew, and pineapple upside-down cake or apple pie, two of our favorite desserts. Again, my mother is absent from my retrovision, either back at Northern State Hospital or fallen into a mine shaft of memory.

My ninth-grade year was jam-packed and I was, as my grandparents sometimes complained, "always on the go" and "never at home." I hardly noticed that Grandma moved less and less often from her sofa, spent more time lying down than sitting up, drank much less bourbon, climbed up and down the stairs for the bathroom with ever greater difficulty.

One day in the spring of 1961, Grandma went to the hospital and was there for about two weeks. I have vague memories of visiting her, and of the strangeness of life without her constant presence in our home. On a Saturday morning, I woke at nine o'clock, panicked that I'd be late for baseball practice. In a few minutes I was downstairs with my ball glove and bat, ready to gobble a bowl of cereal and dash. I was surprised to see Grandpa still home, at the kitchen table looking somber, and not at work. He was wearing yesterday's wrinkled shirt.

"Where are you going?" he snapped, beyond cross.

"Baseball."

"No, you're not. Your grandma's dying."

"But I have an important practice."

"This is your last chance to see your grandma ever again."

His eyes on mine were like touching ice-cold steel on a winter's day.

"I can go right after practice."

"She might not be here by then."

"I promise."

His head pivoted away, his eyes now aimed out the window at the lake and the mountains beyond them and the cloud-dappled, powder-blue sky above.

"Suit yourself."

Grandma was lying in her hospital bed, smiling at me, looking impossibly frail and weak, though her face still had its normal rosy bloom. Someone must have applied her makeup. In her eyes, though, I could still see the grandma who cooked for loggers, planted flowers, praised my school grades and track trophies. I sat down beside her, and she asked me, as always, to tell me about my days.

I rarely needed much prompting and blathered on about Mr. Miller's algebra class, how he would draw *Peanuts* characters with balloons on the board, put a math problem in one balloon, and call on a student to answer in another. How DJ and I planned to run stride for stride in the city's cross-country championship and finish in a tie for first. About rehearsals for Thornton Wilder's *Happy Journey to Trenton and Camden*, in which I had the lead male role. Most of the play takes place during the automobile journey, with the father, mother, and children seated in chairs—the driver's and passenger seats—on a bare stage, bantering and reminiscing. I showed Grandma how we had to bounce, shake, and lurch with the movement of the car and as I shifted gears. Grandma laughed, suitably amused. But her laughter was harnessed, straining.

Grandpa came and went, silent, staying only for a few minutes each time, and spending most of his time pacing or sitting in the hallway.

At some point I ran out of things to say. Grandma lacked the energy to talk. It was so unlike me to sit still and do nothing for any length of time. I didn't even have a book. But I did sit there attentively. I finally realized that Grandma was not going to rise from her hospital bed any day now, come home and lounge on her sofa reading Agatha Christie and watching *Perry Mason*, sit at the piano and sing "That Old Black Magic" and "I'll Be Seeing You." Let alone resume weeding around the marigolds and canning peaches and visiting the cosmetics counter in the Bon Marché in her black dress and high heels.

"I'm afraid your grandma isn't doing very well," she said.

She was sinking into some invisible space inside her body and mind. Like a movie character who has stepped into quicksand, swallowed up to the hips and then waist, then only the head visible, and finally just an arm, hand, fingertips.

As she sank, Grandpa ceased to come into the room.

In a gasping voice, she suddenly asked for the stainless steel, kidney-shaped pan on her nightstand, motioned for me to place it beside her face, under her mouth. She turned her head toward it, vomiting blood. I somehow managed to catch it all in the pan. If there was the slenderest thread of belief that she might recover, at least enough to come home for a while, it was severed like a neck under a broadaxe. What did I do with the blood in that pan?

She was now too weak to recognize me, her mind in thrall to a dying body.

No doctor came by, not one nurse visited, nor an orderly. No one. I was left sitting beside Grandma's bed, as she lost awareness of my presence, as her vision stopped seeing the room, as her consciousness receded from this world. Her eyes were still open, but Grandma was not inside them anymore. For the first time in my conscious life, a person I loved and who loved me had withdrawn forever from my view, and would never apprehend me again, and be forever beyond my reach. For the second time in my life, a mother figure was vanishing from herself, going under, leaving a void above water, where I floated.

Grandma's eyes gradually rolled back in their sockets, waning slivers of old moons. Her breathing quickened, more shallow. Her skin grew sallow, yellowing, with startling speed. She lingered like that, and I thought of the trees her brothers and stepfather cut down. How, she'd told me, sometimes a great cedar or Douglas fir, when the saw had cut through, would stand there for several moments, pausing before its majestic toppling, its thunderous crash. Grandma paused for hours.

It was deepening dusk when Father Kappas appeared in the doorway. I have no idea how he came to be there. Rainier Maria Rilke's *Duino Elegies* are one of my secularly sacred texts. The first elegy begins, "Who, if I cried, would hear me among the angelic / orders?" I don't remember if I had wept visibly during those hours, but my inner cry was somehow heard. And Father Kappas, my earthly angel, gently told me that I had done enough, that I should convince my grandfather to take me home now, where we should stay and wait for the inevitable. Grandma was now, he said, in the best possible hands. He soon left.

I found Grandpa standing at the end of the hallway, looking out a window at the charcoal sky smudging the downtown buildings, at windows being lit with incandescent candles. I stood close behind him.

"Father Kappas said we should go home now."

I expected him to object to being ordered about by my priest, whom he saw as a rival for my affection.

"I didn't do right by your grandma," was all he said.

I waited, and waited, until he turned slowly around, not seeing me, his eyes swollen with pain. Grandpa had always stood and walked straight. Now, I followed his hunched form to the elevator.

I fell soundly asleep on the living room couch, while Grandpa lay on the dining room sofa, which had been their version of a love seat in happier times together, and Grandma's final bed at home.

The phone woke me at two a.m. Then Grandpa standing over me.

"Your grandma has passed away."

There were no other words, and I left him downstairs, climbed into my side of the bed that had once been theirs, and quickly fell asleep, again. Aileen, my grandma, was dead, from cirrhosis of the liver. She was sixty-three.

I have never had any memory of her funeral. I do not know where she is buried. Although one partner after another urged me to track down her cemetery and visit her grave, I have never done so. My facile excuse had long been that I was content with, and preferred, what I could imagine. The unadorned truth is that I was avoiding an experience that would engulf me in forlorn grief.

I also have no memories of my mother during my grandmother's terminal decline and the weeks after her death, though she was very much present in our home. My adolescent mind had pushed her so far into the wings that she doesn't even make a fleeting appearance on stage for an added touch of pathos.

Four years after my grandmother's death, three years after my mother returned home permanently from Northern State Hospital, and one year after I graduated from high school and moved out of my childhood house, I came home one evening for one reason or another and found Harry and Gloria naked together on the dining room sofa. That is one of the last images I have of my mother from my adolescence, before I left Seattle for good. It repelled me back then, and troubled and saddened me for many years after. Now, though there is still pathos, I can envision them, lying there, with empathy and compassion. Not quite with the glow of gazing fondly on lovers, but with a warmth that pleasantly surprises me. They were, after all, not related by blood, but by hardship. My mother had suffered much misfortune and loss, and my grandfather had endured more than his share of heartache and disappointment. Their son—for I was his son too—had not embraced his mother upon her final return. I had not welcomed her into my life and shared mine with her, and had withdrawn increasingly from both of them since Grandma's death, until I used home as "a place to eat and sleep and change his clothes," as Harry said. I had moved out at the earliest opportunity, visited infrequently, then left town, the state, and finally the country. But long before I left the country, they had found each other, and for that I am grateful.

In the early 1980s, when Gloria was living in the Lynnwood Arms Retirement Center in a suburb north of Seattle, she informed me during our Sunday phone call that Mr. Hall had asked her to marry him. To be precise, US Air Force Major Hall, retired. A widower with an excellent pension, he had one of the large private rooms at Lynnwood Arms, appointed with upscale furniture-store elegance. He lacked the use of his legs and needed a wheelchair. A consummate gentleman in his early seventies, with a career officer's correct courtesy and a southern Midwest accent—think Kansas or Oklahoma—Mr. Hall was eminently likable. I'd met him during several visits as one of Gloria's friends for whom she did shopping and laundry, and who reimbursed her rather well. I'd also seen how graciously and respectfully he treated her. Mr. Hall seemed to like me, though I wondered what he thought about me moving to Canada during the Vietnam War. However, his mind had lost a fair bit of its sharpness, and I suspected he was in Lynnwood for his dwindling faculties as well as his physical handicap. Thus, he didn't seem to put one and one together when it came to my anti-war conduct.

"And you said yes, Mom, right?" I asked excitedly, assuming she had.

This was beautiful news. She had this later-in-life (she wasn't yet sixty) chance for a second husband and marriage, with a man she was quite fond of, and who admired and cared about her. She had someone she loved to look after, as the kind of woman and housewife she had learned in her era to be, and he seemed duly grateful. This was hardly the stuff of women's movement discourse in the early 1980s, but for my mother this was, I thought, empowerment and validation, especially with a husband who was physically disabled. My mother might be waiting on him, but that was a form of agency for her. A rigidly limited feminist template would exclude countless women, including my mother. She would have to give up her room, I supposed, but, hey, she'd had roommates, none of her choosing, since she was shipped to Northern State Hospital in 1948, apart from her decade in my childhood home.

Not to mention that this "roommate" had money. (It did, briefly and selfishly, occur to me that I wouldn't have to send her as much.)

Moreover, Gloria would likely outlive him and she would likely have a nice inheritance, which would at last give her the money she'd lacked for thirty-plus years.

All this flashed through my mind in the few seconds between my question and her reply:

"Oh, now, Richard. I wouldn't want to marry him."

"Why not?" Oh my God, why the hell not?

"Mr. Hall is a very nice man, and his offer is very kind. He even gave me a beautiful diamond ring, I think it cost a lot of money, but I gave it back. He was very sad."

"Mother. Listen to me. Why not?"

"Oh, sonny boy, your mother hasn't been married for a long time. I'd have to move into his room, and give up mine. I wouldn't want to do that."

"Maybe you could stay in your room too?"

"No. Your mother's too old to change her ways. I like my independence."

My mother was way ahead of me when it came to women's liberation. Female roommates were one thing, a legally attached male another.

"Besides," she said. "I was married to Harvey. He was my husband. He's your father."

Mr. Hall, she then told me, wanted her to stop doing laundry and shopping for other people after they were married, and that was unacceptable. Maybe she had only half a room, but it was her half, indisputably. She had little money, but it was all hers. She could not avoid having other people sometimes tell her what to do or not do, but she would not risk losing the freedom she did have to a husband. She had been, in a severely circumscribed way, her own person for a long time and would not throw that out the window for a ring, fancy room, and inheritance. I also wondered if the attraction to Mr. Hall, an air force officer, and the refusal to marry him, was connected to her relationship with her military hero father.

As well, she was Mrs. Gloria Lemm and did not want to exchange that for Mrs. Gloria Hall. She was not going to detach herself from her first and only and forever husband. She still loved Harvey and would tell me so until her final days. I suspect that his death so soon after their separation and divorce allowed her to maintain the bond in a way she might not have if he'd gone on living, with a new wife, with more children.

My mother and Mr. Hall parted ways immediately after her refusal, and I saw no more of him. There were no other marriage proposals the rest of her life and no friendships with men that suggested a liaison.

Gloria cheerfully continued to shop and do laundry for her Lynnwood Arms friends. One she especially cared for was another veteran, Ron, a large African-American and a paraplegic in an electric cart. He had been severely wounded in Vietnam, and more than his legs had been damaged. He never talked and seemed to comprehend very little. Yet he often smiled warmly and gratefully at Gloria, and I felt his affection for me. We three would sit in the dining room, which doubled as the games and TV room, and watch a Mariners baseball or Seahawks football game. I believed that Ron sensed the games at a deep level, and imagined he had once been a robust athlete. Three amigos on a Sunday afternoon: the noble warrior, a catastrophic casualty of dutiful service to his country; the draft dodger, no longer constrained by exile up north, able to visit his native land, its tamed west, and thank his lucky stars; the girl of my father's prewar and overseas dreams, a casualty of a magician's trick. A trickster's myth: sawing the nuclear family in half.

4

The Noble Warrior

My first image of my father is of him leaning over my crib and looking down. I say "image" because I was no more than nine months old, and I am not someone who claims to have infant memories. Yet this picture has the vividness and emotional resonance of a genuine memory. I can see him walking from the front door, down a dimly lit, wood-paneled hallway in the tenement apartment, my first home. Perhaps my grandmother told me that my father had visited, bent over the crib, and gazed at the son he'd left behind when he and my mother divorced. His face is lambent with tenderness and contentment, and without any shadow of whatever sorrow or regret he might feel. As if he is blessing me, ever so briefly, with his love. My habit of wishful thinking was already in evidence.

In my childhood bedroom, I had two framed studio photographs of my uniformed father. In the earlier one, taken in Wyoming in 1943 before he went overseas, he is youthfully angelic and dreamboat handsome, with a soft half-smile. The studio has given his face, underneath his tilted khaki hat cap, a creamy, rosy, ethereal sweetness. His eyes gaze directly, intimately immediate, into mine. In the later photo, he wears, at a jaunty angle, the cap of the US Airborne Paratrooper Enlisted Reconnaissance. His head is angled coyly down, as if he is waiting for some pretty woman to place her hand on his cheek. He sports a pencil-thin mustache—think Errol Flynn and David Niven. His smile is still gentle but more knowing.

The hues are a range of light browns and grays, making him more corporeal, belonging to the earthly world with its perils outside the frame. I know he is staring with devotion at my mother, for the inscription in his stylish handwriting is "Merry Xmas to my darling wife. Harvey." But, in my childhood, I needed to believe his loving gaze was meant for me.

Aileen had created a history for me of my father, and the first part, the gloriously honorable part, created the movie reels in my head.

In one reel, Harvey Matthew Lemm, a paratrooper in the US Army, has dropped into the front lines of Normandy, into ferocious enemy fire, joining comrades who have leaped from amphibious vessels and stormed ashore. Flinging himself onto the sand, under the Nazi barrage, my father snakes forward on his belly the way we did in our backyards, through imaginary barbed wire, lifting up now and then to fire at our enemy.

In another reel, having survived D-Day, he has landed in the North African desert and is chasing the tank legions of Rommel, the Desert Fox. In one scene, a movie still, he stands on the desert sands at night. This image was shaped by a poem, clipped from a newspaper, which he had taped to the back of his sergeant's photograph:

All day and all night I long for you.
The stars of the desert night
call out from my heart to you.

A solitary soldier, looking up at the heavens, loving and pining for his wife, perhaps the way I longed for my mother and certainly for my father.

Later, in another reel, he descends through sleet and artillery flak into the mountains of Italy, an epic and decisive battle, battling stubborn Axis resistance in the last year of the war. At the end of the movie, he comes back, alive, unscathed, a decorated American warrior par excellence.

How thrilling these imagined scenes were for a boy who was asked by his friends what happened to his father, and who lobbed dirt-clod grenades from foxhole flowerbeds at whoever's turn it was to play the Germans. With my Bowie knife strapped to my belt and my cap-guns, I could live up to my father's heroics. And when I had to be German, I knew to keep my head down, move stealthily, be extra smart, because Harvey Lemm, the Canadian-born, invincible Yank with the deadly aim, was waiting behind a neighbor's hedge.

I could see my father descending from a wintry sky in his parachute, into frosted trees on a snowy mountainside. I had won my first writing prize—in my high school's Memorial Day essay contest —by describing my father's brave and tragic death in the Italian Alps, after his valiant survival in Normandy. My writing was so passionately persuasive that no one questioned how I could be born two years after his death. I was learning the art of storytelling from a master, my grandmother.

It never occurred to me to ask Aileen the hard questions: for instance, *did* American troops jump from planes in pursuit of Rommel? I devoured articles in my *World Book Encyclopedia*, but I wasn't yet a researcher, not the kind of kid to search for information on paratroopers at Normandy. More than that, I needed those images, those myths of my father. Perhaps my grandmother did too, whatever else she felt about the son-in-law who had left her pregnant daughter and was about to marry another woman. Aileen had, I am sure, moved on, as had all the adults around me, far beyond the gargantuan war that had consumed so much of their lives so recently. Looking back, I have wondered about and marveled at how they were able to let the reality of war slip into the distance and fade into the mythic constructions of *Victory at Sea*, of John Wayne and Cary Grant war movies.

Of course, I have gained some understanding of how and why humans suppress, romanticize, compartmentalize, and transcend such extended apprehension and trauma, just as I have eavesdropped on the lingering, subterranean, overt, and institutionalized resentments that flare again into vicious hatred and slaughter. Still, when I was ten years old and enchanting myself with those images of my father, the war was a mere eleven years in the past. I was born one year after the end of the war in the Pacific, but by the time I was five, so much distance had grown between the war and the favored life we and our neighbors were living. Fitting then, that my father should have been standing in the desert, a yearning and more handsome Bogart outside Casablanca.

"Your father was there, all right," said Uncle Curt. "But he was in the third wave on D-Day. The Allies weren't expecting the invasion to be so successful, and your father was among those who were expected to be drawn into fierce fighting, back-ups to the back-ups, hopefully subduing the last resistance. Instead, he was probably riding around in a Jeep throwing chocolate bars and cigarettes to the French. As for North Africa, I'm not sure what he was doing there. But Rommel was already done for, and your father didn't see any action. He was in Italy too, but just for the mop-up, handling prisoners, that sort of thing. He led a charmed life in the war."

My father, the Camel-and-Mars-Bar-bearing liberator. Mop-up man. Perhaps all he was doing in the desert, after all, was staring up at the stars and missing my mother. This new image of my father tossing candy from a Jeep blended with a minor tribute my grandmother tossed my way when we were making root beer floats together. She was always careful to add ice cream and root beer slowly, in small, alternating portions. "This is how your father did it. He made the best root beer floats." What do we remember most fondly about our departed parents? My father, a Good Humor man.

But I later learned he was doing more in North Africa than gazing at the heavens. He was posted with the Office of Strategic Services (OSS), an American intelligence agency during World War II that coordinated espionage activity. My father the spy.

I wanted to be my warrior father's son, as I crawled on my belly through my neighbors' yards with my plastic rifle and GI helmet. Maybe I was, in a byzantine way, my father's son after all. He had gone to war, played his part in the destruction of the enemy and defense of his country and allies. But he had avoided those circumstances of immediate and overwhelming danger where he might have more readily killed or been killed. That was not his choice, but it was his outcome, the same outcome I would painstakingly choose as a later overseas American war intensified.

At Uncle Curt's funeral in 1991, I waited in the funeral home lobby until almost all the guests were seated for the service. A tall, older gentleman with a Robert de Niro face entered, saw me, looked startled, and quickly approached.

"Are you Gloria's son?" he said with exceptional tenderness.

Now it was my turn to be amazed.

"Yes, how did you know?"

There followed, quickly, a remarkable explanation. Victor Trattorini was close friends with my father in high school, and they were among four school buddies who enlisted in the US Army together and served together in Italy. In high school, Victor was enamored of my mother.

"She was the girl for me. I would have gladly married her. But her heart was set on Harvey. And I knew to step back and leave the way clear for my pal, for the two lovebirds. She was always sweet and kind to me. I was almost as happy as they were at their wedding. After the war, I was single, they were married and we lost track of each other. By the time I heard about Harvey's death, too much time had passed."

He paused, and I wondered what regrets might have now resurfaced.

"I didn't try to contact Gloria. And not long after that, I met my wife." He paused again.

"I saw Curt's obituary in the paper, and I came on the chance Gloria would be here and I could pay my respects. I heard they'd had a son, and the moment I walked in and saw you, I knew you were Harvey and Gloria's."

During our very brief conversation after the funeral, he gave me his business card and said that we should get together for a drink at his favorite bar when I returned to Seattle. His treat. Although I visited Seattle once or twice a year after that, I never contacted Victor. I carried his card in my wallet for a long time, then stored it nearby on my desk. Something kept me from meeting him. I still don't exactly know why I was so reluctant—part of me did want to hear everything he had to tell me—and why, year after year, I refrained from arranging a meeting.

Yet my avoidance of Victor was an evasion of a much greater magnitude. I don't think it was reluctance to have my father-myth further altered by factual information, by another person's memories. Rather, it was yet another shying away from what would have been an intense experience, with ongoing reverberations in my psyche. For years I thought, This visit to Seattle, I'll contact Victor. And now, it's too late.

I knew precious little of my paternal ancestry. Based on memory shards of what Aileen had told me, I'd convinced myself by age eighteen that my father, an only child, was born in Montreal. Later, when I asked my mother, she'd say, "Oh, I can't remember, just that he was born in Canada. But you may be right, they spoke French there." His parents, I'd been told, were German-Americans from

Minnesota who, as I believed, moved to Montreal at some point after 1900 for some inscrutable reason, going against the flow of the Quebec diaspora: over a million emigrants, mostly francophones, including the family of Jack Kerouac, moving south and west between 1840 and the 1930s. I knew that my father and his parents moved to Seattle in the mid-1930s, again the motivation unknown.

In middle-age, I met a Dutch Indonesian brewmaster and hop broker living in England. Sitting next to me on an airplane, he introduced himself as Gerard Lemmens and informed me that he was chief assistant to the world's foremost Lemm clan genealogist, Ruud J. Lem. They were putting the finishing touches on Ruud's masterwork, *Genealogica Lemniana*. Gerard was thrilled to learn that I existed, since my father's death certificate states that he died unmarried and without children.

Ruud later sent me a photograph, circa 1898, of my grandfather, Mathias Lemm, the only visual evidence I have of his existence. Mathias poses dashingly, mustachioed, in the uniform of the 13th Minnesota Infantry Regiment, his handsome pistols drawn and pointed forward and skyward, as if he is leading his swashbuckling comrades into the fray or braced for an enemy charge. He looks more like a cavalryman in old westerns than an infantryman in the Great War that was lurking not far around the twentieth century's corner: his pants tucked into jaunty knee-high boots, fringed scarf around his neck, brimmed hat tilted backward raffishly.

Mathias was one of thousands of American men who answered the call to enlist, to travel over the Great Plains and through the Rockies and across the Pacific Ocean to fight the allegedly cruel Spaniards in the Philippines. He would help vanquish the lingering remnants of the decadent, barbarous Spanish empire and its threat to America's democratic, liberty-loving ideals. Matthias and his fellow soldiers had been rallied to the cause by the purported

Spanish sinking of the battleship USS *Maine* near Cuba, as trumpeted histrionically by Randolph Hearst's and Joseph Pulitzer's newspapers and opportunistic, jingoistic members of Congress. Not to mention specious accounts of alleged Spanish brutalization of Cuban laborers and the sexual humiliation and murder of Cuban women and children. The Spanish imperium was on its knees, collapsing, and the death blows were about to be dealt by America at Santiago de Cuba and halfway around the world in Manila. Enter Mathias Lemm, German-American slayer of evil empires, liberator of oppressed peoples, warrior crusading for American glory.

My grandfather was the son of a German immigrant, Jacob Francis Lemm, who was born in Garzweiler, Rhine Province, Germany, in 1838 and migrated to America, initially to Ohio, in the early 1850s with his parents and his seven siblings.

My great-grandfather and his family were swept to America on one of the huge, continuous waves of German immigration, with over seven million arriving in the United States between 1820 and 1920, nearly one million during the 1850s alone. During this decade, America was afflicted by anti-immigrant racism often referred to as the "Know Nothing" movement. The Irish were the first targets of this fusillade of nativism, and the Germans swelled the resented immigrant ranks. German emigration was propelled by famine in their homelands, along with feudal chaos, revolutionary uprisings, and widespread violence and hardship. And the radiant promise of America. The Civil War soon darkened that promise, yet was an ironic boon for German and Irish immigrants, as tribal loathing shifted to geographic enemies, and as German- and Irish-Americans became Union Army heroes.

In Jacob's obituary of January 19, 1913, I read that "During the Civil War, he served in Company 'G' of the 9th Minnesota Volunteer Regiment." Irish immigrant soldiers were noted for their fierce fighting and flamboyant bravado on behalf of the Northern cause, and this aided their greater acceptance into American society after the war. German-Americans fought no less effectively and bravely, but without the reputed flair of the Irish. Let the stereotypes reign: stolid, methodical Germans and dramatic, audacious Irish.

Another of my great-grandfather's obituaries briefly notes that Jacob "probably shook Lincoln's hand after the Gettysburg Address." There were, indeed, German-American soldiers at the Battle of Gettysburg. That "probably" reference would satisfy no reputable historian or biographer, but for an American-Canadian conscientious objector with profoundly ambivalent attachments to cherry-picked violent elements of my American heritage, the thought of my great-grandfather fighting at Gettysburg (I am, after all, a Northerner) and shaking Lincoln's hand after the Great Speech is too intoxicating to hold at a scholarly arm's length.

That my great-grandfather was a Civil War veteran adds to my have-my-cake-and-eat-it-too identity (some might call it hypocritical) as an American war resister proudly descended from American warriors. Jacob fought in a "just war"—if there is such a beast—to end slavery and save the Union. This also offers a stronger connection between my grandfather Mathias' enlistment in a Minnesota regiment for the Spanish–American War and his generation living in the Civil War shadow of their fathers' generation.

The widespread mood of men who enlisted to fight the Spanish in 1898 was enthusiastic, even exuberant. At last, thirty-three years after the Civil War, a monumental crisis with momentous events— or so it was stridently transmitted and passionately received—would enfold these soldiers in the robes of mythic patriotism and place them on pedestals in the national narrative and history books.

I will never know whether Mathias Lemm, listed as "Farmer" in the field and staff rosters, and as Private "Math" Lemm in Company

M, 2nd Battalion of the 13th Minnesota Regiment, suffered or prospered during the 1893 Depression, the most severe economic depression in American history up to that time. I do not know if he was empowered and inspired by that *fin de siècle* surge of patriotism, or if he felt any need to carve his own niche into the wall of American heroism, as his father Jacob had during the Civil War. I cannot know if he shared in the jingoistic hatred of Spaniards, or the pride in America's first overseas imperialistic venture. I can imagine that Mathias, along with many fellow soldiers, welcomed this opportunity to see the world beyond his small enclave, to travel across western America and, like his father and grandparents, sail across an ocean and immerse himself in a new land.

Mathias' and his comrades' willingness to place themselves in harm's way was also enabled by widespread American antipathy toward Spain and its colonial empire. Americans in the mid-1890s no longer had an enemy threat in its Indigenous population. The "manifest destiny" of continental conquest and expansion was accomplished, and the enterprise of building an industrial and commercial nation on a grand scale was in full swing, not without daunting socio-economic conflicts and social unrest, but peaceful in terms of armed conflict. Indians defeated, gunslingers tamed. Cue the Spaniards. America had, decades before, wrested control of Texas and the southwest from Spanish Mexico, but the villains were hanging around in Cuba, and clung to an outpost in the Philippines that whetted a fledgling American appetite for imperial assertion and swagger. There had been numerous imperial incursions into Latin America, but none across a great ocean.

What I and my schoolmates knew of the Spanish–American War was confined to the swashbuckling deeds in Cuba of Teddy Roosevelt and his "Rough Riders." Roosevelt, from a wealthy Ivy League background, resigned as Assistant Secretary of the Navy to volunteer with the First United States Volunteer Cavalry Regiment.

Most of the regiment were Southwesterners, many of them cowboys, hunters, and prospectors. The tales of cowboys riding to the rescue of Cubans oppressed by wicked Spaniards were fodder for yellow journalism and mesmerized the American public. And schoolboys a half-century later.

The mythic moment we inherited was the Battle of San Juan Hill, east of the Spanish capital of Santiago de Cuba. This was the most brutal and famous battle of the Cuban war, a prelude to the capture of Santiago de Cuba and the Spanish capitulation in the Caribbean. It was also the foremost victory for the Rough Riders, according to newspapers and Roosevelt himself, who used his role to help catapult himself into Great American Hero status and toward the American presidency.

It was Roosevelt, the Rough Riders, and the Battle of San Juan Hill that leaped to mind when I first saw the photograph of Mathias Lemm. Ignoring the inscription at the bottom of the page—"Insignia Left Breast—Co-M 13th Minn-Infantry"—I fixed on the inscription beside the photo—"Uniform of Spanish–American War." He so looked like a cavalry trooper that I ridiculously began to tell people that "my grandfather may have been at the Battle of San Juan Hill." When I later visited Santiago de Cuba, I climbed San Juan Hill, imagined my grandfather charging up on his horse, and had a deliciously mawkish moment at the hilltop monument. Grandpa Lemm might have stood here, near Teddy Roosevelt, a boyhood icon, and an adult hero for his progressive economic and political policies, promotion of conservation as a naturalist and outdoorsman, and friendship with conservationist John Muir, namesake of my elementary school. I had not outgrown the need to identify with my native land's mythology. I could interrogate and deconstruct the mythology of the Alamo, the "Indian Wars," Davy Crockett, and the fur trade.

But I was silly putty—my scholarly training and political morality AWOL—when it came to envisioning a grandparent present at a fabled moment in American history.

Meanwhile, back in Luxemburg County, Minnesota, men were volunteering for a regiment bound for an entirely different campaign across a different ocean. There would be no charismatic leader with an ambitiously brilliant gift for the mythic moment. There were no cowboys. There were millers, quarrymen, broom-makers, bartenders, wagon-makers and teamsters, teachers and students, barbers, bakers, clerks, train conductors, and farmers such as Mathias Lemm.

Although the Pacific and Philippines campaign was secondary, it too was important geopolitically. Many of the American business, political, and military elite believed that the United States must secure territorial bases in the Pacific and footholds in East Asia in order to compete with the European powers, and with the newly expansionist Japan, for markets and geopolitical advantage in China and other Asian regions.

The United States declared war against Spain on April 25, 1898, and that day the Secretary of War issued orders to state governors to raise 125,000 volunteers. Although there was substantial opposition to war on economic, political, ideological, strategic, and/or moral grounds—to expansionist and imperialistic policies, and to foreign military engagements—the majority of Americans supported the war at its onset, much as most Americans did with the Vietnam War in the mid-1960s and in 2005–2006 when troops headed to Iraq. And, as with the Vietnam and Iraq Wars, American opinion and sentiment would shift toward majority disapproval, and more swiftly than in our era.

In 1898, however, most Americans believed that the American Expeditionary Forces were not being sent forth as imperialistic agents of expansion and annexation. Rather, they were charged with the liberation of long-suffering people from the brutal yoke of a vile empire. If I was way off base in seeing Grandpa Lemm at the Battle of San Juan Heights, it was not far-fetched to imagine Mathias seeing himself—son of migrants from tyranny and peril in Germany, and son of a Union Army Civil War veteran—as an inheritor of the mantle of liberator, defender of the persecuted, heroic adversary of despots. An article in the *Minneapolis Tribune* of April 27, 1898, was entitled "Valiant Sons of Valiant Fathers," evidence of the vivid influence of the Civil War three decades later.

Sixty-eight years before I arrived in San Francisco to attend university, Grandpa Lemm and the 13th Minnesota Regiment paused there for several more weeks of training, stationed at Camp Merritt near Golden Gate Park. Whereas I would revel at Grateful Dead concerts and an Allen Ginsberg poetry reading in the luxuriant and fabled park, the soldiers of the 13th languished on the treeless grounds of a former race track, coated in sand blown by ocean winds, shrouded in damp fog, and with disreputable saloons and brothels on nearby streets. On June 25, they boarded the passenger steamer *City of Para*, designed for tropical climate voyages, and Mathias Lemm watched the coastline of America vanish on the horizon.

Unless a diary or packet of letters is discovered in somebody's attic, I'll never know what Mathias Lemm thought and felt about his military and war experience, or the details of his behavior. I know from the Official List of Engagements that the 13th Minnesota Voluntary Infantry "participated in" thirty-six battles, and that Mathias' company was involved in twenty-four engagements. He is not listed among the wounded and did not die of smallpox or dysentery, as did two of his comrades. No doubt he had a less than superlative time with the heavy rains and mud, swamps and insects, and tropical heat.

He would have celebrated when, early in the campaign, the

American forces captured Manila with a token battle and the Spanish surrendered. He might have been dismayed when the Filipino rebel forces, excluded by the Americans from the capture of Manila, attacked the American "liberators," and the righteous war mutated into an ugly, confounding fight with local insurgents. The simplifications of ideological idealism and the strategic assumptions of geopolitical opportunism swiftly gave way to the complex reality on the ground. Foreshadowing later military adventures, facile American victories morphed into a military mess and domestic political crisis. The credibility of my grandfather's and America's supposedly noble actions was quickly tainted and subverted by the specter of Americans and Filipinos shooting at each other and, back home, by the intensified clash of opinions about the war and America's strategic role there and elsewhere beyond its shores. At one end of the spectrum were the expansionists who wanted to annex the Philippines. At the other end, the isolationists. A classic American divide.

As I revisited, in light of Grandpa Lemm's involvement, the history of a largely forgotten war, I considered possible parallels with men of my era enlisting or drafted for Vietnam, and with the ethos of America in the 1960s. For sure, there was patriotic eagerness among many Vietnam-bound Americans, and some young men of my generation, raised as we were in the epic afterglow of World War II and on legends of "How the West Was Won," and permeated by a multimedia flood of tales of valiant glory from Ben-Hur to Wyatt Earp to D-Day to Flash Gordon, saw themselves bound for warrior glory. But the rest of us draft-age men had abandoned our toy six-guns and bazookas for guitars and typewriters, slide rules and stock market reports, power saws and drills, test tubes and semi-conductors, and other implements of peace-time prosperity.

In late 1963, by which time President Kennedy had increased

United States military personnel in Vietnam to sixteen thousand from the nine hundred when he took office, America was still coasting smoothly and contentedly on the road paved by the spectacular juggernaut of material abundance, comfort, and entertainment; on America's technological "progress"; and on its economic and military hegemony on a global scale. The Korean War stalemate was a serious pothole, though quickly paved over, and the intensification of the Cold War and arms race put up road signs—Dangerous Curves Ahead, Watch for Falling Bombs. But even the Cold War had an upside, for some, in the profits, wages, and tax revenues from what President Eisenhower had worriedly labeled "the military-industrial complex." The "fight against Communism" in defense of "the free world" and capitalism also helped keep Americans humming in patriotic harmony, with periodic delicious frissons of war fervor, as they cruised along the highway of American exceptionalism. The Cold War, with its emphasis upon the failures and horrors of communism, drew upon the foundational myths and strengthened the national narrative of liberty and endless opportunity. There was major shifting underground in the tectonic plates of American society, and minor tremors could be felt and warnings were issued, but the earthquakes were in the near future.

As for the men of the Minnesota 13th, Mathias presumably among them, they were treated to numerous banquets and parades with large cheering crowds in their honor shortly after their return. But there were also anti-war and isolationist recriminations, sometimes directed against veterans. Soon, the Filipino–American War vanished from the newspapers and faded from American consciousness. But Mattias Lemm's generation of veterans had won their laurels, and they could resume their civilian lives with some measure of the prestige and self-esteem enjoyed by Civil War veterans. As well, even if the Filipino–American War had lost its luster and fueled a fierce debate, the Philippine archipelago would become a long-lasting base of American influence.

Making the 1890s warmongers seem prophetic, the violent collision between previously isolationist America and imperialistic Japan began at Pearl Harbour, and my Uncle Curt found himself with the Navy Seabees building bases on Pacific islands. The Spanish-American war helped lay the groundwork for the spread of American power and economic interest far beyond the Western Hemisphere and foreshadowed a later conflict that would propel Mathias' grandson to Canada, my father's native land, in a full circle.

Occasionally, when I talked back to my grandparents or had dashed off for the baseball diamond or a neighborhood game of Monopoly without first taking out the garbage or dusting the furniture as I had cross-my-heart-and-hope-to-die promised to do, I would be confronted with the menace of military school.

"If your real grandfather was alive," Grandma or Grandpa would say, "you'd be sent to military school. You wouldn't get away there with back-talk or skipping your chores or making sour faces."

The first few times this threat was uttered, I'm sure my face snapped smartly to contrite attention, stiffened by a surge of fear. This apprehension was magnified when I remembered Grandpa's everlasting disappointment that he hadn't gone to war: "I was too young for the first war, too old for the second," he would lament, then ask, "Do you know how that felt?" What if he decided, in time-honored parenting fashion, to use me vicariously to satisfy his longing, to live out his thwarted dream? What if Grandma wanted me to morph into a junior version of her ex-husband hero? The last thing I wanted was for my blissful world of backyard war games, Marvel Comics, and battle movies to be ruined by the nightmare realm of military school.

As much as I loved my toy weapons and the gunslingers and bomber pilots on the TV screen, my mental images of military school were of fun-destroying discipline and intolerable punishment. Eventually, as I concluded this was an idle threat, my grandparents' harmless way of venting frustration, my expression flirted dangerously with complacent derision.

When military school ceased to be mentioned, I was comfortably left with Grandpa Alexander, clearly a war hero to Aileen and Harry, my mother, Uncle Curt, and yours truly. I don't know what medals or other accolades he might have won, where he served, what battles or campaigns he was part of. Several years ago, I applied to the US government for my father's and both my grandfathers' military records. I was informed that a major fire had destroyed tens of thousands of records, among them those I sought. Grandpa Alexander's obituaries in Seattle newspapers briefly mention his military service, but not his units, providing no link to relevant histories. Genealogy and military websites have come up blank. A person more needful of the facts, a more determined researcher, might fill in the biographical blanks. I have settled on the fragmentary images implanted by Aileen and my mother, and by a photograph of Grandpa Raymond Alexander standing, with a comrade, beside a First World War biplane.

Raymond leans jauntily, one hand on the fuselage behind the propellor. He wears an aviator's cap, a leather jacket, and woolen pants bulging out at the sides, like jodhpurs. When the *Peanuts* comic strip appeared, with Snoopy as pilot battling the Red Baron, my grandmother told me that Grandpa Alexander had flown as co-pilot with the legendary ace Eddie Rickenbacker and that they'd shot down the Red Baron. One day at school, when someone mentioned *Peanuts* and Snoopy during class, I repeated my grandmother's words. I was instantly awash in my classmates' awe and envy. For one brief moment. Then the teacher said, "No he didn't," and gave the class the facts, which did not include any reference to my grandfather. I shrank with embarrassment and my classmates' derision.

Perhaps Raymond did fly on a mission or two with Rickenbacker. Or maybe my grandmother's storytelling enthusiasm and nostalgia had embellished and altered her memory to suit her need, and her grandson's, for potent mythology. His absence from website lists of American aviators in the First World War urges doubt. Yet there is that photograph, and Aileen's, Harry's, and Uncle Curt's— Raymond's son's—confirmation that he did fly in those early warplanes over the battlefields of the Western Front. I also saw hard evidence, in Curt's family records, of Raymond's service, and death, as an Army Air Corps commander and pilot during World War II.

Grandma related how Grandpa Alexander, as biplane co-pilot and bombardier, would lean out the open cockpit and drop bombs by hand on the Germans. Early on, this was, indeed, the method, but bomb racks with release wires were later installed. As a child, my visual perspective was from my grandfather's heroic vantage aloft, looking down at bombs falling on our diabolical enemy, the Huns. I never envisioned the bombs exploding, my sight line following his plane as it veered and climbed away. Years later, exposed to other tales, my perspective shifted to the ground, looking up at a plane buzzing low overhead, the barely visible iron wombs about to give gory birth to people fleeing, homes flattened, bodies writhing, burst open, twisted and motionless on the pummeled earth.

In elementary school, during the Korean War, one of my favorite playground games was "fighter pilot." We'd take turns being American F1 jets and Russian MIGs, swooping toward each other, firing rockets and machine guns, and dive-bomb girls and other boys, our afterburners roaring. When asked what I wanted to be when I grew up, I said, "a fighter pilot." In what seems like another life, as the Vietnam War burst into my consciousness, I developed a moral abhorrence of the fighter-bomber flyboys blasting rice paddies and villages, and even more, a loathing for B-52 pilots dropping automated death from lofty altitudes. They weren't the aerial combat "aces" I'd worshipped as a kid. Yet how much difference was there between a Vietnam fighter pilot such as Senator John McCain and Grandpa Alexander, who was still above the fray, not in the trenches, a newfangled god in his winged chariot.

I know nothing of Raymond before he became an aviator, except for my grandmother's remark that they were newly married and he was working in her mother's and stepfather's logging camp. She'd said that her parents didn't want him to join the military. America entered the war quite belatedly, in the view of allies, and its participation in the Old World's self-destructive follies was a matter of intense domestic and national debate, especially on the far-removed coast of western America. But my grandmother never told me that she objected. Maybe I've forgotten, my need for an aviator hero burying any expressions of her discontent or anxiety. Or maybe her own need for glowing, proud memories suppressed whatever worry and disapproval she may have felt.

After the war, Raymond returned to civilian life, to the logging camp. I have a photo that includes him posing with other lumberjacks. Around 1923, he and Aileen moved to Seattle. As World War II erupted in Europe and the American government commenced unofficial war preparations, he re-entered the service, in the Army Air Corps, as a higher-ranking officer based in Washington State, test-flying and helping otherwise with the development of new planes. In 1943, he and Aileen divorced, and he remarried, and Aileen wed Harry. In 1948, on a test flight, Raymond's plane went down off Vancouver Island, the plane, crew, and Grandpa Alexander vanishing into the Pacific Ocean.

I lost a golden opportunity to know more when Harry died, when I was twenty-three and living in Vancouver. Uncle Curt, cleaning out the basement of my childhood home where so many old possessions were stored, told me there were boxes full of uniforms, medals, photographs, letters. He offered to bring any or all of these boxes to Canada. I was in cold-turkey withdrawal from my past and rejected everything. I wanted nothing. I had immigrated to Canada with only what I could fit in my backpack, and I wasn't about to weigh myself down with artifacts that were emotionally burdensome. Certainly, I entertained friends with stories from my childhood and youth, including the bare-bones tale of my aviator grandfather, but I had no inkling that, decades later, I would plunge headlong into this personal past and remorsefully wish I had retrieved all those boxes full of history.

There is the still-cherished image of my grandfather as a pioneering, heroic aviator, posing beside his plane, in spite of my later knowledge of the damage that warplanes inflicted in a horrendous, arguably pointless war. And my extreme dismay at the ongoing work of his inheritors, the warrior pilots of our era, too often wreaking fiendish havoc on those below.

I also have the story of Grandpa Alexander test-flying new planes for another appalling world war, but one with far more justification than the first, and of Raymond perishing in the post-war service of his country. My admiration for him in that form, my gratitude, leak into my anguished ambivalence about the Allied bombing of Germany and Japan. The firestorms, mushroom clouds, dystopian urban wastelands, and millions of deaths that, so goes the rationale, prevented millions more.

As I left behind those fighter pilot fantasies on the elementary school playground and entered junior high in the later Fifties, airborne warriors were cruising the skies with apocalyptic bombs, and the new Armageddon-tipped missiles did not require warriors at all, only technicians. Perseus at a control panel guiding his chariot.

I was walking down the hallway of Benjamin Franklin High School one day in my senior year when an acquaintance stopped me to ask, "Have you registered for the draft yet?"

"Did what for the what?" I said, or something to that baffled effect.

"The draft. The army. You have to register when you turn eighteen."

I was one of the younger people in my year. With a birthday in early September, I wouldn't turn eighteen until three months after graduation.

"Okay," the guy said, "but don't forget about it when you turn eighteen. You can get into deep shit if you don't register."

He left me to ponder what on earth the draft was, and how it connected to the army.

I was hardly naive about the military. This was the spring of 1964, with the Vietnam War burgeoning and the onset of anti-war protests. A politically-conscious group of us had even conducted an anti-war demonstration in the school hallways and lunchroom that winter, before the first small but significant anti-war demonstration in Seattle on May 2, 1964.

Although our loose-knit, multiethnic, and ever-expanding group endured occasional insults—radicals, beatniks, commie traitors, rabble-rousers—we were largely unassailable for we consisted of varsity athletes, top scholars, class officers, and other well-regarded students. Our "underground paper," *Expression*, was popular at school and earned a minor place in Seattle's protest lore. In 1963–64, we were simply joining a paradigm shift that had been building for over a decade, with foundations much deeper in history. Numerous teachers were supportive and few critical as our focus and values shifted to civil rights, poverty, the peace movement, critiques of "the system" in both the capitalist and socialist blocs, "third world" issues, and what would soon be labeled "counterculture" visions of different kinds of societies. Most classmates, of course, did not share our concerns, critiques, and visions. Most, if asked and sufficiently aware, would have supported the burgeoning Vietnam War and seen us as unpatriotic. Five years later, however, with thousands of Americans coming home in body bags, many of those unsympathetic graduates had joined the paradigm shift.

After high school, though I met up with former classmates for pick-up football and baseball games and apolitical beers afterward, I had been carried fast and far on the new-frontier zeitgeist—thank you, JFK—currents into anti-war and civil rights circles, into homes of older lefties and peaceniks and pads of my counterculture peers, into coffee houses with folk musicians and poets emitting photons of protest and light waves of transformative vision. Among these people were veterans of conscientious objection and rookies like me just taking the field.

Fast forward to 1966. The Seattle military induction center was housed in an ugly cement building among warehouses near the waterfront and not far from the Northern Pacific freight yard where I toiled as a yard clerk on the graveyard shift, adding "worked on the railroad" to my aspiring writer's future book cover bio. I was lined up in a large windowless basement room, in several rows, with dozens of other young men, wearing only our underpants. A military doctor and uniformed underlings with bags of tongue depressors and cones for eye and ear inspections, and with clipboards and pens, conducted and recorded the medical inspection. A bulky, glowering sergeant watched over the proceedings. A few guys, myself included, tried to lighten the mood and ease the nervousness by making jokes, but we were too tense to loosen up, and soon the sergeant barked, "Shut up." We didn't have to obey, but we did.

The final step in the inspection involved each of us, one by one, lowering our underpants to our ankles, spreading legs, and bending over. Every now and then one of the uniforms would snap at some reluctant guy, "Spread your cheeks." It was one thing to have my life-long physician, the kindly Dr. Chesley, take a look back there. Quite another for strange, unfriendly men with a purpose more psychological than physical. But I did feel the comfort of unspoken solidarity from others enduring this indignity. In comparison, however, to the horror stories I've since heard and read about what men do to other men and women in warfare, this was a trivial humiliation. And I even wondered at the time if those guys hated this part of their job.

We were then herded upstairs to a huge space, this one with windows, and joined by guys from other medical inspection rooms, to write some kind of intelligence exam. I remember no specifics, only that it was ridiculously easy, and that I was the first one done in a room full of nearly two hundred men. The only blood pressure-elevating section came after the exam proper. I could choose my preference of branch: Army, Navy, Air Force, Marines, Coast Guard. For a long moment, I was sucked into the nostalgia vortex, on the John Muir Elementary playground during the Korean War, my arms extended in the guise of an F1 fighter, banking and diving, guns blazing, in dog fights with classmates who drew the short straws and had to be Russian MIGs. Or my later love affair with the Marines, wanting their tattoo on my arm and to be called a "leatherneck." I didn't fantasize about being an Army GI Joe or a Navy sailor, but, in my teens, I thought it would be cool serving in the Coast Guard, and, now, it seemed the most morally acceptable choice. There was an adjacent box where one could elect to enlist for four years. This could maximize, maybe guarantee, assignment to the branch of one's choice. I'd also heard rumors that it increased the likelihood of not being sent to Vietnam, or at least into combat.

Still, I declined these options.

Then came the loyalty oath section, where one admitted or denied association with various suspect or allegedly treasonous groups—several specifically named and others generically referred to—and declared one's loyalty to the United States of America. There were boxes to check if one refused to disclose and attest. I checked those. The McCarthy era was still fresh in the American memory, and I'd been meeting people who had been directly affected by anti-Communist witch hunts. I now joined the ranks of people objecting to loyalty oaths; a citizen's loyalty should be automatically recognized. Besides, was an actual traitor going to admit it?

Finally, there was the Conscientious Objection section. I had been doing preliminary work, with a good deal of thought and research, on my CO application for months and was well-prepared for this moment. The easiest choice to reject was military non-combatant. I had already determined that I could not wear a uniform and serve in the armed forces. I had arrived at this conclusion from a combination of: moral and emotional abhorrence of organized warfare, of killing and wounding other people, destroying lives and communities; political opposition to warfare and armed forces as a means of pursuing objectives and resolving conflicts; unwillingness to submit myself to the regimen of military life—I was a product of Elvis the rebel, not Elvis the GI—and fear of being killed or wounded.

I had learned that these non-combatant COs were typically trained as medics and shipped to Vietnam, often with combat units. They had an especially high casualty rate, right up there with chopper pilots. Conscientious objection, legally, had to be motivated by principled opposition to warfare, militarism, and killing, not gut-level fear of injury and death. In that moment, I had to concentrate on my principles. There would be ample time in later years to admit, to myself and others, that I also didn't want to get my legs or head blown off. Or my sanity shattered.

This left me with two choices and boxes to check: complete refusal to participate, or willingness to serve my country for two years in civilian alternative service, for example, as an orderly in a mental hospital, one of the postings I'd heard about. I chose the latter, with a doubled-up pride—I was declaring my conscientious objection and my willingness to serve my society—and with the hopeful feeling that the powers-that-be would smile favorably on my community spirit. Mutual aid rather than homicide and suicide by firefight.

Our papers were collected and we were told to sit tight while all the uniforms left the room. Time passed. And passed. Then a sergeant returned, looking aggravated, and yelled, "Lemm, who's Lemm?" I raised my hand. "Follow me," he commanded. I rose, every face staring at me with curiosity and relief, and trailed him along corridors, up and down stairs, through door after door. With a mixture of self-satisfaction and mild trepidation, I thought of Kafka, including *The Trial*, which I'd recently read. I had just launched myself into the heady atmosphere of genuine, real-world rebellion. I felt proud, modestly heroic, and a tad shaky. I was ushered into a small office, and seated across the desk from a handsome African-American captain, built like a pro-football linebacker.

He was scowling at my documents. The silence dragged on. Finally, he looked up. I expected him to berate me for my patriotic and manly failings. Instead, he wearily said, "Why'd you have to go and do this?"

"Huh?"

"Why'd you have to screw up my day?"

For a moment I thought this was a preamble to a lambasting. But he just looked at me with an irritated dismay that had nothing to do with patriotism or manly virtue, but with a monkey wrench dropped into the smooth administrative cogs of his routine. It was my refusal to sign the loyalty oath that was the problem, not my declaration of conscientious objection.

I succinctly explained my reasons. He listened respectfully, then said, "You know what happens if you don't sign this?"

"No. What?" I was now riding a surge of righteous pugnacity. I was now the pint-sized halfback, fast and tough, keen to deke around or bounce off the burly linebacker.

He opened a desk drawer, looked for a file, and took out a form. "You have to sign this."

"And what if I refuse to sign that?"

He bent down again to his desk drawer and produced another form. "Then you sign this."

"And what if . . ."

"Man, they got another form after that and another. Come on, baby, they got forms keep you and me tied up for a month of damn Sundays. I'm getting a headache just thinking about it. Just sign it and spare us both all the bullshit."

I couldn't help but like and feel sorry for him, even if it was a practiced act. But I politely refused and said that I wanted to talk to the American Civil Liberties Union.

"Suit yourself, man. But you gonna be back here signing one of these damn forms."

With that, I was allowed to leave the induction center, though I did return, on the advice of the ACLU, to sign one of those damn forms, declining the alternative of facing a fine and possible imprisonment.

And with that, I began a process that dragged on for several years.

What I remember of my Conscientious Objection hearing with my local draft board, a few months after my physical, is a windowless room, dimly lit, and a bunch of nondescript men sitting around a long table. I can see myself standing throughout the hearing, not invited to take a seat. There were no pleasantries, and the men were unsmiling and solemn, their faces registering skepticism or disapproval or outright antipathy. There were no kindly or courteous expressions. If there was any sympathy around that table, any tolerance of war refusal, any support for peace activism, it was concealed under judicial neutrality, at best, while several countenances displayed blatant aversion to my presence and plea. On the table before the chairman was a copy of my application with its sixty-plus pages. I was asked to explain the basis of my CO request, in terms of my belief in a supreme being and other religious convictions, and in terms of my views of military service and warfare. I was challenged to elaborate on why I wouldn't serve my country in a military uniform. And I was tossed hand-grenade scenarios and asked how I would react.

"You're walking down a dark alley at night with your girlfriend, and a gang of men attack, intending to rape your girlfriend. You can't flee or talk them out of it. What do you do?"

I would, I said, look for any weapons of self-defense—bricks, trash-can lids, bottles—and counter-attack.

"Would you approve of policemen using force, using violence, to stop those rapists?"

Yes, I declared, that's the job of the police.

"The Russians have invaded and you're visiting your parents. Russian soldiers with rifles are climbing through the windows and crashing through the doors. How do you react?"

I surrender, I said, if there are too many, and plead for them not to harm my family. If there are only a few and they attack with the clear intent to harm us, I grab a chair, a kitchen knife, my old baseball bat and fight.

"Why would you use violence in these situations, but not to defend your country as a member of our armed forces?"

I reiterated what I'd articulated in my application: that I could not participate in organized warfare of any kind, whether the combatants be national militaries or rebel groups and guerilla forces. I could and would, however, engage in self-defense and defense of my family and friends if attacked. There were precedents for this limited pacifism, and well-argued treatises, several of which were referred to in my application. I knew this weakened my position, perhaps fatally. The Seattle draft board had a reputation for die-hard patriotism of the militaristic kind, firmly supportive of the Armed Forces and American military engagements, and hostile to conscientious objectors. The word was that you had to be a Jehovah's Witness or Seventh Day Adventist, and maybe a Quaker, to be granted CO status. I was on thin ice to begin with. They were looking for any pretext to reject CO applications. I knew the logical fault in my position: if I'm willing to defend myself and family against Russian soldiers invading my home, why can't I do so wearing a uniform and using an army rifle instead of a baseball bat? They could use my limited-pacifism response to saw a circle around me on the ice. But, perhaps foolishly, I couldn't lie and claim that I was a total pacifist.

"Your father fought in World War II. Would you have refused to fight against the Nazis and fascists? Do you think your father was wrong, immoral, to have participated in that organized warfare?"

It's hard to say what I would have done, I answered. If I was my father's age at that point in history, maybe I would've joined and fought. I would have been a different person, influenced by different situations, with different beliefs. I can respect my father's decision to enlist and his actions. I can accept that, if there is such a thing as a just war, the Allied cause in World War II was as close to a just cause as one can get. However, I argued to those stony draft-board faces, my CO position is that World War II could and should have been prevented, and my father should not have been faced with the decision to join the war effort and contribute to the cycle of organized, large-scale violence, however just his cause. All wars, ultimately, are unjust. We need to prevent wars, I said, launching into a reiteration of the reasoning in my application, drawn from various anti-war thinkers, that every war, however justified it seems at the time, invariably leads to further wars. We need to stop this process, especially in an age of massively destructive firepower.

"You have friends serving in Vietnam," the chairman said, shooting down my cycle-of-war flight of eloquence when it was barely off the ground. "What do you think about that?"

My first thought was: how did they know this, since it wasn't in my application? Doesn't the FBI have better things to do?

I respect my friends' decisions, I answered, and their desire to serve their country, even if I cannot support the war and participate in the war effort.

As I left the draft board hearing room and building, I felt that I'd acquitted myself admirably and honorably. Those impassive and inhospitable stares, and bluntly belligerent questions, were intimidating. But I'd stood up to them, literally, with dignity and pride in my tiny contribution to the anti-war movement and my ability to speak with conviction in their presence.

I simultaneously felt, as I walked to my car, how insignificant, even ridiculous, my impassioned declarations were, my moral performance. I wasn't achieving anything more than friends who paid psychiatrists to have them declared mentally unfit for service. My draft-dodging was merely elegantly attired in philosophical and political discourse and ethical rhetoric. Moreover, elsewhere in the world, people with my convictions were jailed, tortured, executed, exiled, or endured military service with stoicism or courage. My conscientious objection seemed like another luxurious privilege of middle-class white America.

Even so, I had notably parted company with the myth of the noble warrior. I had broken the chain of patriotic command linking my father, grandfathers Mathias and Raymond, and Great-Grandpa Jacob. Almost all my friends, old and new, were supportive. But then, I had gravitated toward anti-war people, largely leaving behind and avoiding unwavering patriots.

I couldn't avoid Grandpa Harry, who said nothing when I briefly described my actions, but let me know by his downcast expression that I was bafflingly and shamefully turning my back on a path he would gladly have traveled.

5

The Man's Man

During our road-trip pilgrimage with Father Kappas, we stayed in De Pere, Wisconsin, near Green Bay, with one of his seminary classmates. An avuncular host who showed us endless slides of their novitiate together, he had a friend whose luminous earthly light was infinitely more exciting.

When our host learned that Tom and I played football and Tom had a football scholarship to the University of Washington, he offered to take us to meet Bart Starr, the Green Bay Packers' field general, already regarded as one of the greatest quarterbacks of all time. The quarterback position requires substantial intelligence, and Starr was one of the most cerebral, as well as a superbly gifted athlete. He was also a classy player and universally respected on and off the field. The Packers were my second favorite team, and I was now politically attuned enough to appreciate their status as the only non-profit, community-owned NFL team.

In his modest home and binder-lined study, I was struck by his quiet self-assurance, the decency he emanated, and his respectful, gracious treatment of two young men as if we were journalists from *Sports Illustrated*. In a short time, I was deeply imprinted by another role model. Whatever success and authority I might later have, this was the kind of person I wanted to be, the kind of conduct I wanted to be known for. Not celebrity flash, but Starr's subtle, unassuming camaraderie and leadership. He was an athletic counterpart of upright western heroes, but those were mostly rugged individualists, while Starr embodied a much more common and essential reality in American and any society: teamwork and collaborative leadership.

He invited us to a Packers workout, where we not only saw but viscerally felt the strength, speed, and agility of pro athletes. My pie-in-the-sky fantasy of playing pro football came splattering down.

There are the clichés about men "not showing their emotions" and "not showing physical affection"—clichés that apply to some men in certain cultures and eras, but not to countless other men. Athletes such as Bart Starr were allowed, at times, to show a wider spectrum of emotions, including physically. And there was Uncle Curt, a war veteran and aircraft builder, whom I could count on for hugs, an arm around my shoulder. In those years, our coaches and Boy Scout leaders could rely on that arm as part of their mentoring and guidance, without snickers or formal complaints. Grandpa, though, was a man of handshakes, and they came with lessons: "Not too firm and not too soft"; "Don't be a threat, but don't be meek."

Grandpa showed his love by giving me two season passes behind first base for the Seattle Rainiers baseball games, a thank-you reward from his Rainer Beer salesman, and by taking me to Huskies football games with mid-field seats among the well-heeled alumni, another token of corporate gratitude. He shared his love by teaching me how to paint window trim, mix concrete, change the oil in a lawn mower, clean paint brushes, sharpen knives, and drive a nail straight into hardwood, and how to tell which politicians were crooked or clean and which athletes were slacking off or earning their pay checks. Sports heroes were dazzling and enviable but remote. Grandpa's jack-of-all-trades heroics, his manly know-how and savvy were tangible, immediate.

Harry, Grandma told me, had wanted to be an engineer. By the 1950s, engineers had ceased to be heroic figures of the Industrial

Revolution and pioneering geniuses of American progress, but their engineering feats were still moderately marveled at and celebrated. And building "infrastructure" was still politically sexy. The world's first major floating bridge on Lake Washington was visible from our back porch. Grand Coulee Dam in eastern Washington. President Eisenhower's massive program of interstate highways. Boeing's space-and-time-conquering 707s, on which my Uncle Curt worked in south Seattle and spoke of with beaming delight. Grandpa Harry never mentioned his long-lost dream, but I was enthralled enough by engineered wonders and could tell from Grandma's tone of voice that this had once been an occupation with magic appeal and noble prestige for a working-class youth such as Harry. Moreover, he was a devout believer in making a purposeful contribution to society through one's job—absolutely essential to one's self-worth as a man. And that contribution, that worth, in that era was no more visible than in a bridge, dam, tunnel, or new office building downtown.

"But the Depression came along," Grandma said, "and ruined his dream. He went to Normal School for a while to become a teacher, but he had to leave to help support his family." Supporting his family, they both told me, a lot more than once, meant riding the rails in search of work, picking crops, hefting heavy boxes in warehouses, sleeping in hobo camps along the rail lines. And sending his earnings back home to his family. Then driving a taxi for ten long years before becoming head bartender at Green's Cigar Store. Maybe even smoking a little of the wild "tea" that grew along the tracks, I learned one day, when I asked him about the title of a David Dodge mystery, "It Ain't Hay." "Hay and tea are what we called marijuana," was all he said. I was mildly amazed that Grandpa and other hard-knocks men in the fabled Depression might have indulged in something I vaguely associated with drug addicts in flophouses downtown.

Other times when I asked Grandpa about his life back then, all I'd get were taciturn repetitions of how hard one had to work for a plug nickel, how little the fat cats cared about the ordinary Joe without whom they'd have nothing, and the need to pull oneself up by one's bootstraps. And how I needed to feel and show more gratitude for all the luxuries I enjoyed, such as a plate heaped with roast beef and mashed potatoes, and the freedom to dash off to the sandlot and play baseball all day with no more chores than mowing the lawn, doing dishes, and taking out garbage. I could sit on the upstairs furnace grate in my pajamas before school on a winter morning reading *The Three Musketeers*, whereas young Harry had been shivering in a boxcar and, with his lean frame, toting hundred-pound sacks of spuds.

On workdays, he wore one of his starched white shirts, which I or Grandma fetched once a week from the neighborhood dry cleaners, wrapped in blue wax paper and secured with string. There was always a tie with an immaculate four-in-hand knot. I vividly remember him teaching me in front of a mirror, how he stood behind me, his arms around my shoulders, his hands guiding mine until my hands made the proper movements alone. And our pride when I mastered this rite of passage into the prospect of respected success for a working-class male. In that moment, the love between us was at its strongest.

Some mornings he had a bright glow, as if the world was his oyster and pearls were waiting for him on the bus ride downtown and at Green's Cigar Store. Then, he savored his Corn Flakes or ham and sunny-side-up eggs. He might ask what the day had in store for me, and whether I was prepared. "How's band class, been practicing your clarinet enough? You playing baseball after school today, don't go ruining that new pair of jeans, wear something old, we're not made of gold you know and your grandma can't be patching your duds every night."

Some mornings, a glum weariness dulled his face. And my pancakes were greeted with a grunt. One glorious summer morning, when the sun through the kitchen window bounced fruitlessly off his wan face, I eagerly rattled on about the merit badges I was going to earn at the upcoming Boy Scout camp. All I got in return was a leaden "good for you."

Downcast, after he left for work, I complained to Grandma.

"You have to understand," she said, solemnly and gently, about to reveal a secret out of the stunning blue, "your grandpa had another family before me and you. He had a wife and a daughter, who still lived with them when she was twenty-two. One day he came home from work and they weren't there. He found a note on his dresser. 'We've left, for good. Don't try looking for us and don't bother calling the police.' He didn't, and he never heard from them again. He's mostly put it behind him, but sometimes that all catches up with him."

Where did he learn his numerous skills, with hammer and saw, paintbrush and trowel? It's amazing how little I know about the pre-grandson past of the man who raised me. One summer Sunday morning, Grandpa and I were high up on our roof. I was not exactly fearless, then, but I was able to rein in my trepidation and scale the wobbly wooden extension ladders to a height just below the wispy cirrus clouds and step onto the asphalt shingles. There was a thrill inside my trembling, the adrenalin rush, the joy in following Grandpa's nonchalant ascent. Once on our slanted roof, anxiety vanished, replaced by unconscious trust in my high-top US Keds, my shortstop's nifty footwork and balance. And my grandfather's quiet demand that I focus on the task at hand, tarring and shingling a section of the roof. He had rope-hauled up a bucket of hot tar and toted a roll of tar paper. I was careless for one moment with the tar bucket, almost knocking it over, and he chastised me, sternly. I thought it was because I'd almost wasted something valuable. It was drilled into me, by those veterans of war and Depression, logging and hobo camps, not to waste the precious possessions granted us by hard work and good fortune. But, no, not this time.

"That's how the back of my neck got scarred," he said. "Some guy careless and hurrying with a bucket of hot tar up a ladder, me standing below."

"You used to tar roofs?" I asked, impressed. You'd think he'd just revealed that he once played for the Yankees. That morning, I was more proud of Grandpa and to be his grandson than if he had been Michelangelo dangling beneath the Sistine Chapel's ceiling.

Another summer Sunday right after daybreak I was roused grumpy from bed, resentful over Cheerios at the table with Grandpa, my baseball plans ruined by Harry's need to dig a pit for our new oil tank. My first few dozen shovels full of dirt were dug and tossed grudgingly. Then, transformed by the alchemy of purposeful work, I was completely absorbed in this monumental task, forced to pause by Grandma for lemonade. I was digging for treasure, delving for ancient tombs, hollowing out a foundation for Seattle's biggest skyscraper. And then a further transformation: we were digging an astonishingly deep hole, just the two of us, in just a few hours, for an oil tank for our new furnace. I was doing real work and loving it as much as the real work with Grandma of filling the cupboards with the winter's fruits and vegetables.

I see my grandfather behind the long, gleaming mahogany bar at Green's, rows of magical bottles with their rainbow array of liquids reflected in the great mirror, along with his white-shirted back and the faces of his customers enthroned on stools with green and red plastic seats. I see the fresh, companionable visage he would some-how present six days a week to the world of Green's Cigar Store. That affable, welcoming face I would look forward to when I went downtown to Green's and which I simultaneously begrudged. Why was that face not there for me at least six days a week at home?

One Saturday afternoon while I was there, a large man at the bar had downed one drink too many and became loudly belligerent and verbally abusive to Harry and other customers, including rude remarks to women in the booths. Other men had moved away from him. Harry asked him to leave, offered to call a cab, to no avail. Suddenly, Grandpa, all five-foot-six and one-hundred-twenty pounds of him, in his mid-fifties, vaulted astonishingly over the bar. Before the stunned drunk could react, Harry grabbed him by his collar and the seat of his pants, hauled him off the stool, marched the cursing lout out the door, and dumped him on the pavement. He stepped back inside, slapped his hands together like a hero in a western movie, and said, "Good riddance," returning to his station behind the bar. I was in awe. I also knew, approvingly, that he had done this for my benefit. To show me exactly what Harry Osborn, head bartender, was made of—a man I could look up to and emulate. The star of *Barsmoke* and *Have Swizzle Stick, Will Travel.*

Several days after Grandma's death, home from the funeral I do not remember, Grandpa sat in his armchair, stunned and desolate. The front window shades, yellowed from years of cigarette smoke, were drawn all the way down, and Grandpa stared with hollowed eyes through the dim, smudged light at his heart's wasteland. He summoned me to that Stygian living room and said, in a voice submerged under fathoms of murky melancholy, "It was your grandmother that looked after you. You're on your own now."

Nothing more. Dismissed. His gaze returned to the barrens.

My initial reaction was stunned disbelief. How could he say, let alone think or believe, that he hadn't "looked after" me as much as Grandma? And how could he wash his hands of me with such sudden, deadened finality? After all, I was only fourteen.

Then, with equal abruptness and with ebullient, conclusive

clarity, my mind spun one-eighty and I heard a voice in my head say, "You're free." I was, indeed, on my own and overjoyed.

He did not, in fact, wash his hands of me. In his understated, minimalist way—more detached than begrudging—he continued to be a caring and supportive parent until my senior year, when our relationship became too strained and fractious, and I pulled away from his chronic brooding at home, took strong issue with many of his ideas, and wilfully asserted my autonomy. Before that, I still felt his loving guidance, albeit filtered through the thrum and haze of his regret and unspoken self-recrimination.

Three years later, as I was moving out, carrying my possessions from our shared bedroom to my car, Grandpa tried, for the only time in our lives together, to hit me. He took a punch, and I grabbed his wrist and held his arm. He strained against me for a few moments, then his arm went limp and I dropped it. Beaten, he turned and retreated to the living room. I was out the door, hurrying triumphantly down the porch steps to my car. Driving away. Exhilarated by my self-liberation, my first moments as an adult on my own. By my victory over Harry in the hallway.

And then I was distraught. Grief-stricken. Ashamed.

Years later, after I'd told the hallway story for the umpteenth time, a friend said, "He could have hit you if he'd wanted to. He was still strong enough, and maybe angry enough. He let you stop him. He loved you too much, and didn't have the heart to struggle with you further."

Why did he try to strike me? So many possible reasons. Because I was rejecting and deserting him and my mother. Because I had my whole life ahead of me, with an abundance of skills and talents garnered from a fortunate upbringing in bountiful America. Because I seemed cavalier, ungrateful, selfish, uncaring to my closest flesh and blood. And had transferred my affection and devotion to other people. Because he loved me so much, and I so blindly refused his love, that he struck out not in anger but with a broken heart.

When I was sixteen, Green's was sold to a well-known Seattle restaurateur, who promised to retain all the staff, most of whom had worked there devotedly for many years. The new owner soon broke his promise, terminated everyone, including Harry, and brought in his own people. He gutted Green's, eliminating the barber and tobacco shops, the betting counter where customers once placed small wagers on football and baseball games, and the big smoky room in the back where older gentlemen—aging vets, rooming-house residents—played quarter-ante cards and socialized.

For a while, Harry enjoyed freelancing in downtown cocktail lounges and taverns, relying on his excellent reputation and his high standing in the bartenders' union. Then the Sportsman's Café, with a small restaurant up front and cocktail lounge in the back, next door to the former Green's was for sale. Harry re-mortgaged our house and joined the small-business owner class with muted pride and audible schadenfreude as he retrieved his many loyal customers from the revamped joint next door and other haunts to which they'd drifted.

Halfway through my first year away from home, Harry told me he needed a loan to get the establishment over a small hump. He was doing a brisk business in the cocktail lounge but wasn't selling enough food in the restaurant, and the law required his restaurant sales to at least equal what landed in the liquor till. He admitted, in confidence, that he'd been moving money from the lounge to the food till lately and fudging the books. But he didn't like doing this, he'd always been squeaky-clean honest before, and the inspectors would eventually get suspicious. He needed the loan just long enough to build up the restaurant side of the business. Why didn't he get another bank loan? I asked. He didn't want to go back to the bank with this problem.

They might not loan him the money if the restaurant was struggling. He needed five hundred for ten months, and could I afford that? He'd pay me back fifty dollars a month.

I was flattered on two counts: that he'd ask me for a loan, and that he trusted me enough to confide in me, especially when he was violating the law. If I begrudged him my heart at home, I gladly, lovingly, would help him at work where we had our benign relationship. Darlene and I were saving money for a long road trip around America, Canada, and Mexico, and then for some cool college somewhere exciting. I could easily spare five hundred for a while.

After the first month, when I dropped by and asked for the first payment, he politely asked for a month's grace. Business was picking up too slowly in the restaurant. After the second month, ditto. I was getting impatient and told Harry that I needed him to start repaying me.

He said, sourly, "You'll never get that money back. I don't owe you a dime."

I knew instantly to what he was referring. During my junior year dating upper-crust Gwendolyn with her Thunderbird convertible, I felt the need to treat her in high style. Among Harry's convictions was a belief in "cash on the barrelhead." He had no chequing account. The night of his weekly payday, he'd have ten twenty-dollar bills in his wallet. When he'd fallen asleep, either on the dining room sofa or the bed upstairs, he'd leave his pants folded over a chair. A sound sleeper, he was never disturbed by my cautious removal of a twenty-dollar bill. This continued until I began dating Darlene, confessed my theft, and had my conscience slapped upside its head.

Staring at Grandpa's back as he walked from the café to the cocktail lounge, I was mad, but I understood and did not argue. I even left the Sportsman smiling inside, sort of, ironically. He'd waited and got his back when he needed it.

After traveling around North America for half a year, Darlene and I decided to move to California and attend San Francisco State College. For that, we needed to replenish our bank accounts and returned to Seattle. A high school friend, Neil Beck, had been working in the Northern Pacific Railway freight yard in the city's industrial area. He'd been drafted into the army, taken a leave of absence from work, and would soon ship out for Nam. Home before departure, he told me the yard was short-staffed and arranged an interview for me with the yardmaster. I was hired as a yard clerk on the spot. My job was to walk the tracks in all weathers, making lists of cars—a neat trick in the dark in Seattle drizzle—and tacking contents and destination cards on loaded cars.

Working on the railroad was no longer a voguish elective for a bohemian artist's résumé. Freight trains were still crucial to our economy and lifestyle, but emptied of industrial thrill and proletarian glamor and barely noticed as they rumbled across or squatted in urban and rural landscapes. Model railroading was rapidly fading from boyhood. But the declaration that I was working on the railroad and in a freight yard did tap into a vestigial romanticism about trains and elicit a millisecond or two of mild admiration from my peers.

I worked the swing and graveyard shifts and became a votary of the growling locomotives and grimy cars rolling by and clanging together and shaking the earth, of walking for miles up and down the tracks in the chill Northwest winter rain and then the clement summer nights, of the midnight special solitude within that metal and gravel labyrinth, the darkness impaled by a switch engine's brilliant beam or imprinted by a hobo's sudden apparition, of dawn's Impressionist pastels layering the sky and coating the yard. I loved every moment of my time there. Including the rough-and-ready, foul-mouthed men, some with Navy and Marine Corps tattoos, and nicknames such as Lurch (a lanky switchman who lunged with each stride), Fishmeal (who stank from scraping fertilizer from boxcars), G-string (a strip-club habitué who dressed like Chaplin's tramp), and Wrecker.

Wrecker was the original Sears and Roebuck catalog model for a brick shithouse. The foreman of a switch crew, he'd earned his name by inspiring engineers on switch engines to "throw" cars at excessive speeds down tracks, where they would collide with howitzer force against stationary cars. Possessing some mischievous wizard's power, he'd wave his switch lantern and normally placid, rule-abiding engineers —a noble breed sitting aloof in their cabs—would give 'er full throttle. If you were watching, you could be seized with mortal fear at the sight of a DO NOT HUMP sign on the catapulted car or, worse, the additional word EXPLOSIVES.

My first direct encounter with Wrecker happened during my inaugural night as weighmaster. His crew weighed cars on the night shift. After I had proven myself to the yardmaster as more intelligent than the average yard clerk and highly reliable, I was trained to be a weighmaster and entrusted with the fifty-thousand-dollar scale, something unprecedented for a rookie. There was a federal government sign in the weigh shack warning against a variety of abuses resulting in a fifty-thousand dollar fine and/or prison time.

I was about to enter the weigh shack when Wrecker blocked my way. His three crewmen stood behind him.

"What's your name kid?"

"Lemm."

"You one of them anti-Vietnam protestors?"

"I'm the new weighmaster on the night shift," I said, with a firmness and aplomb that surprised me. "We have cars to weigh."

He stepped closer, his face a foot away. "Cut your hair, kid," he growled.

"My father fought and died in World War II," I blurted out with some vehemence. "Killed by the Nazis in Europe fighting for my freedom and your freedom and America's freedom," I went on, astonishingly, with reckless belligerence, summoning that part of me which on the football field relished blocking and tackling the big kids. "He didn't sacrifice his life so somebody could take my liberty away, including telling an American how to wear his hair." I thought of mentioning George Washington's ponytail but didn't.

There followed a brief moment of pride, in my father, in myself, and a feeling of righteous potency. Succeeded by panic and the vision of Wrecker's fist flying into my face.

Instead, Wrecker's face scrunched into a mixture of surprise, confusion, and embarrassment. Then his expression was outright apologetic as he extended his hand.

"Sorry kid, I didn't know. Sorry about your dad." He looked reflective for a moment, then, "Let's weigh some cars."

I was amazed. My dormant thespian gift might dovetail with a future as a creative writer.

From then on, Wrecker was my champion in the yard. "If anyone gives you shit" etcetera, and no one did. I was the egghead yard clerk with sufficient moxie and street savvy, and he seemed to be fondly proud to have me as his little buddy. In a typically para-doxical American way, the freight yard, part of a giant corporate bureaucracy, was nonetheless a fraternity of rugged blue-collar individualism and camaraderie. And I'd passed my initiation with the hardest-nosed switchman that night. He never asked, nor did anyone else at the yard, why I wasn't being drafted. Whatever the reason, apparently my blood was red enough.

Neil, meanwhile, at six-foot-eight and two-hundred-eighty pounds after boot camp, was now a sergeant leading a platoon in Nam. He had two jobs. Salvaging parts from downed choppers, after the body bags were taken away. The other was leading his platoon into Viet Cong tunnels and clearing out the stashed supplies, from ammo to black-market American beer and canned fruit cocktail. One day Neil and his men surprised a Viet Cong soldier sleeping in his hammock, rifle on the ground. After taking his rifle and ammo, Neil let the man, bowing with gratitude, escape. There was no doubt about the color of Neil's blood or his deepest feelings about the war. He told me this story, with immense delight, a year later while waiting in line for the Pirates of the Caribbean ride at Disneyland.

One early summer day in Vancouver, a year after I moved permanently to Canada, my then partner Carol and I returned home from a day hike to the phone ringing, an operator with an emergency message to phone Uncle Curt. I instantly knew something was dreadfully wrong, though my first thought was about my mother, not my grandfather, who seemed indestructible. Depressed for years, yes, and a bit weakened, but physically invincible. I cannot remember him even sick enough to miss a day's work, though he would have gone downtown anyway.

"Something terrible has happened," Uncle Curt said.

Somehow I now knew it wasn't my mother.

"Harry was shot and killed in a hold-up in the bar."

Earlier that afternoon, with sixteen customers seated at tables, four men entered the bar and demanded the money in the cash register. One man had a gun. Harry gave them all the bills. The man with the gun ripped the phone cord from the wall and told Harry not to try to call the police until they were long gone. The other three men had turned to leave, perhaps had left the cocktail lounge, when Harry said to the leader, still pointing his gun at Grandpa's chest, "I'll get you, you dirty n____." There were sixteen witnesses who heard him.

The four men were Black. The gunman pulled the trigger.

"They shot Harry in the heart," said Uncle Curt. "He died instantly."

I was beyond incredulous. My first thought: how could he do

that, say that? Why on God's earth? The men were leaving. The man was pointing a gun at his heart.

When Uncle Curt hung up, I related this to Carol. Slowly, inevitably, we began to talk our way through our disbelief and shock and distress. I said, "But he seemed so content. So much happier than he'd been for years. How could he let his prejudice take over like that?"

After a long, thoughtful pause, Carol answered, "Maybe he was ready to die."

"But he was only seventy, in excellent health . . ."

"You say he'd been happy lately, after being depressed for years. I'm not saying it was conscious, obviously. But maybe a deep part of himself wanted to die, happy . . ."

"With his bartender's apron on," I managed to say.

"And that part of him uttered the necessary words."

Plausible, as a partial explanation. But it was not like him to abandon my mother. And he was anything but a reckless, impulsive man. Even if there was some truth to that suggestion, he had also, in a rare and fatal moment, let old bitterness flare. I think that outburst had less to do with prejudice toward Blacks, and more with the blended residues of his life's disappointments and grievances, personified by those men. The tribulations of the Depression years. The frustration at not wearing a uniform and going to war. My grandmother's alcohol-related death at age sixty-three. A child adopted and raised from age two who had mutated from a dutiful and loving all-American boy into an insufficiently respectful bohemian.

As well, those men were violating much of what he stood for and valued: respect for others and their property, hard honest work for one's money, and the all-important trust and lawfulness which allows people to live together in a community and society. As well, no matter that drinking establishments were sometimes targets for robberies, they were, to Harry, sanctuaries where people could be free for a while from the wickedness of human behavior. Whatever prompted my grandfather's words, those men tapped into more than racial prejudice. I've wondered what happened to the gunman and his companions. I've chosen to imagine that man, not as a sociopath or brain-dead addict, but as an ordinary person, troubled or warped enough to carry a gun, but someone with his own deep resentments, and capable of being haunted by what he'd done. In spite of all the witnesses and descriptions, there were no suspects, no arrests, and as far as I know, my grandfather's murder remains unsolved.

So much of the imagery of manhood and the mythology of masculinity that I had absorbed as a boy involved physical aggression, weapons, and conflict mediated by corporeal violence. This was a salient quality of masculinity for many Americans, especially with its centuries-old gun culture. But it was far from exclusively American and hardly confined to my boyhood. As an adult and a professed conscientious objector, I had not infrequently become engrossed in narratives and imagery of violence and weapons, from Japanese samurai films to *Star Wars*, Zulu warriors to James Bond, *Lord of the Rings* to Indigenous snipers from Canada in the First World War.

The vaster reality, however, has been an ocean of blood—of brutality and suffering—on which those myths and their imagery have floated as beaconed buoys anchored by our need to avoid and transcend knowledge of our malevolent aggression. The majority of masculine violence is not mythic, epic, romantic, heroic, or manly, whatever that means. It is sordid, banal, weak, craven, pathetic. The finest art, such as Akira Kurosawa's *The Seven Samurai*, shows that banality and pathos, and, yes, the mythic deeds of the warriors. But the overwhelming reality is not worthy of the briefest moment on Shakespeare's tragic stage. It is the feebleness of a petty thief with a deadly weapon killing an aging bartender.

6

It's All in Your Mind

Throughout my childhood, I would from time to time be overcome with yearning for my mother and ask Grandma, "Will my mom ever come home?" I don't recall the exact answers, but they were of the "we don't know, we'll just have to wait and see" variety. The waiting to see must have worn my patience so thin, and my persistent asking become so intolerable, that during one visit to Northern State Hospital when I was thirteen, I found myself led between my grandparents to the chief psychiatrist's office. I recall a slim woman with graying blond hair pulled back and definitely, I thought, a German accent, which triggered movie and TV show stereotypes of Nazis, including demonic Nazi doctors. But this was America, and I also knew there were good German refugees, scientists like the celebrated Wernher Von Braun, who had switched sides. It is quite possible that this doctor had fled the Nazi terror, and she might have been Swiss, Austrian, or even Jewish. Still, that "German" accent did leave me feeling suspicious, grim, and rancorous toward her for several years afterward, even when I knew better.

We sat across from her, me in the middle. She was addressing her attention to me, and I knew this had been set up by my grandparents. The doctor examined my mother's chart, shuffling through the papers silently, solemnly. Then she looked up with a gravely clinical expression and fixed her gaze on mine. There was no warmth or compassion, and certainly no encouraging glimmer. I was clinging by my fingertips to hope, but full of foreboding. Her voice slammed down on my fingers.

"Your mother is incurable," she said flatly, starkly. "She will never be able to go home." I did not know that some patients never left that hospital. They died there. Now I knew.

Period. Dismissed. Maybe my memory is doing this doctor an injustice, and practicing psychiatry then could not have been often uplifting. Maybe she was working miracles and keeping a hundred dams from bursting with only ten fingers. Perhaps she was worn to the emotional bone but carrying on, a trooper. But what I received that day from that psychiatrist was a knockout blow. And I knew that's what my grandparents felt I needed to hear: pull-no-punches reality. As we walked from the doctor's office, I asked them if they agreed with her. They had already talked with the doctor, they said, and they wanted me to hear the truth straight from her mouth. I could go home and think the doctor was an ex-Nazi and her manner and attitude cruel, but I did not question the diagnosis and prognosis. She was head psychiatrist of Northern State Hospital, and therefore her word was medical fact.

Traveling home, and for a short while after, I grieved. Felt hollow. I endured a kind of death—not only of a lifelong dream, but of the mother I imagined would one day be part of my daily life. The mother recovered, restored, revivified. My actual mother was incurable, and that other mother was dead.

We need to label what we don't sufficiently understand and what confounds, threatens, or torments us. Labels that keep changing. Nervous breakdown. Transient psychotic grief reaction. Post-traumatic stress disorder. Throughout my childhood, I took it for granted that my mother's "nervous breakdown" had been sufficiently severe and, therefore, an all-sufficient explanation for the decision to send her immediately to a mental hospital and to keep her there for years.

I long believed her breakdown was solely caused by the trifecta of her marriage break-up, my father's car crash death, and her father's war plane plunge into the sea. Many years later, I delved further back, making connections with her parents' divorce and with my "real" grandfather.

My grandmother sat at the kitchen table while I swept the floor after the supper dishes were done. She had taken off her apron and poured two fingers of bourbon. That evening, she was jovial, as she often was, and sweetly nostalgic. Sometimes her nostalgia took a devilish turn.

"Your real grandfather," she began. Aileen often referred to her first husband, Raymond Alexander, that way, even in front of Harry, who never seemed to notice, let alone mind. Still, I flinched whenever she said this, worried that this did wound him. After all, he kept most things bundled deep inside. Expressionless. Buster Keaton, his favorite silent film actor. This served him quite well as a bartender: the taciturn listener. At home, it could be perturbing.

Once I'd said, perplexed and disapproving, "But Harry's my real grandfather, isn't he?" My consciousness wasn't yet expanded enough to remind her that Harry was the one raising me and that I had never met this real grandfather, who was, by the way, dead. "Grandpa Alexander was your blood grandfather," she'd said, and I was expanded enough to think that a blood connection couldn't get out of the batter's box compared to Harry's home run of bringing me up.

"Your real grandfather was quite the disciplinarian," said Grandma, sipping her bourbon. "The military man in him. When your mother and uncle were disobedient, he would sometimes make them stand at attention, and he'd place a broomstick through their arms, in front of their elbows and behind their backs. He'd make them stand like that for an hour or more."

I was resentful of her implication that I might need such disciplining, mildly fretful that this was a veiled threat she would act on if I pushed her beyond her limits. But I had to see what it felt like. With the broom in my hands behind my back, I bent my arms and thrust my elbows as far back as they'd go, then moved the broom handle into the crook of my elbows. My shoulders were pulled way back, chest pushed out, and head jutted forward. Aileen told me to keep my head straight, chin up. Everything above my waist quickly started to ache. My real grandfather made his children do this? For over an hour? Was this military at-attention position? Was I supposed to be sorry and sad that Raymond Alexander wasn't my substitute father?

Aileen told me to hold that position a few more minutes, to know what it's like. I thought of my step-grandfather in his armchair in the living room, a Camel burning in his ashtray, a Rainer beer on his side table, *Gunsmoke* on the TV. The closest he had come to disciplining me physically was the rare threat to take me to the basement and strap me with his belt. Only once did he march me downstairs. He got as far as removing his belt, then said that he couldn't do it, but that the next time I was bad he would, for damn sure, take his belt to me. Now, as the broom discomfort intensified, I was grateful for Harry, the not-real grandfather.

I was, according to Aileen and Harry, often guilty of "talking back." This time, removing the broom and snapping back from that torture position, I said nothing. I was too busy contemplating the bizarre harshness of the punishment—agony to a pampered American child in the 1950s—my mother and uncle endured, and thanking my patron saint, Thèrése of Lisieux, that my grandmother had divorced Major Alexander and married a low-key bartender.

Long afterward, I did ask my mother why her parents divorced. Often. Her memory, her ability or willingness to remember, were far too compromised to be of much help. Yet a few answers came, brief flashes, on occasion, instead of her usual, "Oh, Richard, I can't remember, that was so long ago." These glimpses joined the one thing I recall Aileen saying about their separation:

"I left because of your grandfather's drinking."

"He was the most wonderful man and father," my mother told me, over fish and chips at Ivar's seafood restaurant on a downtown wharf. "A wonderful husband to Aileen."

Then one evening, over bingo cards at Lynnwood Arms: "He was awful to Aileen. He would drink and then he'd beat her something terrible."

"He'd get drunk and beat her?" I said, prodding.

"Oh, no," she said, reversing directions on the gossamer pathways of her mind. "Father could hold his liquor. He would never hurt Aileen or anybody. He was the most gentle, loving man."

Another time, she told me, "I loved my father, but he was very strict. He'd never put up with disobedience."

"How do you mean, 'strict'?"

"He'd punish me. Sometimes badly. He'd get very violent."

"He'd beat you, too, and Aileen?"

"Oh, never. Your grandfather would never get violent. I loved him."

And so those revelations and reversals would appear and just as quickly vanish as her memory closed down.

In spite of my mother's mental limitations, I never knew her to confabulate. And the instant denials, after revelations, fit the familiar pattern associated with physical abuse. I must assume there was physical violence toward my mother and grandmother, if not toward my uncle. If there had been fear of her father, it was deeply suppressed, apart from those fleeting disclosures. In its place, consciously, she adored this father who could be "awfully strict." I chose not to broach this matter with Uncle Curt, who also revered his father, and whose full name was Raymond Curtis Alexander. I felt I'd get nowhere, except thrown out the door.

Now, I wonder why I did not ask my uncle, in later years, for information about Grandpa Alexander, and, instead, badgered my mother's enfeebled memory. Partly, I wanted to know more about her, to recover what I could of this mother who had been unavailable throughout my childhood and earlier adult life.

The last, very tentative, and dangerous piece I have in this grandfather puzzle has to do with my mother's breakdown. My grandmother told me that she was found, several months after her father's death, and a year after my father's, standing in the middle of a Seattle street, screaming at the sky above. Aileen and Harry took my mother to a downtown Seattle hospital. After a short time there, she was shipped to Northern State, where she spent the next thirteen years. Not until my late twenties did I question why Aileen and Harry consented to her long-term incarceration.

I had no other answer until the 1980s, when a female friend who worked with victims of sexual assault wondered if there was any sexual abuse, namely, by my mother's father. That, of course, was putting it bluntly, coldly, in contemporary language and viewpoint. Another way to frame it: was there, in my mother's and maternal grandfather's relationship, an intimate and abusive bond—sexual or not—which contributed to her breakdown upon his death, and partly underlay, albeit unconsciously, my grandmother's consent to her indefinite hospitalization seventy-five miles away? Was this embedded within my mother's contradictory statements to me? Did my grandmother suspect? Was she aware? Did Harry know? Was this also why Aileen divorced the war hero?

I see Aileen, sipping her bourbon, wistfully telling me how heroic my grandfather was. I hear my mother, dipping her fish into the tartar sauce, telling me how much she loved him, how he beat my grandmother, how dashing he looked in his uniform, how stringent and marvelous he was as a father.

My mother and I were sitting in my car on the Edmonds waterfront north of Seattle, gazing at ferries chugging to and from the wharf, scuba divers and kayakers, gulls and cormorants, the San Juan Islands on the tinfoil waters, and the Olympic Mountains behind them in the hazy sky. We were eating McDonald's cheeseburgers and fries and drinking vanilla shakes. McDonald's is normally my least favorite fast-food joint, but I was savoring every sip and bite. This was now my mother's favorite meal, and she was—thank you Ronald McDonald—happy. I allowed myself to share her delight.

In this caloric-euphoric mood, my native land-and-waterscape before me, I asked her what she had wanted to be when she was young. Usually, to such questions she'd say, "Oh, sonny boy, your mother's memory's not so good anymore." This was an exception.

"I wanted to be a dancer."

"Really? That's lovely, Mom."

"And a historian."

"Wow," I said, thrilled by these answers and delighted by the juxtaposition. No doubt there are historians who danced ballet, modern, or folk. And there surely are dancers who studied history. I once sat on a plane next to Canadian figure-skating champion Karen Preston, who was a history major and studying for an exam at the University of Toronto.

"But why did you want to be both those things?"

As always, Gloria had no more to offer. A revelation was invariably a lone lightning flash and never followed by a crash or low rumble of clarifying thunder, let alone the downpour or drizzle of an explanation.

"Oh, I don't know. That's just what I wanted to be. Do you want the rest of my fries?"

Another afternoon on that waterfront, I mentioned that I hadn't found her photo in the graduating class of Garfield High School.

"I never graduated," she said. "I quit school during my senior year."

"But . . . you said, and Grandma said, you were an excellent student."

"I was."

"Then why did you quit?"

"I don't remember. I just did."

I did learn, a few visits later, that by dancing she meant popular forms: waltz, jitterbug, and jive. "I wanted to be a hoofer." She had a gorgeous voice and liked to sing, so maybe a chorus girl. I also learned that she loved all her history courses. But her own history had largely been deleted from or driven too deeply into the recesses of her brain.

I have two stories implanted by Aileen, two movie scenes projected onto my brain screen, of my mother in the days between, as my uncle described it, her stoicism at my father's and his fiancée's double funeral and her hospitalization after her father's death.

In one, she is on the pedestrian walkway of the new Floating Bridge on Lake Washington. She is carrying a baby. The wind is not gale force, but strong enough to whip up whitecaps, push chop against the bridge, and fling spray in the air. Halfway across, my mother climbs up, with her baby, onto the concrete barrier running along the side of the bridge. The top of the barrier is wide enough for her to maintain her balance in the buffeting wind. Cars whiz by, as many drivers tend to do, for their sundry reasons, even when a woman with a babe in arms is perched on a bridge barrier above tossing waves. Before a tragedy occurs, one of those humans who is prone to stop on such occasions does pull over and help my obliging mother, with her infant son, down and into his car, off to the police station and, hence, home to Gloria's concerned mother and stepfather.

How concerned, I don't exactly know, since I remember Aileen concluding this story only with the understatement, "That's when we began to worry something was wrong with your mother."

I don't know whether the tunnel escapade happened before or after the bridge adventure.

We lived on 31st Avenue, along the crest of Mount Baker Ridge. From my grandparents' bedroom window, I had a glimpse through houses across the street of Puget Sound and the Olympic Mountains to the west. From our back porch we had a grand view to the east of Lake Washington and, on sufficiently clear days, the Cascade Mountains and the spectacular dormant volcano Mt. Rainier. We could also see the Floating Bridge. There is a tunnel to and from the bridge under Mount Baker Ridge, almost directly under our house.

One day when she took me for a walk in my stroller, Gloria found her way down the hill from the ridge, and onto the elevated pedestrian walkway inside the tunnel. Somewhere in my psyche are impressions of the hour or two I spent there, made manifest by the times I later walked or biked through the tunnel. The streaming headlights and flashing red brake lights and dull yellowed ceiling lamps. The grimy cold cement dankness and greasy fumes from exhaust. The echoing cacophony of tires and horns. The tomb-vault feeling of enclosure. Who knows, though: maybe I wasn't traumatized, maybe it was thrilling to my infant mind, for I love tunnels, especially ancient and darkened ones, whether clammy or desert dry.

Not thrilled, however, was my grandmother when Gloria

returned home alone, in a euphoric post-walk mood, apparently unaware that she had abandoned her baby, with no recollection of where. She did, Grandma said, become immediately distraught when Grandma dislodged Gloria from her reverie. Aileen phoned the police. We had no car, so Grandpa took a taxi home from work. A search party set out, Harry in a taxi, Aileen and Gloria in a squad car. One concern was that Gloria had left me where I couldn't be seen from a car, and maybe not even by a pedestrian. The search was not going well when a call came through to the squad car from the precinct station. Again, a conscientious motorist had noticed the stroller and braked to a halt—a dangerous thing to do in that tunnel—climbed out into the traffic, scaled the wall and railing, and managed to bring me and my stroller down to his car. If there's a heaven, I hope the tunnel and bridge Samaritans are there. I was presently making my first, or second, visit to a precinct station, watched over I assume by cops of loving grace.

If after the second incident my grandparents were even more worried, they did not act on their concern and seek professional help beyond, perhaps, taking my mother to a family doctor.

What help was there in those days anyway? Now, an accomplished therapist might say to her: Let's see, you're happily married only a couple of years when your husband goes off to a terrible war. Month after month, you worry and wonder if he'll come back to you, and what he will be like if he does. Meanwhile, you're one of those many fortunate women able to use some of their ability in one of those jobs vacated by men and created by the war boom. You drive a little cart delivering mail and packages at the Boeing field and plant. You love and take pride in your work and earning your own money. You are somewhat regretful when the war ends and your job is taken away from you and given to a man. But your husband is home, unharmed in mind and body, and full of energy and ambition. His love for you, conveyed by him while he was overseas, seems strong as ever.

You rent a nice bungalow in the Central District. He starts a movie distribution business, and, contentedly, you work in the office, doing the bookkeeping and looking after the marquee posters. And you're pregnant. You have everything: a home, a loving, handsome, and stylish husband with brains and drive, a job in the burgeoning entertainment industry, and a baby on the way. America is booming, leaving the Depression and war years rapidly behind, and if your husband's in the driver's seat at the start of this glorious ride, you're agreeably riding shotgun and sitting pretty.

Then the car starts to go out of control, blown tires and gaskets, broken steering. Harvey is out too many late evenings, with movie and theatre and nightclub types. You're home alone, pregnant and lonely. Frustrated, perplexed, resentful, and maybe envious. After all, you love to look snazzy and go out dancing as much as Harvey does. And you're perhaps, understandably, fretful—all those attractive, sophisticated women, some no doubt predatory. Harvey, too, is bewildered, frustrated, resentful. The way you spend the money he brings home to you, coming back from grocery shopping with twelve quarts of milk and fifteen loaves of bread. What on earth is wrong with you?

Things go from bad to worse, and you separate, divorce, with you still pregnant, moving in with your mother and new stepfather. Then, with your child only nine months old, Harvey is going to re-marry, a French woman who owns her own restaurant on Aurora Avenue, the main highway through Seattle. On the way to his wedding, they're killed.

You're finding it hard to cope, then your beloved, estranged, and perhaps physically abusive father dies in a plane crash, his body not recovered.

Then you are found standing in the middle of a street screaming at real and imaginary planes in the sky, "You dirty Japs! You killed my Harvey!" And the rest is psychiatric case history.

Did she really shout "Harvey"? I can believe that she used the term "Japs," since my mother, a sweet, gentle person 99.99% of the time when living in retirement and nursing homes from 1969 until her death in 2005, and adored by the multiethnic staff, would on rare occasions viciously lose her temper, cursing and yelling racist epithets at employees of color. She would apologize profusely for these insults, spewed from some vent in the depths of her memory. But "Harvey"? Had her psychotic break conflated husband and father? Had her repressed grief and anger at losing Harvey—to work, another woman, and then death— finally erupted? And why "Japs"? Harvey had been in Europe and North Africa, and her father served Stateside during World War II. Only her brother had been in the Pacific. The unconscious link had to be symbolic: the Japanese attack on Pearl Harbor, the start of the war for America, with the divorce and Harvey's death as the war's private, intimate, tragic conclusion. And Japanese-Americans were a visibly metaphorical presence in Seattle, and at multiethnic Garfield High, with Seattle's largest Asian student population, in a way that German and Italian Americans weren't.

I don't even have the skeletal details of what happened next, I have a fragment of bone. Gloria stayed in the hospital downtown for several days before being shipped north for storage in Northern State Hospital.

Only when I was an adult did I begin to question those decisions. Did Aileen and Harry simply feel they were way over their heads and unable to cope with a gravely depressed and/or psychotic daughter? Were they frightened of the effects on Gloria's young child? Was my mother now an unbearable embarrassment? Were they steamrolled into these choices by a medical-psychiatric establishment grossly understaffed and clinically primeval, and, therefore, prone to hustle the crazies off to loony bins for the long haul, still smack-dab in the era of long-term institutionalization? Was Aileen hiding away the evidence of an abusive relationship between her ex-husband and daughter? Did they know that my mother's unhappy brain would soon be fried?

A gigantic hydroelectric dam had been built on the Columbia River at Grand Coulee, Washington, a big draw in the burgeoning tourist industry, and generating a vast new supply of electric power, quite sufficient to spare a score of jolts for a woman in the throes of a nervous breakdown. My mother, I know from examining hospital records, had a grand coulee total of twenty-three electroshock treatments. She also began a regimen of drugs—antipsychotics, antidepressants—changing with pharmaceutical and clinical fashions, continuing till she died.

Years ago, I immersed myself in the literature and debate about electroconvulsive therapy. I concluded that attaching electrodes to my mother's skull and zapping her brain with electricity was preposterously crude, right down there in the pseudoscientific gutter with phrenology, bloodletting, and ice-water baths and insulin shock therapy (the latter two of which my mother missed out on by very few years). Aliens do this to human brains in sci-fi flicks. The neuroscientific basis was ludicrously primitive.

Whatever the cause-and-effect relationship of ECT, my mother was sufficiently docile afterward. Blessedly, when her affect spiked—and I'm envisioning an oscilloscope which registered her emotions—it was almost always upward, in serene or cheerful zones, not down into the darker states. Psychotropic drugs do, often, work—if "work" at the bare minimum means making someone's moods acceptable and behavior manageable when institutionalized.

I have no images of our visits during her earlier years in the hospital. Our visits to my mother at Northern State Hospital, always on Sundays and no more than once a month, all roll into one experience with a few variations.

My grandparents not having a car until I was eleven, we took train and bus to the nearby town of Sedro-Woolley, and then a taxi to the hospital in its serene pastoral setting: eleven hundred acres on a rise above wetlands with the North Cascade Mountains sculpting the eastern horizon. Externally, it seemed an Edenic sanctuary. The luxuriant grounds were designed by the Olmstead brothers, whose father, Frederick, is considered the father of landscape architecture and designed New York City's Central Park. The buildings, still standing in disrepair, are Spanish Colonial Revival with red clay tile roofs. Northern State was a town unto itself, with forty-five buildings, including the huge two-story main hospital. In the early 1950s, almost three thousand patients lived there. A seven-hundred-acre vegetable farm, greenhouses, dairy, canning facility, and lumber mill enabled the mission of occupational therapy. There were even first-class baseball diamonds, horseshoe pits, and croquet pitches. Upon arrival, I felt I was entering an idyllic realm, though my words then would have been "beautiful," "peaceful," "heavenly." From the long winding driveway, the hospital seemed like a movie set; any moment Zorro would ride up to his hacienda.

The neatness and order, loveliness and tranquility, were in sharp contrast to some of what I encountered inside, on the patients' wards. But outside, all seemed incongruously, reassuringly normal. Patients sitting alone or with visitors in lawn chairs or at picnic tables, or strolling on walkways and lawns. Patients playing horseshoes and croquet. At a relatively young age, I was baffled and amazed that none of them were acting bonkers—no one yelling, waving arms madly, making weird faces, throwing fits, and rolling on the ground. I recall my discovery of male patients—excellent ballplayers—playing baseball.

"But they're crazy," I said to my grandparents, dumbfounded that mental patients could play, and impressively, America's pastime. They looked . . . normal.

"Not everyone here is so crazy they have to be locked up. Look at your mother, she works in the greenhouse and gardens and the Hub. Watching these men, you couldn't tell there's anything wrong with them, could you?"

True enough. There were times I couldn't tell that anything was amiss with my mother, and couldn't understand why she couldn't come home to live with us.

Most Sundays, she wasn't working, and we would meet her either at the Hub, a cafeteria for patients, staff, and visitors, or on her ward, where I disliked meeting her. The ward was hardly a snake pit, but it made me feel bleak, grimy, and contaminated by association with people who were clearly not "normal," who were, as they were publicly labeled, insane.

I see a long, wide corridor of worn gray linoleum, phlegm-colored walls and ceilings, and smoke-sullied windows filtering a sallow light. There are bars or grates on the windows, though I can't see whether they are on the inside or out. Sparsely arranged along the walls are dull metal-framed chairs with plastic backs and seats the color of bread mold. Most of the women who sit in these chairs are chain-smoking, and some of them are tapping their feet or hands persistently. Some are bobbing their heads or rocking their upper bodies forward and back relentlessly. Some are moaning or groaning, or suddenly crying out—words, or gibberish, or just anguished or piercing sounds. Sometimes, one begins laughing—a repetitive chuckle, or a burst of hilarity, or a manic rat-a-tat-tat which strafes us as we walk by. It is a gauntlet we must walk through to reach my mother's room at the end of this long hall-way: of vacant or berserk faces, gaunt, haggard, with unkempt, wiry hair. Thin arms with bony, nicotine-stained fingers reaching for us. Eyes I don't dare gaze into, zombie eyes, empty yet baneful. A gauntlet I must hold my breath through, lest I inhale the vapors from these ghouls.

I cannot bear to imagine that these were real people, with parents, husbands, children, former lives, and homes they might never see again. With sons like me.

I exhale at my mother's door. She is always ready, having waited for us all day, all month, and sometimes several months. I do not remember ever looking inside or entering her room. Gloria is, thank God, nothing like those women in the corridor. Her hair has been newly permed, her lips bright red, her favorite color, her cheeks rosy with rouge, her fingernails and toenails neatly clipped and painted. She had been a fashion plate, still is, within the limits of the inex-pensive clothes we bring or she buys or trades for in the hospital's secondhand store, within the boundaries of what the hospital's beauty parlor has to offer, and within the confines of her ability to conjure the beauty for which she was once known.

"Your mother," she tells me as if speaking about someone gone, "was very pretty."

"Your mother can still look pretty, can't she?" she asks as if trying to summon herself back into a tangible and valid existence.

"I think you're very, very pretty," I say and mean it. Almost. And sort of. For she isn't pretty let alone beautiful the way she was in her youthful photos or the way some of my friends' mothers are, not to mention glamorous and slender Aunt Fern, Gloria's sister-in-law. There's a dowdiness about her in spite of her best efforts to remove or disguise the patina of being a patient in a mental hospital. I can't help seeing a fuzziness in her expression, a faintly blurred look in her eyes. As if a part of her is always off somewhere, dreaming, content never to return.

The walk back up the corridor is quick and I am happy, excited, holding my mother's hand. I'm sure that I'm already babbling, the sluice gates open and all the things a son wants to tell his mother, weeks and weeks of words, spilling out, flooding her mind. She smiles and smiles, squeezing my hand. This is the watering she has needed, her son's voice irrigating the fields, soaking the roots. She is flowering.

We would have lunch in the Hub, or occasionally take a cab to a café in Sedro-Woolley. My mother and I both took exceptional pleasure in sharing a meal together. I was especially fond of French dip sandwiches, a Hub specialty, which also baked scrumptious pies. The food somehow tasted better there, my taste buds and olfactory sense heightened by being with my mom.

I did have to overcome an episode of fear one Sunday when it dawned on me that mad people were working in the kitchen. I wasn't thinking of my mother, who was not demented like the women in her ward's corridor. But sicker patients might be behind those aluminum double doors my mother went through when she was on table-clearing and dishwashing duty. I had ordered a hot roast beef sandwich with fries but suddenly refused to take a bite. I sat there frozen.

"What's wrong?" Grandma said. "Why aren't you eating?"

"Some of the patients work in the kitchen?"

"Of course," she said. "Like your mother."

"Do some of them do the cooking?"

Aileen looked at my mother for information.

"Yes," Gloria said. "They help the hired cooks."

"Are you worried about your food?" my ever-perceptive grandmother said.

"Uh-huh," I said sheepishly, already making the shift from feeling frightened to foolish.

But I couldn't stop myself and I needed to say it. "What if I get poisoned?"

Grandpa, being himself, said nothing and put a large forkful of mashed potatoes and gravy in his mouth.

"Don't be ridiculous," Grandma said. "You don't see us keeling over, do you? Well, do you? Okay, then. People have been eating here for years, and nobody's been poisoned."

We were in Harry's professional territory here, so he spoke up. "They have strict standards and inspections. You're more likely to get sick from a hamburger at Woolworth's."

I began eating, tentatively, and then eagerly, my mother smiling as she always did.

"You have such a good appetite, sonny boy, I'm so proud of you."

She played piano and sang in the dingy recreation room of a mental hospital, not, as I wished, in a nightclub or concert hall. But she was something that many of my friends, when I was young and ever since, longed for: she was unfailingly pleased with me. This wasn't a nauseating "worship-the-ground-her-son-walks-on" and "can-do-no-wrong" kind of pride. She simply took pleasure in however I looked when we visited, and in whatever I told her about whatever I did. She certainly worried about me in normal motherly ways—be careful crossing the street, don't get hit in the head by a baseball, watch out for bears when you're camping, check your brakes before you ride your bike down steep hills. And she could tell me to be "a good boy"—obey Aileen and Harry, do your chores, keep up with your homework, respect your teachers, say your prayers. She could even gently chastise me for not writing to her more often, but that was as close as she came to criticism. Otherwise, I was the apple of her eye.

I was, indeed, what she had to show for the first thirty or so years of her life. Oh, she worked in the Hub, greenhouse, and gardens. She crocheted doilies. But what had she otherwise to show for all that talent, intelligence, athleticism, beauty, vitality, and joy? The son sitting across from her at the café table, in his cowboy shirt, gobbling his coconut cream pie, and telling her about tying knots in Cub Scouts, hearing *Peter and the Wolf* at the symphony where his band teacher played bassoon, getting picked third or fourth (and never ever last) when teams were chosen for after-school baseball. "That's wonderful, my darling boy."

Was I ever proud of her, back then? I thought it was sweet she worked in the gardens, but that didn't seem special—planting seeds, weeding, picking the carrots and beans—those were chores I had to do. But I was impressed about her working in the greenhouse, something a real grown-up would do, not a woman who seemed to shrink into a small child around my grandmother. When we arrived and she was finishing a shift in the Hub, I was less delighted: my mother the dishwasher, nothing I could tell my friends about, the very few friends, that is, whom I told about my mother's whereabouts and condition.

I did, though, love to hear her sing and play in the recreation room, my grandmother often joining her for duets, taking turns, or combining on the keys. I wish I could also remember us singing Christmas carols, a trio of grandmother, mother, son.

This continued year after year, my swelling anticipation during the journey there, from the train station in Seattle to the front entrance of the ward. My head and heart so full of love and delight as we met and hugged. My joy subsiding throughout the afternoon to a plateau of softened contentment mingled with mild disenchantment as I reabsorbed what my mother was—not quite there, not the vivacious, substantial mother I wanted her to be. She was not solid, she was airy, not even liquid, therefore insufficiently nourishing. Then would come the sadness of parting, hers and mine. Even though I had slipped partway from unbridled gladness toward disillusion, I still did not want to separate. But Aileen, with Harry silent nearby, gently yet firmly severed the connection and we were pulling away in a taxi, my mother standing outside the Hub or her ward waving for a little while, then turning away and going inside long before we were out of sight.

How did she feel when we left? Were the drugs strong enough to shield her from heartache? Had the electroshock amply dulled her? Had she learned to wrap herself in a patchwork quilt of stoic resignation as countless people have done who are distanced from those they love the most? Or did she sit at the Hub's counter and stare despondently into a cup of coffee, or walk dismally back to her room and cry? What was it like waiting for however many weeks or months before our next visit? As a child, at times, I felt sorry and sad for her, trapped in that place, unable to leave, to come home. As an adult, I have mourned and vented my anger, in private, to friends and lovers, and in print about how she was imprisoned, sequestered from a chance at a real life and from her son. I entitled my first book of poetry *Dancing in Asylum*, with a six-page poem about my mother.

But there were also moments, way back then, and later, when resentment welled up—at her, for not doing what it took to get well. I've had enough experience with others' mental illness to know it isn't that easy, especially for a woman in that era, institutionalized, shocked, and drugged. But more than one friend, women included, has said to me, unbidden, "She abandoned you. You can't blame it all on society or Aileen. She checked out. She didn't try hard enough to check back in." Other friends are appalled at that suggestion, at placing any responsibility on her. Whoever is right, my moments of resentment were few and brief. Back then, overwhelmingly, I thought of her with only longing, sympathy, and sorrow, in those minutes and hours and days after I'd left her—as I sometimes imagined, and in spite of the ECT and drugs— forlorn, bereft.

My mother's absence presented another problem, namely, at school. While I was popular, never bullied, and rarely teased in a hurtful way, I didn't have the chutzpah to tell schoolmates that my mother was crazy and in the loony bin. Certain insults involved the name Sedro-Woolley, referring to Northern State Hospital. I'm sure that some friends knew, especially from my neighborhood, and they must have told others, but I can't remember being taunted about my mother's illness. In elementary school, I did prevaricate a couple of times when asked about my mother's absence. She was sailing on Lake Washington and struck by lightning. She was bit by a black widow spider. Miraculously, I was entirely spared interrogation and ridicule. Children can be merciless, and merciful.

Six months after that psychiatrist punched the lights out of my dream, I was indoors one summer's day when Grandma went to the front porch to fetch the mail and returned with a letter in her hand and a baffled expression. Her bewilderment was strong enough for me to ask, "Who's it from, Grandma?"

"From Northern State Hospital."

I knew that we never got letters from the hospital, just from my mother. Grandma opened it and her mouth opened, speechless, as flummoxed as I'd ever seen her. I knew nothing bad had happened to my mother, for I'd seen Grandma's someone's-died and someone's-terribly-ill expressions, and this wasn't them.

"The hospital says your mother's cured and can come home."

"Who's it from?"

"The head psychiatrist."

She handed me the letter, with its remarkably brief and official message, and a non-German signature. Sure enough, it said my mother was cured and we should retrieve her as soon as possible.

"But . . . the doctor . . . the hospital . . . they just told us she's incurable and can't come home."

"I know they did, but . . . " and her voice trailed off, and she trailed off into the "back room" beside the kitchen, a repository for heaps of her clothes and purses, her treadle sewing machine and sewing stuff, most of my old and current games and toys and sports equipment, birthday and Christmas presents hidden away, the bottle of Mogen David kosher wine which my gentile grand-parents curiously favored for holiday meals, and which I took the very occasional sip of, and stacks of *Life* and *Saturday Evening Post* magazines that hadn't yet been consigned to the basement. This is where Grandma sometimes went—in cheerful, disgruntled, and weepy moods—when she wanted privacy and to be alone, clearing a space on the sofa or armchair. This is where I sometimes went to find her when I needed to tell her about my day, boast of some achievement, find solace, ask permission to do or buy something. I had been often hugged there, occasionally slapped when she was drunk and angry or sorrowful, and many times entertained and enriched by her stories, enlightened by her wisdom. Now, I followed her with trepidation and stunned confusion and stood in the door-way. She slumped on a pile of clothes, disconsolate.

"What will we do?"

"We'll have to go get her. This Sunday."

Grandma's lack of anything resembling joy and enthusiasm or even mild delight, and Grandpa's muffled look of concern when he came home from work, were signals to me that this was hardly the blessed event I'd waited all my conscious life for. Apart from their apprehension about my mother's condition, and aside from any deep currents of discomfort or aversion going back to Aileen's first husband and Gloria's father, there was perhaps in Grandma and Grandpa's mind concern about Aileen's health, which was showing the early signs of something not right. Another factor may have been their drinking and fighting, which had markedly increased since I was eleven. They'd gone from one bottle of bourbon between them every two or three days to a bottle a day, and the quarrels had gone from sulking disagreements to shouting, cursing, blaming, and threatening. Was Gloria's return something they thought might help calm the waters, or a major stress that could make matters worse?

We now had a car, a '55 Chev, and this Sunday drive I was stretched in the back seat on one of those medieval racks I saw on TV shows. Torn between hopeful anticipation and fretful doubt. Between openness to a miracle cure and suspicion of charlatans. I had read and seen enough about both, the Merlins and the snake-oil salesmen. In novels and movies, the heroes found out before it was too late. I wouldn't know if the wand had Excelsior magic or fake flowers or a fanged serpent tucked inside until we were back home again, the woman who may or may not be my long-hoped-for mother settled in what was my room.

By the time we were carrying my mother's belongings into the house, my brain and its metaphorical heart chose to believe in magic. My mother was home at last, after nearly a dozen years, and I embraced that with a gleeful smile. That doctor, German accent and all, was wrong.

Somewhere in the middle of the night, sleeping on the left side of my new bed, my grandfather on the other side, in my grandparents' room, with Grandma on the dining room sofa, I realized that the German doctor was right, after all, and whoever wrote that letter about her being cured was wrong. Was lying. Was trying to get rid of a patient who'd been there too long and was taking up space needed for another. I was awoken by my mother crying out and whimpering with nightmares. By morning, I was despondent and frightened. I'm sure my grandparents, especially Aileen, tried to reassure me. But I could tell that they were distressed too, whatever worries they had confirmed.

I hear again the voice of an enlightened therapist today: Your mother is going through a tremendously difficult transition. Think of how you feel about her return, and then try to imagine her emotions, coming home after a dozen years. Consider her excitement, joy, anticipation, relief, and think about her fears and insecurities. Appreciate the major changes in her environment, routines, relationships. No wonder she has nightmares. Yes, I'm aware that she has stopped shaving her legs, and they're disturbingly hairy, and that she sometimes doesn't bathe well enough or change her clothes often enough. I know that during the day she sits on the living room sofa with her arms folded or around her knees, and rocks back and forth, and sometimes moans. I understand this can be upsetting for a thirteen-year-old boy who wants a normal mother. And I know it can be uncomfortable when she wants you to sit beside her and let her hug you and stroke your arm and face, this woman with her makeup too thick and smeared.

But consider how strange this all must be for her. Yes, she was under the care and orders of doctors, nurses, and other attendants, but it might be more stressful being under the supervision of her mother and stepfather. The very people who institutionalized her for years. Yes, she has longed to be with her son, but you're in many ways different from the boy who visits on a Sunday afternoon every month or two. Finally, what if there are those dark undercurrents you've speculated about? We know so much more now about the long-term, debilitating effects of violence and sexual abuse. Might that help explain your mother's regression?

Your mother needs weekly therapy or more. Her meds need to be monitored and adjusted. She might even be better off, for a while, in a halfway house or group home, a more neutral, safer surrounding. What do you say?

I say there was no follow-up by the hospital, whatsoever. No therapy, no monitoring of meds. As for her environment, I trust that my grandparents did the best they could, but they were at a loss. My uncle, her only sibling, and his wife lived a few miles away and there were family gatherings, but they had a life of their own, and Gloria was not their responsibility. Meanwhile, her son had quickly decided that his mother was indeed haywire, embarrassingly and repellently so, and put as much distance as possible between himself and both his all-too-palpable mother and his dream of his real mother, sanely, beautifully, nourishingly back home.

I had numerous ways to avoid, ignore, and deny my mother's presence: my church activities, Boy Scouts, school plays in which I had lead roles, the school band, sports, hanging out with neighborhood and other friends, homework and reading for fun, visiting Grandpa at Green's Cigar Store. Who had time for a cuckoo mother who wasn't really my mother after all? Grandma Aileen, I remembered with a vengeance, was my real mother. That person in my bedroom was a creature from *Invasion of the Body Snatchers*.

If I sound awful, I was. But I was also a normal and exceedingly active boy, fleeing my disappointment and disenchantment. Fleeing my disgust, sometimes, in her presence, and my guilt that I felt repelled by my long-awaited and long-suffering mother. My escape took the form of playing clarinet, playing Macbeth, playing soccer and altar boy, all things my mother, I later learned when I was ready to hear and learn, was extremely proud of. Her son weeping when his grandparents told him they had to take Gloria back to the hospital.

I was weeping, not cheering with relief, because all my sadness broke through the dam I'd erected. It's one thing to want someone out of your life, another thing when she suddenly goes. Hauled back to the mental ward, the asylum. The dream not even on life support. The dream as corpse.

There we were driving north again, past the pulp mills and their stench in Everett, past the tulip farms (I like to think it was spring, with at least their brilliant colors), through Sedro-Woolley, along the hospital lane between the lawns and flowerbeds, to the front door. My mother defeated, slumped in her bewilderment and despair in the back seat a few feet away from me. Did I hold her hand? Did I say any reassuring words? Did our eyes meet? Did I hug her before we parted? Did I tell her I loved her?

And then, six months later, we received another letter. Your daughter, it told Aileen, is now well enough to come home permanently.

We really mean it, this time. We do know what we're doing, just a test run last time, adds the son, sardonically, years later.

Maybe they did know what they were doing. When my mother came home the second time, she was shaving her legs, bathing and wearing clean clothes daily, putting on her makeup carefully—if a bit heavy on the lipstick and rouge for 1961—sleeping calmly through the night, sitting on the sofa like a *normal* person watching TV, reading my grandparents' novels and some of the Book of the Month Club selections, crocheting, and never rocking or moaning. She helped Grandma now with the house cleaning, laundry and ironing, cooking, and dishwashing. She went shopping, with Grandma and alone, both in neighborhood stores and downtown. She had ceased to be a scary embarrassment, and I didn't worry about friends dropping by and meeting her. If I was chagrined, when friends were over, about Gloria or Aileen playing piano and singing, it was the nature of the songs—we're talking "Daisy, Daisy, give me your answer true"—not Booker T and the MGs. But my friends simply thought my grandmother was delightful and my mother lovely and sweet. "You have such good friends," Gloria would say to them, and I'd cringe, and they'd be flattered, some of them with mothers they didn't always think were lovely and sweet even if they sang along with Ray Charles.

There was one more encounter with Northern State Hospital. At some point in my junior year, after Aileen had died, my mother had a relapse, not looking after her appearance, not helping much with chores, not reading or playing piano, and rocking once more on the sofa with her arms around her chest or knees. Her deterioration was serious enough to penetrate my absorption in my teeming life away from home. I expressed my concern to Grandpa and strongly suggested that she needed to go back to the hospital for a while, just a few weeks or months. He stubbornly refused to agree, maintaining that she was going through a bad spell and would snap out of it.

I didn't hear any snapping, apart from her sanity and my patience, so one weekday I skipped school and ordered my mother to pack a suitcase. I was adamant. She wanted to phone Harry. I must have been formidably intense, for she complied with my command. Her lifetime of being under other people's thumbs now included her son's newfound authority. In later years, while she could firmly refuse my requests or suggestions, she invariably treated me as the authority figure, asking me for things and apologizing and worried about my disapproval like a diffident, meek child. And I too often treated her like a child. Indeed, there was something childlike about her, especially her fear of abandonment—a child's ultimate fear—that she would be forsaken by her son. So my docile mother pathetically climbed into our '55 Chev, the keys to which were always hanging on a kitchen hook. Slumped in the passenger seat, depleted, crushed, she rode north in silent surrender beside her grimly determined son.

Arriving at the hospital's reception area, my mother in tow, I dumped my distress and demand at a nurse's feet. She left me and my mother in a sparkling new waiting room. After a half-hour, I was led, by myself, and to my amazement, to a brand new building and the head psychiatrist's office. I was defiantly prepared to confront the German shrink. Take her back and make her right this time, I would say, no more bullshit.

The woman who greeted me had shoulder-length fair hair, a youthful, lovely face with a warm, kind, sympathetic expression. She had me sit down, my mother's chart before her, which she didn't open.

"As you'll understand," she said gently, "I've had only a few minutes to glance at your mother's history. But from what the nurse told me, it does sound as if your mother could benefit with a few more weeks here. I'll need to examine her, you understand, before we can admit her. I'll do that right away. We may need to adjust her medications, and there are several new, more effective ones available. I see that Harry Osborn is her guardian. Is he with you?"

I explained, honestly, what I'd done, and why. I steeled myself for her negative reaction. Instead, she said that she understood the situation, and that, once she'd seen my mother, she'd phone Harry and get his approval. My astonishment kept growing.

"I don't want her in that awful old ward." When I'd ordered her to pack and get in the car, I wasn't thinking about the disagreeable things that awaited her. Only the possibility of reversing her latest decline.

"We don't put patients there anymore. It's closed down, in fact. Your mother will stay here. I'll show you around later."

"She won't be kept here . . . again . . . for years?" I heard myself say that, feeling sadness shoving against the relief I felt. And guilt. Even if I'd kept her as far to the sidelines of my life as possible, 1 didn't want her locked away for years again in an asylum.

"We don't like to keep people here any longer than necessary. For one thing, the state doesn't want to pay for long-term care. But, mainly, that's not how we treat people anymore. I can't make promises, but I think we can help her be better when she goes back home."

I totally trusted and believed her. I needed to. And she inspired faith.

The new building was still institutional, but no worse than your average new school or medical clinic. The patients weren't locked in their room, they had a kitchen with snacks and beverages they could access day and night, and a spanking new recreation room with a piano, pool table, television, and stereo.

My mother was interviewed and cleared for admission. Harry was phoned and, though sorely disgruntled, he consented. When Gloria saw the facilities, and when the doctor and I reassured her she'd be there no more than two or three months, her spirits lifted considerably. She even looked grateful and promised me she'd "work really hard to get better" and that she would come home "a brand-new person."

"I want you," she said, "to be proud of your mother." I told her that I already was and would be, and left with both of us feeling hopeful. Harry gave me hell when I returned home, but not as much as I had expected. He was no fool, even if his stubborn individualism made him think he could handle or at least endure any situation. Even more, I think, he was afraid of losing his only companion for years, forever. As promised, my mother was back in less than three months, much improved, and would not relapse again. The keys remained on the kitchen hook.

7

The Dutiful Son

There are different kinds of cruelty, and the passive ones—like Christianity's sins of omission—can be as hurtful as the active ones, the sins of commission.

My mother is a minimal presence in my high-school years' memory. She took her mother's place on the dining room sofa, and Harry often sat there with her. Meals were almost always eaten now on TV trays or at the dining room coffee table, which I'd made for Grandma and Grandpa in junior high woodshop. I was often the only one at the dining table, reading a book while I ate, oblivious to the evening news and other programs, or I took my supper to my room, having come home late from football or track workouts. More and more I was at friends' homes or at St. Clement's Church, and with my girlfriends. When I needed parental permission, for instance, traveling across North America for half the summer with my priest, my mother sat silent while I negotiated with Harry. Occasionally, when Harry wasn't home, she tried to be a more engaged parent, telling me what I could or shouldn't do, and trying to back up Harry or chastise me when he and I clashed. But I paid her no regard, not even courteous lip service. She was irrelevant. I might have been her son, but she was not my mother.

This was no more evident than when I brought my new girlfriend, Darlene, up to my bedroom, that is, my half of the bed, on afternoons when Harry was working. It became necessary to drag a dresser in front of the door, to keep Gloria from pushing her way in, while she voiced her disapproval through the door. I did not feel disrespectful, did not think my conduct was shameful in my mother's presence. I was, rather, indignant at this intruder. Go away, I thought, I'm having sex with my girlfriend. Who do you think you are? Leave us alone. I then left home, Seattle, America, and my mother behind.

When my mother hadn't arrived and was an hour late for Thanksgiving supper at Uncle Curt and Aunt Fern's home, Curt became worried. Harry had died less than two weeks before, and Curt had checked on her in person and by phone several times before and after the funeral. She'd seemed all right and to be taking care of herself. She wanted, of course, to stay in our home, and while Curt was skeptical that she could manage, he was giving her some time before he made a decision about selling her home. Although he was sure that the house and property were too much for her, and that he couldn't take on the task of caretaker, he didn't want to hurry her out. It had been her home for ten years. And there was the problem of finding her a suitable place to live. But her failure to arrive for supper set off an alarm.

Curt drove into town from his suburban home and found her in a deteriorated state, both the house and her a mess. The night before, she'd cut her hand badly while opening a tin of pork and beans, and wrapped her hand in a dishcloth, now stiff with dried blood. The kitchen was a disaster zone, and she herself was bedraggled, unwashed, and disassociating. Curt's family doctor interrupted his own festivities to see her in his office, then asked Curt one question: "Has your sister ever been treated or hospitalized for mental illness?"

My mother was stunningly fortunate to be seen by a doctor who took the time to look beyond the wound and be sufficiently concerned about her condition to probe deeper; who knew and cared enough about the mind as well as the body to take on Gloria's case himself. This involved my mother not only being with the right person but also at the right time.

This doctor just happened to be friends with a social worker couple who had recently leased a seven-story, ex-dormitory building from Seattle University, and turned it into a residence with skilled therapeutic staff for people who could not live on their own: former mental patients, recovered alcoholics, people who had lost their caregivers. People like my mother.

There is a great deal I owe Uncle Curt, for which I thanked him infrequently and most inadequately. Perhaps chief among my debts is the care he assumed for my mother on that occasion and during the months that followed. I was out of the picture, with the convenient excuse that I was now living in Canada, a fugitive from American justice, wanted by the FBI for draft dodging and unable to return safely to Seattle. There were draft dodgers who risked their freedom, crossing the border for family emergencies. I was not one of them. What good would I be to my mother in prison?

Yet I was not exactly phoning and writing her often or checking in periodically with Curt. I was a prolific and long-winded letter writer in those years, and I want to believe that some of those letters were addressed to her. I remember Carol, my wife then—and subsequent partners throughout the rest of my mother's life—reminding and urging me to write my mother, to send her birthday and Christmas cards on time. I can physically feel, even now, the effort it would sometimes take to fill a greeting card, when I could keenly fire off three single-space pages to close friends. How much of that exertion stemmed from the lack of closeness with her when I was a child, and how much was owing to half-buried resentment? And there was self-reproach, which can make one bend over backward to be responsible or can fuel one's evasion of responsibility. Guilt may have contributed to my enormous relief that Curt and his doctor placed Gloria in a suitable home.

Marycrest Villa, on Capitol Hill in Seattle. The first of my mother's three residences where she would spend the remaining thirty-six years of her life. She had been there, happily, for almost four years when I made my first, and legal, journey to visit her in 1973. I was greeted in the Marycrest lobby by a dapperly dressed, older gentleman. He was wearing a top hat, a collar with a golden stick pin, an elegant gray and lavender striped tie and matching vest, a black frock coat with tails, black pants with a razor-edge crease, and shiny black shoes. He led me to the receptionist and bade me a grand day, telling me to buzz for him should I need anything.

"Wow," I told the receptionist, "my mother's residence has the most debonair doorman."

"He's one of our residents," she said. "He loves to do that and he's very good. Some of our residents volunteer for duties and others, like your mother in the cafeteria, earn a little money. He does it for free."

Instantly, Marycrest Villa seemed like a kind of carnival, or like that French village in the bittersweet movie *King of Hearts*, set at the end of World War I. The residents, including the nuns who run an insane asylum, abandon the town before the Germans' arrival, leaving behind the inmates, who take over the town, dressing up as the barber, mayor, and other notables.

I never went upstairs to my mother's room at Marycrest or met any of her roommates. We spent almost no time there, since I was eager to combine my time with her and visiting my favorite locales in Seattle such as Pike Place Farmers' Market and Lake Washington Boulevard. I would cruise these locales with Gloria beside me, and in the backseat usually a very supportive and bolstering wife—supportive of Gloria and bolstering me. For I still suffered, and would suffer for years, from my impatience with my mother, my frustration that she wasn't the mother I wanted. All the intellectual and artistic attention I paid to her kind of circumstances and fate didn't prevent me from checking my watch to see if I'd spent enough time with her and could drop her off and resume my non-Gloria life. My friends were impressed with my learned and empathetic knowledge of my mother's condition, but only my wife *du jour* knew about my guilty relief when Gloria said she was tired and wanted to return to the home.

During those first two years of visiting her in Seattle, I was working for the Vancouver General Hospital Child and Family Psychiatry Outpatient Unit, immersed in psychiatric literature and discussions. I spent one weekend afternoon reading about syndromes that might apply to my mother in the *Diagnostic and Statistical Manual of Psychiatric Disorders*, the bible of the field. But it was one thing to contemplate Gloria clinically and another altogether to be with my flesh-and-blood mother. Let me, then, more honestly state that I also cruised around Seattle with my mother so that I wouldn't have to focus all my restless, somewhat disheartened attention on her. I could distract myself with sightseeing and memories, with pointing out this and that, and telling stories to the backseat wife, who would often remind me to pay more heed to my mother. I wasn't behaving badly, but I was far from the dutiful son I let most friends think I was. The devoted son in my mother's uncritical, ever-grateful eyes.

I eased my conscience with mitigating factors: my mother's energy faded relatively quickly and she became irritable if she was gone too long from the comfort zone of the home. Between visits, during every phone call, she wanted to know when I'd next visit. She'd ask how many weeks and days until we'd be together. Her eagerness would grow. "I can't wait to see you, sonny boy." We'd plan our outings: a drive up to Snoqualmie Falls in the Cascade Mountains; a ferry ride on Puget Sound; a movie, a baseball game, a bingo hall.

But her eyes were bigger than her stomach when it came to outings. In our thirty-two years of visiting, we went to one Mariners baseball game and one movie. She would be too tired by the end of supper and, fatigued, the thought of a crowded movie theatre or giant stadium made her anxious. Similarly, the thrill of thinking about a ferry ride or drive to the mountains—which we also did only once each—altered into: "I don't think I want to be in the car that long." Her safe and cozy places were our old neighborhood, a picnic table by the lake in Seward Park, Pike Place Market, where she preferred to sit in the car while I roamed and reminisced with vendors, breakfast at the IHOP and supper at The Yankee Diner. Then there was shopping.

The first places we went during my visits were a supermarket and drugstore. Gloria's tastes were as fixed as the sacraments in the Anglican church, and she took the Ritz crackers, Vanilla Wafers, and chocolate kisses off the shelves with the reverence of someone receiving the holy wafer and chalice. When I think of the word "brand" in relation to my mother, branding iron comes to mind. Certain brands from her youth were deeply embedded in her brain, and it was virtually impossible to buy her anything else. She loved Nabisco Vanilla Wafers and Keebler's vanilla, strawberry, and chocolate Sugar Wafers, Brach's Mandarin Orange Slices and Butterscotch Discs, and Kraft Caramels before she had dentures. She did love bananas, too. With my "pretty wife" along (all my wives were "pretty"), whom Gloria always wanted to please, she would allow my partner to buy her strawberries and grapes and flowers. At the drugstore, there were the unvarying cosmetics: fire-engine red lipstick, light beige face powder, scarlet nail polish.

Then we went to Value Village, which originated in the Seattle area. When I started making more money, I offered to take her to J.C. Penny's, but she loved Value Village and felt comfortable there. I bought her dresses, sweaters, and coats, and found myself Harris tweed jackets and Pendleton wool shirts. Then she was through shopping, in two or three hours flat, until my next visit.

Living in her next home, Lynnwood Arms Retirement Center, she was within a few blocks of supermarkets, drug and liquor stores, and the endless strip mall that Aurora Avenue—once the main highway through north Seattle and where my father had died—had become. She earned spending money by shopping for less mobile residents. But the hunting and gathering she did with me, always in the first hours of the first day of our visit, was a sacred ritual and mission, and an intense devotional energy suffused her. Long gone were the days of bringing home fifteen loaves of bread and a dozen quarts of milk. For one thing, she had very little space in her room, and for another, unlike her son, she could be remarkably disciplined and make a box of Ritz crackers last for a week.

I also reflected, during every visit, about my mother within our materialist, consumerist society, and as a relatively poor person during those years of a swelling, thriving middle class. She had been excluded from the post-war boom during her hospital years. Finally allowed to go home, she lived with Harry and Aileen's contentment with modest comfort. They jumped on the bandwagon of affluence for the shortest of rides: a new living room sofa and armchair, an ersatz Persian rug, a two-year-old '55 Chev, an oil furnace to replace the coal burner, a new gas-powered lawn mower. They rarely ate out, indulged once every week or two in take-out Chinese food, and drank cheap bourbon. We played albums on a dinky Peter Pan three-speed record player. They were hardly subjects for J.K. Galbraith's *The Affluent Society* or Vance Packard's *The Status Seekers*.

I once took Gloria to a new, voluminous Fred Meyer but she soon wanted to leave. "There's too many things here, I don't need all these," she said with visible agitation. The consumer realm was an Eden from which my mother had been sadly expelled or was blessedly exempt, take your pick.

After Gloria had lived seven years there, Marycrest Villa was forced to close. The cost of maintaining a seven-floor residence, with a sizable staff including health professionals, was unsustainable, and the heroic couple had finally been forced to throw in the towel. There was the small matter of the big lease with Seattle University, which had its own financial needs, and the usual dearth of government funding for mental health projects.

I vented my indignation to wife and friends about society— meaning taxpayers and politicians—turning a blind eye, their fear of and contempt for mental illness, their unwillingness to make mental health and treatment a salient priority. While I indulged in my armchair fuming up in Canada—and armchair it was, for I didn't hustle down to help—Uncle Curt once again, along with those saintly people running Marycrest Villa, rode to the rescue. That social work couple found every resident an acceptable new home. My mother's was more than acceptable: Lynnwood Arms Retirement Centre. From a renovated high-rise university residence to a brand-new, suburban, middle-class retirement home with fake velvet plush wallpaper, landscape and still life reproductions on every wall, chandeliers, a state-of-the-art rehab and exercise center with several rehab specialists, a moderately fancy dining room, and an even better piano in a much larger rec room. Still, I missed the *King of Hearts* ambiance of Marycrest Villa, and I asked Mom, during my first visit to Lynnwood, if she missed her old home too.

"Are you kidding?" she said. "Look around you, boy of mine, your mother's living in the lap of luxury."

For sure, after Northern State Hospital, Marycrest Villa, and even my childhood home in the glum and dingy years after Grandma's death, this was opulence. Even Aunt Fern, who hadn't been keen on visiting Gloria in Marycrest Villa with its harlequin cast of oddballs, felt that Gloria had arrived in a tolerably middle-class world.

Half of Lynnwood's residents had troubled mental histories. The other half were senior citizens ready for a retirement home, or younger people with serious physical disabilities. There were a few severely disabled Vietnam veterans. And, memorably, a young bearded man, Rory, quadriplegic and unable to speak after his girl-friend, during a dispute, shot him in the neck, and who raced his electric cart along the corridors in a silent rage. My mother, invari-ably kind, spoke sweetly to him:

"Hello, Rory. My, aren't you looking handsome today."

"Rory, be careful you don't hurt yourself going so fast."

He glowered at everyone else but nodded politely to Gloria.

My mother lived there for sixteen years. I observed and remarked to others that the longer she was away from Northern State Hospital, and the longer she lived in a more salubrious and socially rich environment, the saner she was: the more mentally alert, emo-tionally resonant, and verbally engaged and expressive.

When I thought and said this, my mind skipped over the decade she lived with us and then alone with Harry, not wanting to dwell on my own inaccessibility and inability to help her be more "normal." My rejection of her as my mother, my discomfort with her as a misfit. How could she blossom to any impressive extent, spending almost all her time with Harry in that dusky house—the living and dining room curtains usually closed—with no visitors, ignored or treated as a pariah by her son?

At Lynnwood Arms, my mother became the life of the party, or at least one of the main sources of vibrancy and bonhomie. I witnessed the Gloria Lemm—when she was sixteen and nineteen—I'd heard about from Grandma and Curt: cheerful and friendly to staff and residents, concerned about others, brimful with enjoyment and gratitude, keen about bingo and other games, euphoric when playing the rec room piano.

"Everyone loves your mother," receptionists, nurses, orderlies, physical therapists, cooks, the laundry lady, and the center's accountant and manager would tell me. "She's so kind to everyone and helps people."

Some of that help, I was pleased to learn, such as doing laundry and shopping, earned her pocket money. I was beginning to send her money and leave money with her during a visit, but not large amounts. For one thing, the process of embracing my mother went on for many years, and my stinginess with money when it came to her reflected that. A typical conversation with a wife toward the end of a visit or when I was writing a check to mail:

"How much should I give my mother? Twenty dollars?"

"A hundred."

"Fifty?"

"Hundred."

"But she'll give it away, you know she does. And buy people candy and cookies."

"So? Doesn't she need to do that too? Give people gifts?"

"But then her money will all be gone."

"So, send it to the front desk, and they'll give it to her in installments."

I'm positive that if it had been my grandmother living on, I would have been readily more generous. Written more often. Visited more frequently and longer, and been enthralled by our conversations, not needing to drive all over hell-and-gone, as Grandma would have said I was doing. And not just because Aileen's mind was so much more intact—but because she had raised me, she was my actual mother. As for Gloria, the conundrum mother, I begrudged the money I would give her until it was sent, and then I felt like a better son—even if it required a wife's prodding. Then guilty I hadn't sent more, yet repeat the internal and marital dickering for years. The amounts did grow, and the staff would release that money a bit at a time. This became essential in the 1990s, when the staff learned she was giving most of the money I sent to several residents, "friends," who had finagled their way into Gloria's gracious heart. "Your mother's a saint," a staff person said, "most of the time, anyway. And saints get taken advantage of."

Along with the renascence of her cheerful, kindly, and popular personality, I also saw more evidence of her industriousness and capability: of the person who had been an eager and strong student, who had loved her wartime job at Boeing and her work with Harvey in the movie distribution business. I was aware of her ability to work when she was in Northern State Hospital, but didn't appreciate it adequately. Now, I was proud of her role as a go-to person for other residents at Lynnwood Arms.

I thought back to the time I found her a job at Goodwill Industries, the year after my high school graduation. In a brief burst of interest in her well-being, I decided that having a job would help Gloria's mental health improve and make her happier and more fulfilled. Someone had put the idea of Goodwill in my head, since they took on people with my mother's kind of background. I met with the supervisor, brought Gloria down, and she was hired. She lasted a bit more than a week. Her job was to iron thirty-five dresses a day. She could manage only twenty-six. When told she had to pick up the pace, she ironed twenty-eight one day. They let her go. When I stormed into the supervisor's office, he very apologetically told me that employees did have to do a minimum amount of work for Goodwill to survive as a charitable business and that thirty-five dresses was manageable. I steamed away mad and received the sympathy of female friends who thought the quantity was not very manageable. I've always loved to iron clothes and vowed then to try ironing thirty-five dresses in a seven-hour stint, but have yet to test my ability to meet that quota.

Even though I was still a good distance away from a lovingly enthusiastic son—especially the kind who relocates his life to where his mother lives, or who moves his mother into his own home or vicinity—I was pleased as punch with this preferable reincarnation of my mother in Lynnwood Arms. Living not far away, in BC, I traveled to Seattle and saw her every two or three months.

In 1984, I received an emergency phone call from Uncle Curt, at my home, now in Prince Edward Island. My mother had suffered a stroke. She was in the Swedish Hospital in north Seattle, unable to speak, and paralyzed on her left side, leg and arm. She was conscious of her surroundings but in a daze. When I arrived the next day, Fern was there (Curt was at work), with their daughter, Myrleen, and son-in-law, Bruce, sitting around the bed. Bruce, a husky chap who had endured childhood polio, was the miracle worker that day, boosting my mother's spirits with gently humorous teasing infused with empathy.

Once I was alone with my mother, my brain hovered under dull clouds of disbelief—that my mother was lying there in a state of motionless stupefaction. It was one thing to have spent a lifetime bemoaning the disappearance of Gloria's early intelligence, talents, and charms into mental illness, electric shock, and medications—that loss of the mother I never knew. But it was worse, now, to envision the disappearance of everything else in my mother apart from her heartbeat and breath, and her eyes fixed on mine—mystified, imploring, seeking reassurance and the sheer presence of my love.

I knew, absolutely, that her eyes were asking, not only about her own fate, but how I was doing. For thirty-five years she often asked me, as an adult—and I'm sure when I was a child and teenager as well—"Are you all right?" "Are you doing well?" "Is everything okay with you?" She would worry about me if I let slip that I was going through a bad patch and didn't sound sufficiently reassuring. Nothing unusual here, but rather, the love of a mother for her only child, perpetually unconditional love in her case, who lived far away and, since I'd moved to the east coast, visited only once or twice a year. And of a mother for whom so much else had been taken away, had been impossible to achieve. Now she was lying in hospital, with everything else stolen except her vital signs and dazed consciousness. And the small remains of her once large extended family. And her son.

Day by day my mother's condition improved, until she had her speech completely back after two weeks, along with full use of her right arm and leg. Mentally, she was no worse for wear; I joked with her, quite seriously, that she was sharper and more alert than ever. I had worried she would be left with chronic depression, since I'd witnessed that in the stroke-victim parents of a couple of friends. Blessedly, her sweet disposition fully returned.

But she was now in a wheelchair. She was also making twice-daily visits to the excellent physical rehab room at Lynnwood Arms, working with its therapists. Although she wasn't a practicing Christian, Gloria believed in the Christian God and expressed her thanks to him for restoring her right side, speech, and mental powers. Me, I wanted her to pay more attention to her physical therapists, who believed that Gloria was quite capable of regaining enough strength in her left leg and arm to move with a walker, even to continue her trips to the stores. She probably would not regain the use of her left hand for tasks such as playing piano, but she could be mobile again, her freedom of movement restored.

Gloria, however, had discovered a wondrous new form of mobility: the freedom to wheel around Lynnwood Arms, and faster than she could walk. She earned the nickname "Roadrunner." She also became Lynnwood's "one-handed pianist," merrily picking out tunes to the delight of residents who thought she was the bee's knees.

She did continue with her rehab for several months, but complained to me, on the phone, about how hard it was, how much she didn't like it, and how she didn't need it, thanks to her wheelchair. On a visit during this period, I went to the rehab center with her twice a day to cheer her progress. As I lifted weights and stretched with such ease, I strained emotionally with the immense effort and patience it took her to move ten feet between parallel bars. I ached over her frustration and discomfort and with her pleas to the therapist to let her stop for the day. My heart lurched when her strength gave out and she slumped and the therapist caught her. Then, during a phone call, she told me she was not going to physio anymore. She'd thrown up her stubborn wall, and the therapists must have reached that point where even the best health professionals can do no more. She fretted that I'd be disappointed in her. I told her firmly and honestly that I was proud of her and understood. In her shoes, would I have persisted and endured?

Rejoicing in her wheelchair, Gloria was active as ever at the home, though she did not want to venture out into the sidewalks, streets, and stores on her own. Her favorite activity was bingo, and she won often. "It's not hard to be a winner," she once said to me, laughing and tapping her head. "So many of them, you know, aren't really here anymore. They don't hear all the numbers or they forget to put down their markers, and the aides can't help everyone at the same time." My mother, the Bingo Queen among the senile and shell-shocked.

Before my mother's stroke, I decided that Gloria might like to play bingo in a fancy establishment. The place I chose was on First Avenue, the original Skid Row, in an old former movie theatre across from Pike Place Market. Talmud Torah Bingo. A fundraising venue for one segment or another of the Jewish community. As soon as we entered, I could tell that my mother was overwhelmed by the vastness of the hall, banks of flashing neon lights, rows and rows of tables populated by bingo aficionados, each of them with a dozen or more cards, and, bordering their cards, good-luck troll dolls, and daubers.

We found seats and mooched daubers off a huge African-American man in his mid-forties, another Vietnam vet it turned out, with his platoon of pink- and green-haired trolls. Moving briskly among the tables, wearing yarmulkes, were young men with stacks of bingo cards, money belts and coin clips around their waists. My mother, used to the solicitude of the staff at Lynnwood Arms, was cowed by the methodical alacrity of these young men. The caller read off the numbers so swiftly that I was having trouble keeping up with my cards, let alone helping my mother. The veteran next to us was daubing with the speed and accuracy of a sharpshooter with an M16.

Across the street, two blocks down, there was Central Loan and Gun Exchange, my Boy Scout master Gerson Goldman's legendary and respected pawn shop, now owned by his son Alan Goldman, one of my closest elementary school friends. We had been a great double-play combo, he at second base, me at shortstop, at John Muir Elementary School. Both of us saw ourselves wearing pinstripes, turning double plays, in Yankee Stadium. My mother suddenly seemed like some hotshot ballplayer who'd been lighting up a dinky park in some dingy small town, yanked overnight to the Show and shriveling under a million watts of stadium lights. Strike three, yer out, next batter. One of the yarmulke men impatiently demanded that we pay for the next game or give up our seats to people waiting at the door. As we rose to go, the vet said, "You folks needs to bring some trolls next time."

Back at Lynnwood Arms, I had the unsettling ability to become instantly absorbed in bingo. Unsettling because it was such a mindless game of complete chance. But that was also its attraction: pure luck, no skill and minimal concentration required. It was an activity where the American democratic ideal truly reigned. In most cases, equal opportunity was a myth. In bingo games, it was a reality. Anybody, regardless of genetic endowment, education, or socioeconomic fate, could win at bingo. Later, playing bingo with Gloria in Pinehurst Park Terrace Nursing Home, her next and final residence, I could feel guilty, winning quarters among people whose minds had moved into another dimension. Quarters I always gave away, of course, to my mother for Cokes.

Gloria found a way to make money at Pinehurst Park Terrace, sitting cozily in her wheelchair. "I'm selling the candy cart now," she told me one day on the phone. Here was a mother after her son's heart. Both of us with famous sweet tooths. The candy cart was rolled out into the main lobby of Pinehurst for a few hours each day and was festooned with Milky Ways, Mars, Three Musketeers, Snickers, M & Ms, and much more. She sold to residents, staff, and visitors. Part of the profit went to the recreation director for games, puzzles, painting supplies, and other entertainments. My mother could keep a small portion of each sale.

My mother felt not only pride in her work with the candy cart but also satisfaction in supplying people's candy needs. Immensely popular with staff and residents at her new residence—"Everybody loves Gloria," I often heard again—she didn't need this part-time job to boost her popularity. But she did value the income. Too much, in fact.

During one phone call several years into her stay there, she informed me that she wasn't "selling the candy cart anymore." I was quite surprised, but she wouldn't tell me why, beyond "I just got bored." When I next visited, the kindly receptionist informed me that my sweet and sweet-toothed mother had been skimming part of the profits and, found out, was relieved of her responsibility.

At some point, Gloria became devoted to watercolor painting. The painting sessions were organized by Ardis, the long-time recreation director, one of those countless unsung heroes who lovingly dedicate their working lives to the unglamorous care of aging and infirm fellow humans, for pitifully small wages and none of the public acclaim directed, for instance, at heart surgeons or celebrity psychiatrists. The skills that Ardis brought to her work rivaled those of a sawbones or shrink. She belongs in a Caregivers Hall of Fame. Ardis photocopied scenes from coloring books—birds, flowers, landscapes—and residents painted between the lines. I would sit with my mother at one of the tables, resisting her invitation to paint. Why? I felt an embarrassment about joining an activity geared toward little children and old people who'd lost most of their marbles. Indeed, many early childhood teachers had abandoned such coloring book confinement of the imagination and emergent skill.

What, however, was the difference between playing bingo and painting between the lines? Bingo was a game, and I've always been a sucker for games. Painting was an art. My resistance was part snobbery and part a feeling of inadequacy dating back to my C-plus in eighth-grade art class. I'd loved painting and drawing and other kinds of art projects until then. But my first "serious" art class hobbled me with a sense of deficiency that remains. Painting between the lines felt like a demotion to kindergarten. Again, it was a wife who urged me to overcome my reluctance and wounded ego—was the activity room full of sneering art critics?—and make my mother happy.

Thus, one day, the three of us opened our little trays of paint, dipped our brushes in cups of water, and began coloring sunflowers, robins, and mountain lakes. I was immediately transported back to sublime hours of childhood. Sitting there, between my mother and wife, I was blissfully absorbed with coloring these simple images. And I was suffused with warm delight at sharing this with my mother. I admired her work out loud, and she praised mine. From then on, I painted with her, and Gloria would say, "Everyone's finished, you have to quit, Ardis has other things to do." My paintings hung on her wall, hers in my study.

Gloria's art gallery was confined to the space over her bed and small night table or over the dresser beyond the foot of her bed. Over the years, when I visited my mother or thought about her from a distance, my mind would stop in its tracks to marvel, dismally, at how her personal space had been reduced since her mid-twenties to the equivalent of a small bedroom, with a single bed, and always with a roommate, never of her own choosing. The few times I asked her how she felt about this, she replied either with cheerful gratitude—if she liked her roommate—or with serene resignation. Leaving aside the effects of drugs and electroshock, she had adapted in classic human form to the severe circumscription of her personal space.

There were moments, however, which threatened to break my heart and sabotage my growing sense of being a loving and dutiful son. She would say, "Maybe I can come live with you and your wife someday" or "It sure would be nice if I could live with you." Once she asked if she could live in a nursing home near me. Even though I had grown more affectionate and caring toward her over the years, my feelings were hardly strong enough to take her into my home—even if my wife were willing—to alter our lifestyle to accommodate and financially support an aging, handicapped parent.

Guilt nipped and snapped at me from time to time, but it took little effort to shoo it away on most occasions. When it persisted, I'd think of people I knew who did have aging or infirm parents staying with them. Of more traditional communities—the way Prince Edward Island was not that long ago—when elderly parents were cared for in the home more often than in retirement and nursing homes. Even if it was impractical in terms of her caregiver needs to have Gloria living with me, even if it wasn't fair to ask my wife to share life with my mother, and even if I had every right according to contemporary values to sustain my lifestyle, why couldn't I find the means to lodge her in a PEI nursing home?

I had an answer for that, which I presented during one phone call to Gloria: "But you wouldn't have your many friends and acquaintances. You wouldn't have your bingo games and other recreation. All those people helping look after you. Ardis. The preacher you adore, who comes and sings on Sundays. Musical groups. There's so much for you to do, every day there's something."

"I'd give it all up in a heartbeat," she said, "to be with you, sonny boy, and your wife."

Touché, straight through the heart. What made her response even more exquisitely painful was that she wasn't a guilt-tripping parent, not in the slightest. I'd gather myself and say, "It's just not possible, Mom."

"I suppose not, sonny boy. But you know how your mother gets a little lonely here sometimes. But I'll be fine. Don't you worry about me," she said with not one ounce of self-pity, with utter and crushing sincerity.

There's the punch line of the joke about how many mothers it takes to change a light bulb: "That's all right, son, you go out and have a good time tonight. I'll just sit here alone in the dark." Even when my mother sounded plaintive, there was no blame in her voice or mind, only the sweetest, loving-hearted longing. Life had somehow dealt these cards to her long ago, and her son didn't have the will, the sufficient desire, to deal a new hand. Still, every now and then she had to ask, hoping wistfully for a miracle.

I would tell myself, and tell friends when the subject arose, that I would have brought my grandmother to live with me, or at least to a nearby home. I convinced myself that this was not emotional legerdemain, a con game my mind played to let me off the moral hook. But it was a comforting tale I told myself: a facile belief, with Grandma long dead, while my mother lived on and on in a nursing home, her only sibling deceased, with occasional visits with her sister-in-law and Fern's children and grandchildren. And her only child on the other side of the continent.

In my self-defense, she did have a relatively rich life at Pinehurst Park Terrace. That richness owed a great deal to her numerous friendships with the Pinehurst staff. I say "friendships" because many of the staff referred to Gloria as their friend. In the first place, she was one of the relatively few residents who were fully aware of their surroundings, capable of engaging conversation, able to reason cogently, and interact in a deliberately thoughtful way. Moreover, she was the "favorite" resident for many staff because of her kindness and warmth, her "sunshine disposition," as one receptionist described her. In a home full of people whose faculties were seriously dimmed or virtually extinguished, Gloria's were as keen and lively the week she died, at age eighty-three, as they were when I began visiting her from my Canadian home in the 1970s.

The staff blessedly told me how good I was to my mother, how devoted a son I was, how caring and generous. Huh? I was tempted to say, you've got to be joking. You're being ironic. Sadly, they weren't, for many of the residents had no visitors. None. Ever. And most other residents had rare or infrequent visitations. Sons and daughters visiting every few years, or merely sending cards. And when they visited, appearing on only one day, going for lunch or supper and maybe a bit of shopping. Siblings showing up only for a deathbed farewell or a funeral. When I first heard this, I was incredulous. In the eyes of the staff, my traveling once or twice a year to spend several days with Gloria was an admirable act of filial fidelity. And to phone her every Sunday was, they said, remarkable. Not to mention sending her a check every few months and a package with food, clothes, and costume jewelry. And nobody else joined the bingo games or watercoloring afternoons, or sat with their parent in the dining room to watch a Mariners baseball game with popcorn and Coke. This did make me feel better. I wasn't about to refuse a gift from the guilt alleviation section of the emotional department store.

There was no assuaging the guilt I felt and still bear for not being with my mother when she died. In fall 2005, Gloria told me about a lump on the top of her head, which steadily grew larger during the following months. It wasn't painful, and she was asymptomatic, but she was referred to a neurologist the next spring. When she finally saw the specialist, in mid-summer, she was diagnosed with a brain tumor. Because of her age, eighty-three, and the low probability that surgery would extend her life significantly, the tumor was deemed inoperable. The prognosis was that she had six months to a year to live.

I had plans and a flight reservation to visit Gloria in later September. My latest marriage had ended the previous January, my partner of eighteen years wanting to live alone as she struggled with a severe recurrence of her adolescent anorexia. As partner and caregiver, I'd been under considerable strain, and her illness had taken a toll on me too. I'd been the steadfast companion for my wife which I would not be for my mother. For months after our separation,

I was breathing and exhaling an atmosphere that was equal parts sorrow and euphoria. I was both grieving and healing, rediscovering and restoring myself, which included partying with friends, especially on my sixtieth birthday.

My mother's usual drug-bolstered equanimity seemed only mildly and briefly disturbed by the diagnosis and her prospects. The few times she referred to her fate, during phone calls, she alternated between wistful irony—"Well, your mother isn't going to reach one hundred like your great-grandmother"—and plucky optimism: "You can never count your old mother out. I'm a tough old weed, I just might live to be a hundred."

A week before my birthday—September 7—I spoke with a Pinehurst nurse who advised me that my mother was quickly growing weaker, that the prognosis had now changed from months to weeks, and that I should rebook my flight to arrive within the next two weeks. Would she last that long, I asked, and was assured that she would. I changed my ticket to fly down a few days after my birthday, after the celebrations I'd planned. Two days before my birthday, Pinehurst phoned to say my mother was declining rapidly, and that the neurologist wanted me to phone him.

"Your mother," he said, "won't last more than a few days. If you want to see her, you should get here immediately."

"But the nurses said she has several weeks to live."

"Well, they're wrong. If you want to see her alive, catch the next flight you can."

I talked to a nurse again, who felt that my mother would hang on until I arrived, but she stressed that "it's up to you, of course."

I did not change my plane reservation. I would be in Seattle in five days and convinced myself that she would still be alive. After all, she sounded encouragingly strong and cheerful on the phone. Although she was now bedridden, she was completely without pain, and more concerned, as usual, about me than about her imminent demise. She keenly awaited my arrival, of course, but didn't press me to come sooner. When she said, "I can't wait to see you, sonny boy," her voice was so soft, unbeseeching. Cottonwood fluff drifting in a mild breeze.

I spent my birthday in warm sunshine and then in evening afterglow at outdoor cafés on Charlottetown's Victoria Row with a succession of friends. At home, afterward, I had a pleasant conversation with my mother, stressing that I'd be with her in a few short days. I thought I heard—I wanted to feel that I heard—the depleted yet mellow voice of my mother serene in the knowledge that I'd soon be with her.

When I phoned her the next day, her voice had, overnight, weakened terribly, words coming with great difficulty and extended silences. My mother's brain waves decaying, her mind drifting beyond this world's frequencies. Taking leave of this realm.

"Your mother's dying," she said. "I wish you could be here."

There were other words, but those are the ones I remember.

"I am there, with you, Mom," I told her, my feeble, pathetic attempt at comforting her and myself. Her fragmentary responses told me there was some comfort in my voice, if not my words.

"You've been a wonderful son to me," she said.

A son so wonderful he could not cancel his birthday celebrations with friends to hop on the next plane to sit with his mother during her final hours on earth.

A phone call from a Pinehurst nurse the next morning told me that she had died peacefully in her sleep during the night. The last flickering dreams of the beautiful girl who wanted to be a dancer or historian, of the cheerful roadrunner in her wheelchair, of the woman whose love for and delight in her only child eclipsed all her losses and heartaches, were extinguished. She died peacefully, in a building full of caregivers and residents, and alone.

After my great friend, chosen father, and mentor of forty-five years, Bob Grimm, died in 2011 in Ashland, Oregon, in the motel room next to my partner's and mine during our annual pilgrimage to the Oregon Shakespeare Festival, I flew back across the continent two months later to be part of his memorial service. No hesitation, no ambivalence. Nothing else mattered. The only place in the known universe I wanted to be. Two decades earlier, I had been on the first plane out of Charlottetown for Seattle after learning of Uncle Curt's death. My reluctance to drop everything and hasten to Gloria's side was the final surfacing of my lifelong ambivalence about my mother. Not flying immediately to my mother's final hours and death bed was not only the result of this ambivalence and my shallow selfishness. There was also, perhaps, the subterranean memory of those last hours with Grandma. And something more powerful: a geyser of emotions I wished, once again, to avoid.

When I phoned the Pinehurst manager to suggest a memorial service in the home, I half-expected her to scoff sarcastically: What? You were too busy partying to come sit by your mother's deathbed and say goodbye to her in person, and now you want to host a celebration of her life at Pinehurst? Aren't you a piece of work.

Instead, she said, "That's a fabulous idea. We all loved your mother. You just tell us what you want, and we'd be more than happy to arrange things."

That Saturday afternoon, the main dining room beyond the main lobby was decorated with balloons and streamers. The dining tables, each with a little vase and flower bouquet, were surrounded by residents, while staff stood around the room near the walls and windows. The retired Presbyterian preacher, who for many years had performed Sunday services and visited residents often during the week, and whom Gloria dearly admired and platonically loved, sang two hymns, thanked the good lord for the gift that was Gloria, and said prayers for her soul.

I told a brief version of Gloria's life, from her bright and hopeful youth, through her darkest times and long incarceration in a mental hospital, to her reasonably contented years, albeit lonely for her far-away son, at Pinehurst Park Terrace. I spoke of how much she valued the staff, how she considered many of them her friends and all of them her kind helpers, and I added my own gratitude and praise.

"You were her family," I said, "as much as I was, and perhaps more, since you were with her every hour of every day."

As I concluded, I looked slowly around the room at the faces of that family and was suffused with the warmth and fondness they felt for my mother. Then, finished, gathering my notes from the lectern, I watched the staff quickly turn to their duties, and knew that Gloria would swiftly fade from their consciousness, the space she had occupied immediately filled by other residents, including the next new admission assigned to my mother's room. This was hardly callousness on their part, but rather, the nature and necessity of their work. And because, while I needed to see them as my mother's family, she wasn't part of theirs. She was a client, a patient, and although she was one of their favorites, she wasn't blood. I was.

I was the one who would collect her ashes at Washelli Cemetery, where my father and her father were buried under white crosses in the military section. I was the one who would contemplate, in the presence of patient cemetery staff, whether to place her ashes next to the husband she never stopped loving. I was the one who would decide to carry her ashes with me across the border, waiting for the right time and right place to scatter or bury them. Sonny boy finally bringing his mother back to his eastern Canadian home.

8

The Land of Opportunity

It's a summer day and normally I'd be outside, but *Queen for a Day* is on and I never miss sitting beside Grandma, as riveted as I'd be with Grandpa at a UW Huskies football game with the score tied in the fourth quarter. This is a game show like no other, where women compete for prizes by telling us—by vividly creating pictures in our heads—of their and their families' tragedies and suffering. Host Jack Bailey introduces the three or four female contestants. One by one, the women share their heartbreaking stories with the audience, persuade us of their spirited efforts and resolve to triumph over misfortune, and tell us what they long for to lessen their pain and hardship. Between stories, we are shown the prizes—a cornucopia of American plenteousness and triumph: gleaming and labor-saving appliances, whiter-than-white detergents and toothpastes to keep the germs at bay, and a lifetime supply of breakfast cereals and never-run nylons. Grandma and I ooh-and-aah at the loot. We hold hands during the tales of woe and longing—shock, wonder, mesmerizing sorrow, and sympathy flowing from our hearts to our palms and fingers. Jack Bailey draws out their stories, smiling like my uncle grilling burgers on the Fourth of July. Finally, the audience applauds for each contestant, the Clap-o-meter gauges the response, and a radiantly transformed winner is crowned. Grandma and I hug and wipe away tears, unmindful of the other women slumping offstage.

That weekly hour with Grandma sits prominently in my mind because every molecule of her compassion and yearning rose and swirled around us and enveloped me. Years later I would see the profound flaws in *Queen for a Day*, its exploitation of those women, and the American myth of individual opportunity, hard work, and success: not everyone was rewarded for pulling herself up by the bootstraps. Most of those women were not, and walked away with a year's supply of Cheerios or a vacuum cleaner, sloughed off by people clapping for a bogus machine. But while Grandma was clearly swept up in the winner's reversal of fortune, for almost all the show she had melded with each of those women, their undeserved misfortunes, and their desire to transcend their damaging and anguished lot. The brevity of that melding belied its depth.

As well, in the show's defense, most of the contestants were working and lower-middle class, including women of color and immigrants, grossly under- or misrepresented in popular culture. Their problems were often caused by husbands' flaws and failures. Typically, the women had to assume responsibility for their families. The show unveiled a different American reality for my young mind.

I'd been raised on the celebratory and proud assertion that America "is a nation of immigrants"—ascendant immigrants. I was steeped in the history and mythology of one wave of industrious, ambitious immigrants after another, working tirelessly at low-paying jobs, prevailing over hardships and prejudice, and scaling the ramparts of occupational status, economic well-being, social respectability, and prestige.

Europeans, including my paternal ancestors, migrated by the millions to America in the 1850s. My German heritage, fascinating to me now, was largely absent from my public schooling, focused as it was on the "melting pot" rendering of American history. The American ethnicities that jut out from my childhood memories of

TV shows and movies, family gossip and schoolyard banter, sports heroes and politicians, and textbooks are Irish, Scots, Italian, Jewish, Chinese, Japanese, and, of course, English. African and Native American were present but grossly misrepresented.

I did not learn, for instance, that half the wagons used for westward migration—the westward ho! pioneering wagons that were so much a part of American history and mythology and of my youthful imagination—were made by Studebaker, a company founded by five midwestern German-American brothers, and which later became the automotive giant. The Studebakers were also members of a conservative German Baptist religion, the Dunkard Brethren, who viewed war as evil. When I worked in that Seattle freight yard after high school, I did not know that my employer, Northern Pacific Railroad, was once led by a German immigrant, Henry Villard, who strove to settle German farmers on his company's vast land grant. Babe Ruth and Lou Gehrig are rumored to have spoken German in the Yankees dugout. German-Americans succeeded so handsomely, it seems, that their ethnic identity eventually fell largely outside the realms of both demonization and romanticization.

I've also come to appreciate a viewpoint expressed by author Timothy Egan, a fellow native of Seattle: "I never cared for the 'melting pot' metaphor, in part because it treats a nation of immigrants like a stew with all the cultures cooked out of it . . . I prefer 'the American experiment.' . . . The audacious idea that people from all races, ideologies, and religious sects would check their hatreds at the door after becoming citizens is our sustaining narrative." As Egan knows, the enactment of that narrative throughout America's history has been far from ideal, and the telling largely excludes, for example, the hatred and persecution of Indigenous peoples. Omar El Akkad, an Egyptian-Canadian writer living in America, writes of "a country that purports to be a melting pot but is in reality a crucible, a vessel of fierce and fiercely luminous burning." Yet a good deal of the hatred has, over the years, been checked at the door, the crucible escaped—at least by most white European descendants— though far less so by Americans of African, Jewish, Asian, Middle Eastern, and Hispanic descent. My German-American ancestors, subject over the centuries to Europe's tribal rancors, were, after initial nativist resentment, beneficiaries of America's foundational myths. There is no need for German Lives Matter protests on behalf of America's largest ethnic group.

I sometimes imagined *Queen for a Day* when I visited my mother in her final residence, Pinehurst Park Terrace Nursing Home. But a revival in which nearly all the contestants were Hispanic immigrants and immigrants of color.

As America grapples with "illegal immigration" and white nativism, and focuses on Hispanic and immigrants of color, the staffs of nursing homes such as Pinehurst provide another tableau of America's ever-transforming ethnic identity, not to mention its socioeconomic configuration. There were people from Nigeria, Ethiopia, Kenya, El Salvador, the Philippines, Thailand, and more. As the cliché goes, "they were doing the work that *n*th-generation Americans didn't want to do." Especially European-descended Americans. Caring for the elderly. And doing so for wages close to the minimum. There were also second-generation Vietnamese, Korean, Mexican-Americans, and African-Americans. Many were working their way assiduously up the socioeconomic ladder: enrolled in post-secondary diploma and degree programs while working full-time, and in most cases raising children. Orderlies studying to become licensed practical nurses, who were working to become registered nurses, who were earning business degrees.

During some visits I chatted with an African-American woman, the coordinator of rehabilitation services, and followed her progress to a bachelor's, and then a master's, in social work, with the goal of managing her own nursing home.

For years, there was Joseph, a registered nurse from Nigeria, who adored, teased, befriended, and superbly cared for my mother, including lifting her spirits when needed. My mother adored and flirted with Joseph in return. He did management studies and moved into the assistant manager's position. But he was unhappy there, missed the hands-on work with residents, and returned joyously to his lower-paid work as a nurse.

There were two sisters from Ghana, licensed practical nurses, who told me how caring for the infirm and elderly within the family and village was an essential part of life where they'd grown up. They were as tall and thin as runway models, yet they frequently lifted and transferred women and men from bed to wheelchair to bathroom and back. They could have done construction work and been paid a lot more. Short, stout women from Central America told me the same stories of looking after aging parents and grandparents. They never tried or intended to make me feel guilty, though guilt did flicker through my mind as I listened, quickly replaced by the evidence that my mother was blessed with care, respect, and affection as first-class as wealthy residents received in a luxury nursing home.

The optimist in me viewed the Pinehurst staff as evidence that the American Dream still had legs, and wasn't yet arthritic and wobbling toward bitter nostalgia. This was still the land of opportunity, and these immigrants were the latest godsend for cultural and economic renewal. Then there was my caustic perspective. Almost all the residents were white. The warehousing of the elderly and severely infirm involves a variety of occupations we hold in relatively low esteem. Who better to employ and exploit, there, than the latest immigrant wave? The reality, of course, is a weaving of both: the warp of exploitation and the woof of opportunity; the shamefully low status and the laudable value of this work. Moreover, with few exceptions, the Pinehurst staff seemed to enjoy, even love, their work and the residents.

I grew up in multiethnic, multicolored Mount Baker Ridge, or just Mount Baker as we called our neighborhood. From my street, the ridge sloped steeply west toward Rainer Valley. Beyond that, the industrial heart of Seattle with its warehouses, machine shops, and rail yards, and further, Elliott Bay and the wharves, Puget Sound and the San Juan Islands, and the mountains of the Olympic Peninsula. The families on the west slope of the ridge tended to be poorer, the houses dingier, the yards scragglier, the dogs mangier, and my friends and I knew few of the kids there and were oblivious of them at school. We did not yet know such jargon as "socio-economic class." We were vaguely aware of the "poor kids" who lived only a baseball's throw away, yet their realm was one we rarely ventured into or thought about.

We gazed and roamed eastward, down the three blocks to Lake Washington, with Mercer Island and the Cascade Mountains beyond, and the snow-capped majesty of Mt. Rainer to the southeast on days not overcast. With each block downward from my street atop the ridge, incomes rose, job status elevated, prestige in the social hierarchy ascended, and homes, yards, and vegetation became lovelier, then grander, until the climax wealth of mansions along Lake Washington Boulevard. Eastward down the ridge, but above the Boulevard, all the kids went to my schools, and so I knew them, played football and baseball with them in the side streets, Monopoly and poker in their basement dens, went with them to Boy Scout meetings and camps.

Up on the ridge, most of the families were "respectable" in the eyes of families in the zone between ridge and boulevard. I had close friends in that zone and was often in their homes and yards. Those families shopped on my street, at Henry's Meat Market, Mr. and Mrs. Lee Him's Grocery, Barney Dahl's Pharmacy. The families in the mansions on Lake Washington Boulevard were another story. I can't remember being invited into those homes, though some were inhabited by classmates. I and several friends, in our early teens, earned money mowing lawns and tending flower beds at those mansions. Their owners paid well. Youthful unknowing Marxists ("from each according to his abilities"), we would charge the mansion owners the enormous sum of twenty dollars for a half-day's work, but five dollars to a kindly elderly widow on the ridge. In my naiveté, I told my grandfather how generous the mansion owners were. Not generous, he said, skinflints. How so? They'd have to pay the Japanese gardeners twice or three times as much. Ah, yes, the Japanese gardeners with their wonderful pickup trucks full of gardening tools racked upright and lawn mowers and bags of cuttings and leaves. And the calm, delicate intensity of their work, as opposed to our rambunctious energy. My grandfather wanted me to earn money and "learn the value of hard work." He was pleased in his taciturn way, so he didn't add, in his union-man voice, that I was taking jobs away from hard-working men. Perhaps he was glad I was taking work away from, as he called them, "the Japs."

My own class bias wanted me to believe that the mansion owners never drove or trundled up the ridge to peer into Henry's meat display. I imagined they shopped in exclusive stores in the wealthy neighborhoods further north up the lake. At Henry's they would have had to rub shoulders with my bartender grandfather, the kind of man they'd hire to moonlight at their parties. With Emma Gayton and her husband Leonard, once a jazz musician, and of the esteemed Gayton clan, among Seattle's Black pioneers, but back then an outdoor billboard sign inspector. Or Annie with the frizzy gray hair, who owned a house across the street with perennials run amuck, vines strangling the house, a moss-mottled roof, Christmas ornaments dangling year-round in the windows.

An elderly Japanese couple lived directly across the street from my house, and during the warmer months, the gentleman was outdoors but invisible within the tall fence around his garden. Briefly, when the gate opened, I caught glimpses of his reverent artistry. Although my grandfather held Pearl Harbor and the Pacific war against all people of Japanese descent, he instilled in me respect for their industriousness and meticulous skill at whatever they undertook. In later years, I would read about Japanese-Americans and Canadians, their early decades in the Pacific Northwest, the discrimination, devastation to their lives and communities, theft of their property and livelihoods, internment camps, and triumphs over adversity. My mother had many Japanese classmates at Garfield High before the war. I played football and studied math at Franklin High with the children of those Japanese gardeners, vegetable growers, and fishmongers, who went on to Stanford and MIT and leadership roles in Seattle.

We knew our immediate neighbors very well. To the south, Mrs. Schmidt, a sweetly benign widow and my primary babysitter, deep-frying donuts for me, with her trunk full of metal soldiers and artillery and wooden blocks to build castles and forts. She would sit in her living room armchair, contentedly watching my fantasies of medieval and modern warfare.

Behind us, a retired couple with a magical goldfish pond and a flower-sprayed rockery cascading steeply downhill. Next door to them, their widower brother, who kept a chicken coop and supplied eggs to his immediate neighbors when the city still allowed that. He also, less agreeably, burned his dog's droppings in an incinerator barrel. Then he died and, mysteriously, his old house was demolished, leaving his relatives with a larger yard for me to mow when I was old enough to earn spending money, imagining myself as a modern-day version of my favorite TV western hero, Paladin: Have Lawn Mower (Gun) Will Travel. Below these neighbors were the Ferraras, who owned a construction company, hence, the neighborhood's only swimming pool, and a gym with a basketball court in their basement where the future Lakers great Elgin Baylor once practiced while playing for Seattle University, making their home a shrine into which I and my friends were never invited.

To the north, the Petronis and my close friend Dean, a year younger, another only child. Mr. Petroni worked in a fruit warehouse in Seattle's industrial zone, slinging boxes and crates on and off trucks. The neighborhood's only basketball hoop was nailed to their garage, and their driveway was our court. Baseball, however, was America's sport, not basketball or football, and Dean and I spent countless hours honing our catching and throwing skills in each other's yard. Even after we had a vicious argument and I bit his ear and we were forbidden to play with each other, we quickly made up and played catch over the fence until the grown-ups relented.

A wide street below ours was our baseball diamond and football field. Apart from a baseball sandlot a few blocks away, the nearest sports fields were a mile off at Franklin High. But we didn't feel disadvantaged. We reveled in snagging flyballs while leaping over a low hedge into a flowerbed, in snaring footballs over a car hood, in the wounds from the pavement. I think I made the football team partly because I learned to catch balls while running full speed, heedless of danger, among parked cars, fire hydrants, and telephone poles. Almost all the neighborhood adults endured the noise and minor damage as an acceptable price to pay for the wholesome activities of boys, most of whom would become varsity athletes, several in universities.

When I remember such delights of the neighborhood, I must guard against nostalgia—good-old-days romanticization, atavistic belief in the superiority of some idealized and "traditional" past. There were boys less gifted at sports, less keen, confident, and reckless, who tired of dropping fly balls and passes, of being ridiculed, of face planting on concrete or being blocked into car fenders, and drifted away from our glorious circle. Some of whom then sank beneath the academic floors of our high school, where the varsity athletes all dwelt, into the basement catacombs of "Industrial Arts," or disappeared altogether before graduation. While the lucky ones reappeared at class reunions as teachers, sports journalists, and lawyers, others resurfaced in stories of petty crime and jail time, booze and drug addiction, their photos taped at later reunions on the "In memoriam" poster, dead before age sixty. There we stood, the lucky gray-haired winners, gazing sadly for a brief moment at the ill-fated losers, the separation beginning decades earlier in Mount Baker's streets and yards.

And in 1950s Seattle, not every neighborhood possessed the charm, modest comfort, ethnic tolerance, and intimacy of Mount Baker Ridge. I was most fortunate in my grandparents' choice of a home to buy in 1950, and in the physical talents and psychological makeup that allowed me to play with the winners. I gave little or no thought to the darker sides of our neighborhood—lonelier or grimmer realities that were concealed or to which I was blind as I bounced along in my cheerful, eager, and lucky-stars way. And I never encountered, or recognized, the racism in the neighborhood that Tom, the Gaytons' oldest son, who became a civil rights lawyer and poet, later wrote about in his memoir.

One autumn evening when I was reading on a living room window bench, I saw Brennan King, my football coach, drive up in his Impala convertible and park in front of the house across the street, formerly owned by the elderly Japanese couple and now inhabited by a single African-American mother with several young children. The garden was neglected and gone to seed, the yard untended and littered with toys. The woman often went out at night, with different men, leaving her children in the care of . . . we weren't sure.

I idolized Coach King, the State of Washington's first African-American high school head baseball and football coach, from whom I was learning about selfless devotion, discipline, victory over inner and outer obstacles, camaraderie, integrity. What was Coach doing there, the woman descending her steps in a tight red dress and spike heels, climbing into Coach's car? Coach glanced straight at my window—did he know I lived here?—as he closed her car door, and left me fretting for days after, especially at football practice, that Coach would not be happy that I'd seen him with a woman my Black friends said nasty things about. Class prejudice and sexism had no racial borders.

Mr. Petroni was promoted to supervisor at the fruit warehouse, and before long they fled our increasingly Black neighborhood for the white suburbs. Dean and I had drifted apart. A couple of years before, we'd found another basketball hoop after Dean, who went to a Catholic school, made it clear that I could shoot baskets in his driveway, but not my Black friends. When I started worrying that we'd follow the Petronis to the suburbs, dragging me away from my beloved neighborhood and Black friends, I was relieved to hear Grandpa declare, "No coons are going to drive me from my home and neighborhood. Over my dead body." For once, I didn't seethe at his racial slur. Now, the Petronis were replaced by the Walkers, our new "colored" neighbors, as Grandpa politely called them.

Grandpa was talking over the fence and drinking beer with Mr. Walker, a high school band teacher. The Walker family, Harry had observed, were quite well dressed, and they'd beautified the yard beyond the Petronis' meticulous standards. Yet Mr. Walker, Grandpa said, wasn't "uppity," rather, was a down-to-earth fellow without any pretensions. "Give them an inch and they'll take a mile," Grandpa would complain and warn about Black people. Mr. Walker, apparently, wasn't taking more yardage than he should.

I was leaning on the fence listening. They glanced at the woman across the street, her kids and all that clutter.

"Darkies," said Mr. Walker, "if you know what I mean."

Grandpa nodded his understanding.

This was an early conscious experience with intra-racial class prejudice. Later, I read about established families of Harlem during the Great Migration northward of southern African-Americans from 1916 onward: listening to classical music and reading Shakespeare, polishing their Standard English, distressed by southern Blacks arriving with their jazz and blues and wild dancing and "Negro" accents. I'd become more conscious of the class differences among the Black students at school, sometimes based on gradations of skin color. And my neighborhood friends would, in our last year of high school and soon after graduation, divide into those confident of success on their horizons and those already seeing failure in their future—the African-American or Black achievers, and the ones who started referring to themselves by the "n" word as a defiant, ironic mark of anti-heroic, doomed honor. The "n" word had been used earlier in our neighborhood, but only as a verbal weapon of last resort reserved for the most heated moments, such as one too many elbows in the face during hoops.

One night during my senior year, I returned home from a date to find a half-dozen police cars and an ambulance, lights flashing, and a couple of dozen neighbors on the sidewalks—everyone's attention focused on the house where the single mother lay dead on the floor, gunned down by one of her boyfriends. I joined the crowd and watched the children be led to police cars and driven away, then the body carried down the steps and slid into the ambulance. I went to sleep with red and blue lights still flashing through my bedroom window.

Our neighborhood's watering hole was hardly a swinging hot spot. In O'Leary's Tavern next to Henry's Meat Market, regulars sat in a cheerless gloom, to my youthful eyes, hardly mitigated by the blue and red lights—like cop cars'—around the bar's mirror. I was the child of a bartender, but Grandpa's place of employment, Green's Cigar Store—named by its Jewish founders Green and Birnbaum in 1903 when Seattle was the staging ground for the Klondike Gold Rush—was a carnival of delights for a kid, so much more than a cigar store, whereas O'Leary's was funereal. Those many times I glanced through the open door gave me a lifelong distaste for what seemed sepulchers for the melancholic. But those people may well have loved the neighborhood as much as I did: O'Leary's their sanctuary just as consecrated as St. Clement's Church.

St. Clement's, a half-block from my home, became a vital haven when I was eleven, as my grandparents drank and fought more, and a refuge after my grandmother died and mother came home, a grave disappointment and loony-tunes embarrassment.

Grandpa and Grandma had sent me to St. Clement's the Sunday after they announced I would not return to Our Lady of Mount Virgin School for first grade. I had wanted to attend kindergarten at John Muir Elementary School, about fifteen blocks away. I have no idea why; my best friend, Dean Petroni, went to the Catholic school. My grandparents decided to send me to Mount the Virgin, as I learned from older kids to call it, because it was only three blocks away. They felt I wasn't old enough to take the bus to John Muir. A salient aspect of my upbringing by grandparents was that they seemed more protective—over-protective, I thought, because they were "old-fashioned"—than my friends' younger parents. Paradoxically, being old-fashioned, they were more trusting of me within the boundaries they drew. They wanted me in kindergarten close by. But if I wanted to explore the off-limits woods and old shacks below the school with friends, I would tell my grandparents I was going to a friend's house, and they would never check up on me.

I loved Mount Virgin and my beautiful-in-every-way young teacher, Sister Carmella. I still have a crush on her. So many people have cruel nun stories, including the horror stories of First Nations survivors of residential schools. I have kind, gentle, nurturing stories, including Sister Carmella's skill at throwing and catching baseballs. She was my first coach. And an early moral guide. She once caught me and a classmate sneaking into the kitchen to steal cookies. Rather than punish us, she sat us down at a table and gave us each two cookies and a glass of milk. This time, she said, you can have them, but never do this again. And I didn't. How could I betray such sweet forgiveness and pleasant remonstrance?

I was cast out of Eden when I came home excitedly during the last week of school, announcing to my grandparents that, next year during first grade, I would take catechism and be confirmed. I can see Grandma's face scrunch into a worried expression, and Grandpa's go dark with ancestral gall. Faces don't go dark, someone once told me when I used that expression. Oh, yes, they do. A slate gray storm cloud swept into view just under Grandpa's skin.

"You're not going back there," he said. "We're sending you to public school next fall."

I saw that my grandmother was not about to disagree, and her stiff posture, standing in the dining room, told me there would be no appealing this time to her more tender emotions.

"But . . . you said I was too young to take the bus."

"You'll be old enough in September," Grandpa said firmly.

How could I become old enough in just four months, I didn't dare ask. But I had one more card to play.

"But where am I going to go to church, to Sunday school?"

"You can go down the block, to St. Clement's."

I was left to mourn the loss of Sister Carmella, a victim of the lingering effect of Protestant hatred and fear of Catholics. My grandmother was a lapsed Methodist, my grandfather an expired Lutheran. They did make sure I said my prayers every night, Grandma often kneeling and reciting them with me, and they made sure I faithfully attended Sunday school whenever my devotion flagged. I do remember a red-letter edition of the King James Bible in the house, but I never saw Harry or Aileen crack its covers.

St. Clements had once been a favored church for Seattle's white Protestant establishment. My first priest there, Father Colburn, referred to himself as a "minister" and wore a gray suit with a gray clerical collar. A plain wooden cross hung over the altar, and apart from Stations of the Cross on the walls and impressive stained-glass windows, there was nothing that would offend the sensibilities of low-church Protestant Episcopalians. The church was not even half-full most Sundays. On Easter and Christmas, when the pews were jammed, most of the worshippers were unfamiliar faces, people who had roots in Mount Baker but now lived in wealthier, white-bread neighborhoods.

Then, when I was eleven, Father Kappas arrived from the Anglo-Catholic diocese of Eau de Clair, Wisconsin. From the start, I was favorably disposed to Father Kappas, who called himself a priest and wore black instead of gray. Instead of Sunday Communion Service, we had low mass at seven a.m. and then high mass complete with incense, not to mention Sunday afternoon Benedictus and weekday afternoon rosary.

The first Christmas Eve high mass under our new priest's shepherding, Father Kappas ascended the pulpit to deliver his sermon, and silently, painstakingly gazed at his parishioners, one after another. Finally, rather than announcing the biblical text for his sermon, he said, "I don't know most of you. I have never seen most of you in this church before. Most of you I haven't seen in this neighborhood. I don't want Christmas Christians or Easter Christians. If you come here only on Christmas and Easter, I don't want your tithe in the offering plate. I want parishioners who are here on Sundays." He paused, letting his words sink in, then said, "Where are the people of this neighborhood? I look around and see a church full of white faces. But the neighborhood has many Black and Asian faces. Where are they? I want to see the faces of this neighborhood in these pews. You are, of course, very welcome every Sunday."

Then, without skipping a beat, he read the text for the day and began his sermon, while his altar and choir boys behind him, me among them, looked at each other in amazement, and while those white faces we never saw on other Sundays were frozen in looks of outrage, resentment, or sheepishness.

Permeating everything about this revitalized neighborhood church was the profound religious devotion of its priest. Whereas St. Clement's under Father Colbourn seemed like another social obligation with religious overtones, the parish was now a vibrant spiritual presence and a vital center of social life for many in the neighborhood. Moreover, Father Kappas, without being preachy or overtly political, and with his every word and action, modeled equality, justice, and compassion. Although the neighborhood Catholics went to Our Lady of Mount Virgin and some Black families went to the

First African Methodist Episcopal Church in the Central Area, and a few families attended the Greek Orthodox church or the synagogue, there was respect for St. Clements and Father Kappas as sources of nurturing and social justice.

As my friendship with Dean Petroni waned and then went cold turkey, I gravitated to the Gaytons, who became my second family through junior and senior high. Earlier, I was close with Lonnie, my age, and then in high school with his year-older brother, Tom, who became my athletic, intellectual and racial justice mentor. I spent countless hours in Tom's room discussing everything from Nietzsche to Hugh Hefner's "The Playboy Philosophy" column, Richard Wright's memoir *Black Boy* and novel *Native Son* to James Baldwin's barrier-blasting essays. I also ran endless pass patterns while Tom, the football star, threw me passes, preparing me for my varsity tryout as well as the intellectual life and racial justice enlightenment.

My grandparents' record collection contained white jazz musicians and vocalists, from Benny Goodman and Glenn Miller to Bing Crosby and Patti Page. The Gaytons' albums initiated me into the temple of Black music with its high priests Duke and Count, Bessie and Billie, Louis and Ella, and Mr. Gayton's holy of holies, Dinah Washington. His tastes ended before bebop, Miles, and Coltrane, but he tolerated our youthful devotion to Ray Charles and Jackie Wilson, the latter, I learned in their home, a serious influence on Elvis.

Midway through my high school years, a new family moved into the neighborhood, the Owens. Their porch became our hangout, along with the Gaytons' dining room where we played Risk and whist in between ball games, and Dexter "DJ" Jarvis's waxed rec room "dance floor." Mr. Owens was a merchant marine and devotee of the blues and R & B. Mrs. Owens was a fine down-home cook and a big-hearted, ebullient host who loved parties and having us kids hang around. For years we'd benefited from Mr. and Mrs. Gayton's largesse, and the latter's wizardry with waffle and pancake griddles and soup and stew pots. Now, we scarfed Mrs. Owens's fried chicken and baked ribs and candied yams. Mr. Owens treated his albums with the same sacred love as Mr. Gayton, and we sat with equal reverence at his feet as he exclaimed, "Heed this righteous sound, baby," adding Otis Redding and Lavern Baker, Muddy Waters and B.B. King, Ma Rainey and Lightning Hopkins to the pantheon.

Ron, the Owens's child my age, had superb athletic talent and was recruited by the track coach, Frank Ahearn, to run sprints and by Coach King as a running back. He stuck with track but not football. Ahearn was famous for his high standards and success—numerous championships and star performances. But the sprinters' workouts were less demanding than King's football practice, and Ron wasn't inclined toward intense sessions, especially in the mud or sleet. Too, he was a smoker and drinker. None of my neighborhood friends and fellow athletes indulged, at least to my knowledge. Not until Ron arrived. Lonnie and DJ, the son of elementary school teachers, were the first of my neighborhood friends to shift, or let drift, their devotion from sports to hanging out with Ron and his vices.

Tom Gayton was always the golden boy, and his brother Lonnie lived in his shadow. Lonnie's caustic humor—think Richard Pryor—and smartass retorts dated back to his childhood, and were the reasons, I'm convinced, that our fifth-grade teacher delivered the severe blow of failing him for the year, in spite of his sharp intelligence, and Lonnie never regained his stride. To my discredit, I gradually distanced myself from him and gravitated to golden Tom, who welcomed me as a protegé, a surrogate younger brother heading for praiseworthy distinction and not delinquency.

We all liked Ron: he was generous, funny, cool, happy-go-lucky, and a warm, devoted friend. His attitude was the opposite of Lonnie's increasingly surly, fatalistic, and resentful demeanor. But several of us saw Ron leading Lonnie and DJ down a self-destructive path. DJ had been a star athlete, strong scholar, dazzling dancer, and class clown of the upbeat, delightful variety, the kind the entire class and teachers cherished. We thought he would shimmy and jive his way into a bright future, sunshine crowning him. Now, a wistfulness infiltrated his disposition as if he sensed his best days were behind him, and he seemed to be cringing at a premonition of his future.

By the last two years of high school, we were going our separate ways. Friendships remained, but now in twos or threes through mutual interests and in wider circles at school. Tom and I were the only ones listening to jazz and discussing Black authors with Mr. Gayton. We were the only altar boys who would visit Father Kappas on Saturday afternoon to discuss Christianity and social justice. Apart from my many hours at the Gaytons', I was hanging out with old and new friends from other neighborhoods, and with my year-older girlfriend from another high school near the University of Washington.

But we all did get together on occasion, and ironically at the Owens'. One of those gatherings was on their front porch a few days after graduation. Tom was now a first-year student at the University of Washington, on his way to a law degree, and active in the Black student society. There was David "Duke" Dupree, an academically stellar student with an athletic scholarship to a major California university. As I recall, his father drove a library bookmobile, and one evening as I walked by their house, I heard classical music—a small ensemble—and saw through the living room windows David and his family playing. Both Tom and Duke had no end of confidence and aplomb.

Then there were DJ, Lonnie, and Ron, smoking.

And me.

The lighthearted, lackadaisical chatter floating in the afternoon summer air suddenly nose-dived into dark waters.

"We nothing but spades, man," DJ said with spirited resignation, "gonna end up on Jackson Street with rags on our head, shuckin' and jivin' in Angelo's Pool Hall."

"That's bullshit," Duke said, disgusted. "You can be whatever you decide to be."

Tom launched into an impassioned, eloquent sermon about our friends' abilities, the opportunities they could seize, and the necessity of avoiding the dead-end, degenerate fates of those brothers in Jackson Street dives. He concluded with an inspired crescendo about the worlds they could embrace. I was mouth agape, deeply moved. Not, however, our three brooding friends.

"All well and good, Tom," Ron said, his voice gently sorrowful. "You some kind of super dude intellectual, got no shortage of swagger, you gonna take the world by storm. Duke, man, you this all-around brain, not to mention bold as brass. And Rich, well, he's white."

The fabled end of one's innocence, for most of us, accumulates in stages. But there are thresholds one may suddenly cross or be shoved over, sometimes with a painful crash-landing, into a more complex awareness—a less innocuous, more troubled reality. Ron's declaration thrust me out of the comfort zone in which I'd managed to separate my experience from the racial inequality and distress of which I was increasingly aware, intellectually. None of my Black friends in the neighborhood had ever referred to me, in my presence anyway, as white. When insults flew, including the "n" word, I kept quiet, exempt, an innocent bystander. Now, in this moment of rhetorical sundering, Tom and David were deemed to be among the blessed, destined for success, because of their intelligence and confidence, whereas I would succeed because of my color. There was no rancor in Ron's voice when he said that, no put down, just a sweetly sad statement of fact.

I prefer another memory of Ron. Five of us were competing for the four spots on the mile relay team—the glory event at a track meet's end—at the city championships. Our collective speed guaranteed first place. Ron was faster than me. Rounding the last turn, he faded and I secured a spot. I knew his "failure" wasn't from smoking.

Once we'd caught our breath, I said, "Why'd you let me win?"

"I'm in the hundred and two hundred. This is your race, baby, you've worked your ass off all year, you've earned it. Not me."

When, running anchor, I broke the tape at the finish line, there was Ron with a huge grin.

After graduation and until we left Seattle, Darlene and I were befriended by Ron's parents and invited to their parties, a young white couple warmly embraced by all their older Black friends. Mr. Owens even offered to secure me a merchant marine's ticket and immediate passage on a ship to Saigon. But I have no recollection of seeing or speaking with Ron after that day on the porch. I've blanked him out.

A year later, Tom Gayton and I both drove up to the pumps at our old neighborhood gas station at the same time. He was in second year at university, an active member of the Black students' society, and we hadn't seen each other for twelve months. I greeted him enthusiastically. With a large Afro and wearing sunglasses, looking over my head, he raised his fist and said, "Black power, baby," and started pumping gas. Devastated, I got back in my car and drove off. I did not speak to my once-best friend for twenty-five years.

In 1992, visiting Gloria, I saw an obituary in *The Seattle Times* for Emma Gayton, Tom's mother. I phoned the number I'd dialed hundreds of times and Tom, now Tomás, back from California for the funeral, answered and warmly told me to hurry right over. When I arrived, his first words were "My brother" as he tightly embraced me.

At Green's—"Seattle's leading sporting center" boasted its match-book covers—I sat in the barbershop, while Tommy the shoeshine boy bent over my dress shoes on those Saturdays I went shopping with Grandma, followed by a haircut and lunch in a Green's restaurant booth.

Tommy was no boy; he was the only Black person working at Green's, a friendly, mild-mannered, unassuming, gray-haired "colored" man, as my grandfather called him. Or Tommy the shoeshine boy. When Harry was in a grumpy mood about Black people and race relations, about more African-Americans moving into our neighborhood, about civil rights boycotts and marches, he'd talk about "darkies" or "coons." In a foul mood, the "n" word. There were, however, "good colored people." Like Tommy. "I'll take a good colored person any day," Grandpa said, "over most white people." Unfortunately, it seemed, very few Blacks qualified as good in Harry's books. I've wondered since about Tommy, what he was like, who he was, away from Green's. What was his life before Green's, and how did he become part of the Green's family? How did he feel being the only "colored" person working in an establishment where I can't recall seeing any customers who weren't white or Asian-American? What did being called "shoeshine boy" do to his insides?

Harry's occasional anti-Semitic remarks were much milder than his anti-Black slurs, and heavily outweighed by his respect for Jewish achievements in America, a success story he would wield as a weapon, during our arguments, against Black Americans. His favorite musician was Benny Goodman and he loved the Marx Brothers and Dinah Shore. He had nothing but respect and gratitude for Mr. Green and Mr. Birnbaum, sons of the founders.

A half-dozen years later, my grandfather, ensconced behind the Sportsman's bar, was far more content than he had been for a long while after my grandmother died and I'd absconded. I was now living in Vancouver, and valuing an infrequent but affectionate and respectful correspondence with Grandpa. We were gradually becoming closer again, more trusting, more grateful for each other.

At the opposite end of the galaxy from that flawed or broken soul who shot and killed my grandfather in his bar was a glorious spirit I met in the San Francisco Airport. He had been a hero of mine and my Black friends as Cassius Clay. In 1966 he was now a hero of my non-violent resistance to war, after declaring himself a conscientious objector. Waiting for a flight to Portland and Christmas with the Grimms, I saw Muhammad Ali standing right in front of me.

I rose, greeted him, and said as succinctly as possible that I, too, was a conscientious objector, and that I deeply admired his principled conduct. He politely and briefly shook my hand, said nothing, and gazed over my head, his expression aloof and guarded. There was no warmth, but he was not impolite. From what I later read, in this early phase of his devotion to Islam, and to the Nation of Islam with its more extreme view of "the white race" as perpetrators of genocide against African-Americans, Ali minimized his contact with white people. This was not the Ali who, after his 1972 pilgrimage to Mecca, converted to mainstream Sunni Islam, dedicated himself to unifying and helping humanity, and converted to Sufi Islam in 2005.

I sat back down in my airport lounge seat, Ali still standing nearby.

"Ali, man, is that you?"

I looked up and saw a middle-aged, gray-haired airport janitor, African-American, with his mop and bucket. Ali's face transformed with shining eyes and that radiant smile. "Brother," he said, and gripped the man's hand warmly. Somehow, my pique instantly evaporated. There was such loving-hearted intimacy flowing from Ali to this admirer. This was the man who would survive the ire of so many Americans and become, arguably, the most revered human on the planet in his later years, the foremost ambassador for the human race. A new and uplifting American myth.

Another mythic figure did not survive the wrath of one hateful American. Daylight was fading outside my room on Steiner Street in San Francisco, where I was studying and listening to jazz on Pacifica Radio. The tune stopped abruptly and an announcer's grave, incredulous voice was reporting the murder, only a few hours before, of Martin Luther King Jr., as he stood on his room's balcony at the Lorraine Motel in Memphis. I sat stunned and frozen, listening to reports of the aftermath. The beginning of the manhunt for the assassin, unrest or eerie quiet in Black neighborhoods. Statements of shock, anger, bewilderment, despair, grief, and also of reassurance, of the need for calm and unity and hope—of how Dr. King himself would react, how he would want us to respond to his death and to each other. The first assessments of what this would mean for the civil rights movement, race relations, America.

I was alone in my apartment, light from the streetlamps no longer soothing, but mournful. Suddenly, the only place I felt I could be was the hickory-pit barbecue on Fillmore. There was no reasoning involved, it just felt right. There were a half-dozen other customers, solitary men eating or sipping coffee quietly, and me, the only white face. A black and white TV was on, the volume almost inaudible, post-assassination urban scenes and talking heads from around the nation. Customers looked up at the screen now and then, stared, looked down at their plates and cups in eerie silence. Sam, the barbecue wizard, usually bantering jovially with customers, stood stoically behind the counter.

What had I expected? Dramatic and memorable expressions of outrage, violated hope, and inspiring resolve to transform this profane tragedy into further gains for justice, equality, dignity? The numbed silence, the faces and eyes so uncannily muted, were as powerful as any words. They said: this is what a lot of white people have done to a lot of Black people in America for over four hundred years. Elsewhere, there were people screaming their anger and pain in the streets. But there were far more people, I realized, sitting and staring benumbed into the void where Martin Luther King once was, only hours before.

The American Dream could swiftly turn into the American Nightmare. The land of opportunity was also the land of oppression, thwarted ambition, devastated hope, and grievous sorrow. The day that Dr. King was killed I already had in my wallet my Canadian immigration card. My insurance of safe passage from the carnage of Southeast Asia and America, into the golden opportunities of another, northern land. I felt prodigiously grateful. I felt worthless, craven, a deserter, not from the military and war, but from the gargantuan challenge to help redeem my native land from its catastrophic racial history. I felt a small comfort in Sam asking, in a kindly voice, "Can I get you anything else, son?"

9

The True North Strong and Free

Mathias Lemm, newly minted American hero, and his wife Rosie left the United States for Canada two or three years after his Philippine excursion. But my long-cherished belief that my father was born and raised in exotic—to a Seattle lad—and cosmopolitan Montreal went up in Alberta campfire smoke. I am the son of a western Canadian. Now, with archival evidence, I can place Mathias and Rose within the historical flux of Americans and Canadians moving back and forth across that relaxed western border in the late nineteenth and early twentieth centuries, seeking land, economic opportunities, and adventure. Both nations wanting settlers, laborers, entrepreneurs.

There were practical reasons for the migration of a war hero and his new wife. Apart from the severe depression of the early 1890s, the end of the century was a stressful time for many Americans, with work plentiful but often temporary.

Mathias and Rose might have experienced this economic instability and moved north with some anxiety or desperation. Or maybe they had a comfortable life in Minnesota and thought the grass was even greener north of the border—and the snow and cold less onerous. Perhaps Mathias' huge dose of adventure had made him crave another, albeit one less remote, strange, and dangerous: one comparable to his experience in Minnesota. Perhaps he felt some bitterness about his war experience, the American masters of war, and the way many in his country had turned against the war and its veterans.

In a 1903 letter to the editor of a Stearns County, Minnesota, newspaper, "Math Lemm" writes from "Wetaskuwin, Alb.,Can." Wetaskiwin, which means "peace hills" in Cree, is some distance south of Edmonton. "I noticed by a recent issue of your paper that Stearns county parties have been in Western Canada. They reported as finding it extremely cold. I therefore wish to correct the impression they have given out. I can truthfully say that, so far, I have witnessed the mildest winter I have ever experienced. The thermometer at no time has been lower than twenty-two degrees below zero, and that was only for about five days. The balance of the time we have enjoyed mild weather . . . Cattle can be seen on the prairies throughout the winter grazing. The ranchmen up here do not seem to wish to build places of shelter for their stock as they do further south. This does not look as if the winters here were very severe. I hope such reports of the country here will have no effect upon those who are contemplating coming to Canada. They should not, for I can say that Canada is the coming country."

Mathias was hunting coyotes for their pelts in Alberta and working as an auctioneer. His brother William joined him there, hunting, selling horses to the army, and raising cattle. William was joined by Mary Jacobs, a native of Washington State, who had moved to Minnesota and become a Lemm family friend. They married in 1906 and lived for years in Alberta, William and Matthias hunting coyotes, silvertip foxes, and wolves. In a family reminiscence, one of William and Mary's grandchildren writes, "They had lots of fun up there . . . They sold furs, made moonshine and anything else to make money. They also had big barn dances. This was real rough and tough country-style living. It was very hard to survive." In 1919, after two childless decades, Matt and Rosie finally had their only child, my father, Harvey Matthew Lemm.

I have sometimes relied on "My father was a Canadian" to assert my belonging in this country when someone tries to diminish my status by pointing out my American background. I can now play the "My father was a Prairie lad" card to western Canadians.

I have only three other documentary references to Mathias and Rose between 1903 and his death in the Seattle veterans hospital in 1936. They returned to Minnesota from Manitoba on June 24, 1922, at the Noyes, Minnesota, border crossing. A data bank of "Border Crossings from Canada to the U.S. 1895-1954" records that my father, age two years and eight months, entered the United States for the first time. His "Race/Nationality" is listed, quite curiously, as "French." Where had they been living since my father's birth? In a Franco-Manitoban community? My father's US Army enlistment documents and death certificate indicate that he was a Canadian citizen. A US Army record from the US National Archives & Records Administration unhelpfully lists my father's "nativity" as "British North America or Canada or Labrador or Newfoundland." Again curiously, he never took American citizenship and died a Canadian.

An obituary in the St. Cloud, Minnesota *Daily Times and Daily Journal* states that "Math Lemm . . . moved west, living at Grand Birch, British Columbia, before moving to Seattle about six years ago." However, there is no Grand Birch, BC. Most likely, Matt and Rosie migrated from Alberta. In Mathias' mother's obituary on July 27, 1929, in the *St. Cloud Times*, "Mathew" is listed in Holden, Alberta. It is likely that they moved to Seattle because Mathias was critically ill, thus transplanting my Canadian father onto American soil.

As an individual act of war resistance during the Vietnam era, transplanting myself to Canada seemed inconsequential. But as tens of thousands of Americans moved north of the border during those years, emigration became a factor in the anti-war movement. Such a sizable exodus had not occurred before, not since the British Loyalists, along with five thousand African-Americans, fled revolutionary America. All these modern-day Americans turning their back on The Greatest Country on Earth and the American Dream, choosing another country as a better homeland in crucial ways. The media and Americans were taking note, and this did have an impact on shifts in American attitudes. Enough for the emigrants to be considered minor heroes or traitors.

Canada had not yet introduced its point system. Instead of praying to be granted the necessary points for language skills, education, employment, and other factors, Darlene and I had to write essays explaining why we wanted to emigrate from our native land and immigrate to Canada. This was my sweet spot, and I swung away enthusiastically, putting lots of spin on the ball. I wrote about my great-grandmother's migration across the continent and pioneer life on the west coast, helping to build a newer nation. About my paternal great-grandparents emigrating from Europe and helping create America's plenitude in the nineteenth century. About my paternal grandfather and father migrating to Europe to fight for freedom and the well-being of humanity. Now it was my turn to migrate, be a modern pioneer, and contribute to Canada's bounty and munificence.

Did anyone read those essays? Did someone laugh hysterically or yawn, jaded, at mine? Was someone sucked in and moved by my words, impassioned and mostly earnest, but also embellished with buffalo shit? Or did officials simply think, "Good, two more young Americans for our economic growth and professional class"?

A half-year later, re-boarding the Greyhound bus on the Canadian side of the border with my temporary but official Canadian immigration card snug in my wallet, I rejoined the distinguished-looking gentleman in a well-tailored suit whom I'd sat beside in silence from Seattle to the border.

"You've just immigrated, haven't you?" he said cordially in a British accent.

"How did you know?"

"It's quite obvious to any other immigrant, such as myself. You're looking rather rapturous."

He shook my hand warmly.

"Let me tell you about Canada in a nutshell. It was intended to possess British governance, French culture, and American know-how. Instead, it has American culture, French governance, and British know-how."

When Canadians asked, as they often did in my early Canadian years, what differences I saw during my early days and months up north, I remarked on the feeling that I had time-traveled back to pre-Beatles, pre-Dylan Seattle. I expected to hear the Lennon Sisters on people's radios, not John Lennon, Bing Crosby instead of Crosby, Stills, and Nash.

On that first day as an immigrant in Vancouver, I checked into the YMCA and set about exploring my first stop in my new land. As I strolled downtown, I thought, where are the Black people? I knew enough Black history to explain their absence, and my American travels had taken me to plenty of white-only regions, including lily-white Seattle neighborhoods. And those football games where we'd lined up against the blue-eyed, blond Swedes from Ballard High. But I hadn't imagined that Canada's major west coast city would be so devoid of Black faces.

The displacement, though, was relatively mild. I think of all the refugees and immigrants before and after, from China and Poland, Chile and Syria, and all the advantages I had by comparison. I spoke fluent English. My skin color was the same as almost everyone's, albeit the lighter northern European shade. The landscape was gloriously known: mountains rising above water, verdancy of conifers and deciduous trees. The customs of this new home were almost identical to my own, Vancouver and Seattle being part of a cultural continuum. And while I was escaping unwanted military service and the possibility of imprisonment, I wasn't fleeing the traumatic experiences of war zones, brutal regimes, dungeons and torture, ethnic and religious and gender persecution, drought and disease. My family and friends weren't huddled in bombed-out buildings or refugee camps, or buried in mass graves. I felt lonely, but it was the loneliness of a stranger in a familiar land. And permeating my solitariness was the euphoria of the border crossing, my new status and identity, and the miraculous Landed Immigrant card in my wallet.

In late afternoon, hungry, I looked for an appropriate eatery for my first meal as a Canadian immigrant. What should I discover but the Sportsman's Café, as if it had been transported by a jinn from Third Avenue in Seattle. I might have been unable to open myself emotionally to Grandpa the night before, but I was immensely grateful to sit at a Sportsman's Café table and order from a menu almost identical to my grandfather's: a hot roast beef sandwich with gravy and fries, followed by apple pie à la mode. I silently voiced a bittersweet "thank you" to Grandpa, pointless to him, but not to me. And vowed to write sooner rather than later.

After supper, I resumed my walkabout and spotted, in front of the Hudson Bay department store, a young man with very long blond hair and granny glasses, selling the local underground newspaper, *The Georgia Straight*. Here was a San Francisco apparition I didn't hesitate to discover was real.

After introductions, he explained that the paper was new,

founded by a collective in May, and the latest edition had been banned by a judge for obscenity. In fact, in the authorities' eyes, the offensive materials were articles critical of local politicians; the obscenity charge was a cover. A fundraising rally for legal costs and moral support was planned that evening in one of the union halls near the waterfront. Would I like to attend? You bet your life.

Soon, a black Mercedes-Benz sedan pulled up. Not your normal activist car. But my brief Seattle left-wing experience had shown me that, along with the Corrs in their older VW van, there were moneyed people who drove fancy cars to peace marches. The owner and driver was Harry Rankin, a criminal and labor lawyer who helped establish BC's legal aid system, and an alderman who served on Vancouver's city council for over two dozen years from the mid-1960s to early 1990s. When I met him, he was already legendary as a popular and effective left-wing figure in the city and province.

Sitting next to Rankin was a man with a large head, rumpled hair, and craggy face, wearing khaki work clothes exactly like Bill Corr Sr., and smoking a large Cuban cigar.

"This is Milton Acorn," Rankin said, "one of the co-founders of *The Georgia Straight* collective. He's also one of Canada's finest poets and a prominent nationalist and socialist. A poet of the people."

With that pronouncement, Acorn swung his head and face toward me with the psychic weight of a wrecking ball.

"You a draft dodger?" he demanded in a startlingly high and squeaky, but nonetheless forceful, voice—the power coming from a deep, resonant place inside, like a seer's cavern, walls vibrating with ancient pictographs.

In spite of this company, my years'-long anxiety about my freedom and fate bubbled up from its own dark cave, and I hesitated to answer. What if this was an elaborate trap sprung by Canadian customs in cahoots with the FBI? I swallowed that irrational fear.

I was going to be asked this question often by Canadians, and I couldn't have asked for more sympathetic people to break the ice.

"Yes, I am."

Acorn's head whipped forward and he pounded the dashboard with his cigar-free hand.

"Goddamn those Yankees. Damn their capitalist war," he bellowed and then fell silent.

I was home. Free.

At that union hall in Vancouver, I was barely a neophyte poet on the first day of my Canadian novitiate. But garbed in mythic cowboy denim and lumberjack plaid that passed muster on both sides of the border, and raised by a logger's daughter and people's bartender, I felt a camaraderie with Acorn and everyone present.

I was standing alone in the back of the union hall when *The Georgia Straight* vendor approached me with a burlap bag. Would I, at his signal during the rally, make the rounds of the now-packed hall and collect donations for the legal costs?

"For sure," I said, honored to be asked, feeling purposeful again and not an outsider, and amazed that I, a total stranger, was being trusted. Welcome to Canada, indeed. When the rally ended, I sat at the back with the bulging bag, watching people exit, waiting to hand over the hefty boon. Before long, the hall was empty, and there I lingered with *The Georgia Straight*'s legal defense fund and future. I went outside and saw the vendor, Rankin, and Acorn talking with a few other people. The vendor looked at me quizzically. I held out the bag.

"The money," I said.

"Oh, shit. What're you doing with the money?" It wasn't so much an accusation as a look of bewildered panic.

"You asked me to collect it. Remember?"

"I did? Oh jeez, yeah. I totally forgot. Thanks." He had the look of someone who realized he might have fucked up royally but got lucky. "Thanks a million."

Rankin and Acorn were now walking toward the car, and the vendor turned to join them, leaving me alone in an empty parking lot. Canadian trust had suddenly morphed, I thought, into Canadian thoughtlessness.

The vendor turned back. "Need a ride somewhere?"

I smiled, my boyhood Canadian hero from the fifties TV series come to life: Sergeant Preston of the Yukon wouldn't leave a traveler stranded in the Canadian urban wilderness, after all.

After several days at the draft dodgers' crash pad, I rode another packed Greyhound bus, this one heading north through the BC interior in a driving rainstorm, and my war-fleeing self sitting in soaked Levis beside a badly leaking window, and beside me a young man talking incessantly about his boring highway construction jobs, pick-up hockey games in late-night arenas, and boozy barroom weekends shooting pool and getting into fights with loggers. One kind of quintessential Canadian, I thought.

Somewhere north of Williams Lake, the sky cleared, and the landscape was illuminated by a full moon. Then I noticed, through the windshield, a cluster of headlights ahead and the flashing lights of a police car. The bus slowed to a crawl as we passed a sizable biker gang—Hell's Angels from California on a run—the hirsute men patiently waiting while a lone Mountie checked their ID. Here was another mythic Canadian moment—in the middle of nowhere, a fearless Mountie doing his duty and the outlaws respectfully obliging.

Next, I was stowing my gear at St. Joseph's School in Vanderhoof in a cabin occupied by Lance and a Quebecois religious brother who loved our taste for Cutty Sark scotch and had been, he said proudly, a draft dodger during the Second World War.

Since Lance was working as one of the school's handymen and a recreation leader, I was allowed to stay as his assistant. In the handymen's shop, I took over the unskilled jobs: floor sweeping, simple sawing and nailing, hauling whatever needed moving. Lance loved the power saws and miter box. I loved pushing a wheelbarrow full of bricks and gravel.

In the gym or on the sports field, I was in my element. Soon, Lance and I had several dozen boys learning how to throw and catch footballs, block and tackle without cracking their skulls open, and work as a team with formations and plays. When Lance first arrived, the nuns—their teachers—told him that the kids, especially the Indians (as they were called), weren't capable of learning a complicated game like football. Moreover, they (meaning, really, the Indians) were too undisciplined and too "rough"—translation: chaotically violent—and would only end up seriously hurting each other and getting into fights. Lance and I were also sure that the nuns didn't want Indian kids tackling white kids. "Sure, winning isn't everything; it's the only thing," a dictum made famous by legendary Green Bay Packer coach Vince Lombardi. We were determined to win our argument with the nuns.

At first, the boys were chaotic and clumsy, on the verge of catastrophe. They were also keen, quick learners. The racial divide, there at the start—"we ain't playing with them"—swiftly vanished. Every scrimmage, every game, the teams were mixed and remixed. No Indians, no whites, just teammates. Like at Franklin High, we told them, describing our African-American coach Brennan King and our multiethnic squad, our band of brothers. We would help them become a team that could whup the asses off any team from Prince George to Prince Rupert. We taught them how to hit and be hit so that injuries were minimized and minor—especially since there were no helmets or pads—fewer than in their untutored and often bellicose "games" and fights. The nuns left us alone. We thought it was because they'd heard, or observed from afar, that the kids were transforming into disciplined, skilled athletes.

One day, during football practice, Mother Superior, the principal, approached the field, no doubt to heap praise on the boys and congratulate us. She watched for a while. The boys were a long way from catching the eye of an American university scout, but Coach King would have been impressed by how far they'd come.

Mother Superior strode over to us.

"How dare you," she snapped. "We did not give you permission to make these boys beat each other up."

I was flabbergasted. I could see that Lance's blood was about to boil, but he held himself in check. He could do that: feel sudden outrage yet keep it on a short lead while he tried to reason. He began to point out that these boys were learning, with amazing speed, to play a complex game involving intelligent teamwork.

She would hear none of that and cut him off. We were "disobedient," and "unleashing violent behavior," which would "lead to serious problems." This football mayhem must end immediately. We were put on warning.

We gathered the boys together and said how proud of them we were. That we hoped they would take what they had learned about their individual potential and their ability to work together as a team and use it in the rest of their lives. They listened glumly, their resentment directed at the principal striding back to her command post, at an adult world that once again made no sense and seemed unjust, and then retreated into their segregated cliques and days ahead without this game that, for a time, enhanced their self-worth and mutual respect.

One of my other tasks was to make lunch for children without their own lunches or lunch money. Almost exclusively, these were the Indigenous kids, who made up half the student population. The federal government paid the school a quarter per student for lunch. Every day, I boiled water in a huge kettle and poured in several packets of Lipton's Chicken Noodle Soup. The nun in charge of the kitchen chastised me one day for using too many packets, and thereafter kept them under lock and key and handed me three every morning. For a ten-gallon pot and over a hundred hungry kids. The soup had the faintest hint of Lipton's chemicals, a scattering of ersatz noodles, and the power of suggestion in the word "chicken."

I also made them peanut butter sandwiches. Two slices of Wonder Bread per student, with one swipe of a knife in a margarine tub and a scoop into the peanut butter. I tried to maximize the results of those swipes and scoops, but again I had Sister Pennypinch doing spot checks and castigating me if I exceeded her limits, as if the Church's economic survival was at stake and I was dooming the Indigenous kids to the Third Circle of Hell in Dante's *Inferno*, the one full of gluttons.

I'd recently read Solzhenitsyn's *One Day in the Life of Ivan Denisovich*, and wondered if gulag prisoners ate better, especially when one lucked out with an eyeball in the fish broth soup. If the lunches weren't quite at that level of abuse, the treatment of the Indigenous kids in the hallways and classrooms sometimes was. Lance witnessed that, not me, since he helped on occasion as a teaching assistant.

The nuns' weapons of choice were long rulers. The white kids must have been wondrously well-behaved, for the sisters whacked only the Natives. Or perhaps the Indigenous students were blessedly shriven of their sins in a manner denied the white kids. Lance deferred to the nuns' authority as long as he could stand it, then, one day seeing a nun wallop an Indigenous student repeatedly, he intervened. He summoned his own formidable moral authority, based not in robes and religious orders and racist hierarchies and a perverse theology, but in a profound understanding of justice. He told her that her conduct was immoral, lacking in intelligence, and destructive. And that she obscenely dishonored Jesus.

Lance was speaking, however, to a consciousness thick as the cornerstone of a cathedral. In that nun's airtight reality, Lance was mouthing impudent nonsense. What was Lance thinking? That the bride of Christ would snap her ruler in two and ask for sweetgrass and a sweat lodge?

After other impudent behavior, the nuns sent me packing, but retained Lance's essential handyman services, on strict probation.

This was my first direct experience of the racism and oppression inflicted on Canada's Indigenous peoples. I knew almost no Canadian history and assumed—more wishful thinking—that Indigenous peoples had suffered less in Canada than in America. That racism was less intense and pervasive. I soon learned that, when it came to Canada's First Peoples, their experience was a long and chock-full saga of horrors, of endless racist maltreatment.

With no job, and with my CO appeal, however hopeless, still in the system, I decided to return to San Francisco State College for one more semester, knowing I could easily find part-time work on campus, and for one last feast of American culture, San Francisco-style. I would come back to Vancouver in the summer, well ahead of any draft notice and warrant for my arrest, flashing my get-out-of-jail-free card at Canadian customs.

Soon after returning to Canada, I walked into Duthie Books in downtown Vancouver with the pipedream of working in a classy bookstore—me and *beaucoup* others. I was in the right place at the right time. Duthie's was opening a glamorous large store on Robson Street, which would become a cultural heart of Vancouver. I was hired for a week to help schlepp and shelve hundreds of cartons of books. I worked my *derrière* off and was rewarded with a full-time job in the basement paperback section.

One day after a few weeks there, I was shelving newly arrived books in the American and international fiction section. Bill Duthie, founder and owner, came up behind me, observing. Bill, I'd been told, had attended Toronto's Upper Canada College, a boys' private school and training ground of the establishment, and then the University of Toronto. His manner was warm, urbane, and suavely relaxed, but his Upper Canada accent was laced often with wry and sometimes sardonic wit. He was already a legend in the Canadian book industry, having previously been the premier western Canada sales rep for McClelland and Stewart, Canada's flagship publishing house.

"Why are you putting that in American fiction?" he asked.

The book in question was *Beautiful Losers* by Leonard Cohen.

"Cohen's an American folk-singer. I didn't know he writes fiction."

"Leonard Cohen, young Richard, is Canadian. One of our finest poets too. He took up the guitar and started singing after he'd published poetry books. You have much to learn about Canada." Cohen's publisher was Bill's close friend and former employer, Jack McClelland, who provided a publishing home for so many Canadian authors. Names that meant nothing to me, but soon would: Pierre Berton, Farley Mowat, Margaret Laurence, Margaret Atwood.

Bill had, he said, "a puzzling habit" of hiring American draft dodgers and deserters, some of whom, I learned, never came to work but used the Duthie job offer to help them immigrate. His paperback manager and old friend, Binky Marx, was the first Jewish person to graduate from Upper Canada College and, said Bill, "probably the only graduate to become a Marxist." They were a wonderful odd couple: the dapper, genteel Bill and the rumpled, proletarian Binky. Two years into my tenure there, Binky, contemplating an early retirement, asked me to be his successor. Bill approved. Deeply honored and tempted, I nonetheless declined that alluring career and role in Canadian culture to take my chances in academia.

Resuming my studies at Simon Fraser University, while working part-time at Duthie's, I had a significant encounter with another Canadian writer helping rediscover Canada's history and re-envision its identity, while conjuring his own mythic status.

I signed up for a seminar on Canadian poetry with Al Purdy, SFU's writer in residence that semester, one of the luminous poetic stars in the nascent "CanLit" firmament. There were no Canadian literature courses at SFU then, so this was the token CanLit gesture. In his early fifties, Purdy had been publishing poetry for over twenty-five years. I'd gleaned this from Binky Marx, who was especially supportive of poets at Duthie Books, along with the appealing fact that Purdy was a "working-class poet." Without a university education, said Binky, Purdy was one of the best-read people in Canada. After serving with the Royal Canadian Air Force in the war, and working at a variety of jobs, he now supported himself as a writer. This was the résumé, sans military service, I'd once desired.

Purdy began our first class by announcing that he hated teaching, didn't like academia, and was doing this only because he and his wife, Eurithe, wanted to go to Europe. He then opened his old leather briefcase, took out a Labatt's Blue and church key, and said, "I brought only one bottle. So if you want a beer, you'll have to come down to the Cariboo Pub with me." He put the bottle and opener back in his briefcase, snapped it shut, rose, and left. Most of the students followed him out the door and down to the pub. I sat there, indignant. Yes, I applauded and venerated certain rebels and nonconformists, fancied myself one at times. And, yes, Purdy came as advertised. Wasn't he showing himself to be the kind of poet I'd signed up for? Didn't I use to brag that I felt more comfortable in working-class taverns than in trendy joints? And didn't Purdy, in his white dress shirt with sleeves rolled up, remind me of my grandfather? The academics were now sporting plaid, khaki, and denim, while the blue-collar poet had white-collar class.

However, I'd inherited my grandfather's adamant belief that if you accept a job you do it. Purdy, whatever he was, had an obligation to stay in that classroom and be our teacher. That was the blue-collar way, too. I wasn't going to sit around a pub table and listen to a self-appointed iconoclast and a shirker spout off about poetry. While I stayed in the course and wrote the one paper he required, I boycotted the weekly pub sessions. Biting your nose off to spite your face, my grandfather would have told me. And more fear of being found wanting by a top-grade writer, one who nurtured and published many of Canada's finest younger poets. I've regretted my asinine choice ever since.

During those immigrant years before citizenship, I lived in a cottage on Tsawwassen Beach, a mile south of the BC Ferry wharf for Victoria and Gulf Island sailings, and the colossal Roberts Bank coal terminal spewing black dust into the sea winds. This location was, for me, ironically appropriate. A quarter-mile south of the cottage was an international border marker. When I walked beyond it on the beach, I was in the United States, a fugitive from Uncle Sam on American sand. The forty-ninth parallel intersects a small peninsula, with Tsawwassen to the north and Point Roberts to the south. Fifty years later, when I silently recite those place names, "Tsawwassen," which means "facing the shining sea" in the Hul'qumi'num language, sparks a warm glow of safety and serenity, while "Point Roberts" still casts the cold shadow of a threatening metallic presence.

In 1970, I learned that my CO appeal had been rejected unanimously by the President's (now Nixon) appeal board. A flood of panic subsided as I walked south on Tsawwassen Beach, and, as I reversed direction at the border marker, turned into a wash of tranquility. I do not remember receiving a draft notice. But I can see myself hiding our small stash of marijuana under bricks in a basement crawl space in the bizarre event that Mounties had nothing better to do than bust and deport draft dodger immigrants for simple possession.

Just as I'd feared, an RCMP officer in full dress uniform did knock on our door one day. To inform me, however, that the FBI had contacted the Mounties about my draft evasion and status as a fugitive from American justice.

"We are required to ask if you intend to return to the United States," he said soberly.

"No, sir, I do not."

He then broke into a wide smile, shook my hand, and said, "May you have a very good life in Canada."

My proximity to America was also perfectly symbolic as my identity gradually morphed from that of an American in Canada to that of a Canadian permeated and inflected by my American past. A lifelong process for most, if not all, immigrants, and certainly for me. I would never be able to say, as did Prime Minister Wilfred Laurier, "I am a Canadian. Canada is the inspiration of my life." But I was moving in that direction. However, though the thought of Point Roberts gave me the heebie-jeebies, I was still potently attached to many aspects of America, even as I slowly absorbed Canadian values, perspectives, traits, and emotional sensibilities.

The views from our windows and deck, and my beach walks, sustained me in this transition: a Pacific Northwest coastal landscape that made me feel absolutely at home. The Canadian Gulf Islands replicating the American San Juan Islands in my consciousness and dreamscape—the Strait of Juan de Fuca blending into the Georgia Strait (now the Salish Sea) without regard for human boundaries of arbitrary, transient nations. Vancouver Island's mountain range evoking the Cascades and Olympics of my American youth. The ferries coming and going from the nearby Tsawwassen terminal reminding me of ferries on the Seattle waterfront and plying Puget Sound. The beach redolent with cedar driftwood and kelp, gleaming with opalescent shells. But this consciousness and its deep knowledge went beyond staying in touch with my American roots while becoming Canadian. I was still living in the embrace of my native landscape, still in my home region, my place, blessed with its bountiful gifts.

My partner Carol and I wanted to explore the province. She was a schoolteacher and counselor with two months of summer holidays, and I took time off from Duthie's. We were a few years ahead of the quantum leap in wilderness adventure, and backpacked the West Coast Trail on Vancouver Island in near solitude before it was discovered by hordes of hikers, the back-country wilderness of Banff and Jasper when you could still trek all day and count other hikers on one or two hands, and the beaches of Haida Gwaii. We visited Carol's Indigenous students, daughters of a Nisga'a chief, at New Aiyansh (now Gitlaxt'aamiks) and chanced into close friendships with back-to-the-landers from California on Malcolm Island in the Queen Charlotte Strait, with its history of the Finnish utopian colony of Sointula.

Although summer holidays were over, for some forgotten reason I was riding the small ferry to nearby Alert Bay and Sointula on September 28, 1972. We were chugging along, plowing through a steady drizzle in choppy, slate-gray waters, with the captain periodically making announcements over the intercom. Gazing raptly at the seascape, I paid no attention, oblivious of the sudden silence and intent listening of other passengers. Whatever the captain was saying, people were not reacting as if we were floundering. No one was donning life jackets.

Then, the boat lurched and dipped to the left, rocked back, and plunged to the right, while the captain's voice yelled, "Henderson scored, Henderson scored!"

Young and old were bouncing up and down, arms raised to the heavens like the souls being saved in Michelangelo's "The Last Judgement." Then, having arrived in heaven, the passengers were hugging, not with polite restraint, but passionate joy. The boat continued to veer and lunge. I looked up at the bridge and saw the captain and a crew member embracing. Who cared if we capsized and drowned in the Strait's frigid waters? No one. Henderson had scored.

I was being hugged too, vigorously, by men and women, some of them strong enough to squeeze the air from my lungs.

"Who's Henderson?" I finally managed to say audibly with all the shouting and cheering. "What did he score?"

"You don't know?" said a gray-haired woman holding me by the arms. "We beat the Russians. We've won."

"Won what?"

"The summit."

Decades later, "Henderson scored" and "We beat the Russians" are mantras for a threshold moment in Canadians' self-discovery and Canada's assertion of prowess on the world stage. There was Canada's coming-of-age during the First World War and there was the Summit Series victory. It was a shot heard round the world, at least the hockey-playing world. A moment that burst our spirit's sleep and united us, Newfoundlanders and Albertans,

Francophones and Anglophones, European descendants, Asian immigrants, First Nations. If the Americans had a surfeit of mythic moments and Canada seemed to have so few, we now had this monumental one. They had Babe Ruth pointing to the center field fence and hitting a home run there. Jackie Robinson's first at-bat with the Dodgers. Mildred "Babe" Didrikson winning gold medals in track and field at the 1932 Olympics. Amelia Earhart flying solo across the Atlantic. Lincoln at Gettysburg. Washington crossing the Delaware. We had Henderson's winning goal. Threshold moments for a nation, a culture, a people can take many forms. One of ours, inevitably, was hockey.

In the fall of 1973, I walked into a federal government office in downtown Vancouver to apply for citizenship. I had the same tingling excitement and nervous jitters as I'd felt while driving Grandpa's '55 Chev downtown to *West Side Story* with Lulu Mae Paborsky, my first-ever date, beside me. Or on the first day of tryouts for my high school football team. Failure, I then believed, could have dire consequences for the rest of my teenage years, and perhaps lifelong. Success would place me firmly inside the entrance of the promised land. Denial of citizenship would leave me vulnerable, however unlikely, to deportation and arrest, whereas citizenship meant the burial of that worry, barring Canada's conquest by the US Marines.

The clerk's weary and rote manner reassured me. She could have been issuing dog licenses for all her enthusiasm. But I didn't relax entirely as I filled out the application form. Lurking cleverly within her blasé behavior could be a fierce guardian of Canadian identity poised to strike, and she might somehow sense a threat to those mythic qualities of Canadians: polite, modest, apologetic, tactful. Maybe I seemed, even unobtrusively, too American.

As she reviewed my completed form, she paused, looked up, and said, "What's your ethnic origin?" In that box, I'd written "mixed."

"Heinz 57," I joked, "melting pot."

She did not smile. "We don't accept 'mixed.' You need an ethnic origin."

"American," I said, still trying to be funny, but with an incautious edge this time.

"That's not an ethnic origin. What's your parent's ethnic origin?"

"My mother's Scottish, Irish, English . . ."

"Your mother doesn't count. I mean your father. Last name, Lemm."

Too taken aback and cautious to challenge this rampart of the patriarchy, I stammered that my father was born and raised, as I then thought, in Montreal.

"Another French-Canadian," she said with wry satisfaction and turned to her desk and typewriter. Her response might have been due to the influence of the Trudeau government's bilingual policies. The Official Languages Act had been passed four years earlier. Was she under orders to bolster French-Canadian numbers to help justify bilingual services? She crossed out "mixed" and typed my new ethnicity onto the form and official status.

When the clerk returned with the paper, her signature affixed, she said,

"Since your father was a Canadian, you didn't have to wait five years to apply. You could've come in after one year, and it's automatic. You don't have to write a citizenship test or be interviewed by a judge. I can process this now, and you'll be called to the ceremony."

I considered this briefly, then said with conviction, "Thank you. But no. I want to go through the process like other immigrants." I wanted their experience to be mine, including studying the book

I was given full of facts about Canada and being interviewed by a citizenship judge. My nervousness about being sent packing had vanished when her signature on the form appeared. It had transformed into a strong desire to earn my citizenship, to prove my worth as other immigrants must. The whole nine yards of becoming a Canadian.

I set about memorizing the citizenship handbook—which I believe was over two hundred pages, jam-packed with history, geography, politics, economics, and culture.

The applicant was required to take two character witnesses to the interview. I chose, first, my closest Canadian friend and fellow draft dodger, Michael Goldberg, who was the recreation director at the Jewish Community Centre. My other witness was Dr. Carl Kline, a prominent psychiatrist and my primary supervisor at Vancouver General Hospital. Carl, his educational psychologist wife, Carolyn, and their draft-age sons had immigrated from America a few years earlier. Carl and Carolyn were pioneers in the field of learning disabilities; I had been hired for their pilot project of therapeutic tutoring and became team leader.

I do not remember the judge's last name, but his first was "Babe"—at least that was how he was known. As soon as we walked into his office, he looked at my witnesses and said, "Carl, what are you doing here?" and "You, too, Michael?"

The judge was the chair of the board of the Jewish Community Centre, and he and his family lived next door to the Klines, good friends as well as neighbors. Any tension in my body and mind evaporated, and I relaxed while they shot the breeze. After ten minutes, though, I began feeling impatient. All this information bottled up inside me was now fizzing and pushing the cork out. Hey, I thought, you talk often with the judge, this is my showtime. Right on cue, the judge said, chuckling, "I suppose we should pay some attention to Richard. This is, after all, his interview."

He began asking me standard questions. The provinces and territories. Dates of Confederation and completion of the transcontinental railroad. The three major political parties and their leaders. The main economic activities of all ten provinces. This went on for about ten minutes, and I was having a grand time firing off replies, ready to name the Group of Seven and Canada's key battles in the First World War, when the judge said,

"You've obviously memorized the handbook and know your facts. It's seldom I get someone who's so knowledgeable and articulate, that is, in English or French, and I can have a conversation with. Usually, I'm satisfied if people know the Prime Minister's name and the national capital. I'm going to ask you some questions far more interesting to me. Let's start with what you'd do about French and English relations in Canada, especially Quebec."

Oh. My. God. This was not in the handbook. This was highly unfair. I froze momentarily. Then realized that the judge, leaning back in his chair and smiling happily, wasn't grading me. He genuinely wanted a more stimulating discussion, and perhaps to test my mettle for the sheer pleasure, not to evaluate my candidacy. I knew enough about the French–English question to talk for a long time. The judge, however, interrupted me after less than a minute and launched into his lengthy analysis of the problems and his remedies.

"Let's get more local," he said, having solved the challenges of bilingualism, Quebec–Canada relations, and other grievances arising from Canada's French and English heritage. "As you know, we've recently experienced a BC Ferries strike, and we've had strikes and lockouts with postal workers. What would you do about labor relations in Canada?"

Now, this was even more up my alley. I had a slight worry that my pro-union position might not please the judge, but knew how to modulate my answer. I didn't have to, since the judge again quickly interrupted me to wax eloquent on this topic. As I listened politely, I was aware of Dr. Kline's growing restlessness, his glancing at his watch. He had appointments, and he'd heard this all before, no doubt. Michael, who thrived on discussions of social issues, was enjoying himself, though I could tell he was chomping at the bit to join in.

When the judge had resolved Canadian labor strife and began asking me what I would do about "the crisis with our Canadian Indians," Dr. Kline loudly cleared his throat and declared that he had patients waiting. The judge apologized for "rambling on," thanked us all, told me what a pleasure it was to speak with such a well-versed applicant, and announced that he would recommend me without reservation for citizenship. "A done deal," he said.

A few weeks after my meeting with Babe, I stood in the citizenship courtroom with dozens of other immigrants about to become Canadian citizens. From my high school senior year onward, as a political protest I had stopped singing "The Star-Spangled Banner." Now, all my pent-up, frustrated, disenchanted American patriotism, and all my newfound Canadian loyalty burst proudly forth with "O Canada." No rockets' red glare and bombs bursting in air. Rather, The true north strong and free / Il sait porter la croix. I had carried my cross to freedom and planted it, that moment, with all the strength of my voice in the glorious true north.

Then my brain heard the judge say, "Every new wave of Canadians, once they are established in Canada, wants to have the door closed behind them."

Had I heard the judge correctly? There was now an intensity in his voice and face, replacing the boilerplate dignity of his earlier statements.

"The Scots arrived and, when settled, said, 'Keep the Irish out.' Then the Irish said, 'We don't need any more immigrants. They take our jobs and their values are different. Send those Jews and Italians back to their homes.'"

The judge paused, slowly gazing around the room at our expectant faces. And then his eyes fixed on some point above and behind us.

"The Second World War ended and there were waves of Ukrainians, Poles, and others from war-ravaged Europe. The Italians, Jews, and Greeks said, 'Close the door. We can't afford any more immigrants.'"

Another lengthy pause, several deep breaths. "Then came the Hungarian Revolution and Soviet occupation, and Hungarians fled to Canada. 'Close the door' said the Ukrainians and Poles, 'we have our own mouths to feed.' Then the democratic uprising in Czechoslovakia, and the Hungarians said, 'Close the door before we're overrun by those people.'"

The judge scanned the faces in the room again. So did I, and the expressions on many faces—of those people who could understand English sufficiently—were solemnly intent. Mine, I think, showed amazement at the judge's speech—and wondrous gratitude. He had become an animate Canadian Statue of Liberty. The words of Emma Lazarus inscribed on that statue, from her poem "The New Colossus," sprang into my head: "Give me your tired, your poor, / Your huddled masses yearning to be free . . ." The judge's voice pulled me back from New York Harbor to that Vancouver courtroom.

"You are all grateful for the open door that welcomed you to Canada. As with groups before you, the temptation will come to demand that the door be closed. The door was open for you. Do not close the door, ever, for those who come after you, seeking their new home and citizenship in Canada. Do everything in your power to keep the door open."

My pride in this new citizenship further transcended my elation at being securely free of the American government. This nationality embraced humanity in all its crazy-quilt reality, at least according to our judge. Of course, I knew this was an imperfect and incomplete embrace, which the judge had acknowledged as part of his appeal. I had been learning about Canada's ignominious treatment of Indigenous peoples and its residents of African, Chinese, Japanese, and Jewish descent. I knew that bigotry was alive and well in my new land. But the variegated faces around the room were vibrant evidence that the doors were now much more widely open.

As the judge administered the citizenship oath, I felt myself become Canadian. A transformation spreading from my exhilarated brain throughout my tingling nervous system. Of course, I was merely experiencing an electrochemical rush triggered by potent stimuli, but what a blissful rush. At the moment, it felt as if my Americanized character had been swept away in a flash flood of Canadian identity. My Daniel Boone costume was stripped away to reveal a Hudson Bay trapper. The truth is that my American identity was only hip-checked aside for the briefest of times and soon sidled back into its prominent place in my brain.

Four years later, I was teaching Canadian history in a high school in the Cariboo country of British Columbia. Some of my students, white and Indigenous, complained about the "Pakis," South Asian immigrants who were "taking jobs away from Canadians" and "lowering wages" in the logging camps and sawmills. I explained that they should direct their ire at the company owners who want cheaper labor and to bust the unions, not the workers who were only doing what my students' own ancestors, even some of their European-born parents, had done: worked hard to secure a better life in a new land. I thought of that judge and said, "Don't ever close the door behind you." One of my Indigenous students said, "We shoulda slammed the door four hundred years ago. But," he added, "since it's open, leave it open."

Several months after I became a Canadian citizen, a draft-dodger acquaintance in Vancouver told me of a group of liberal-minded lawyers based in San Francisco who were working pro bono to investigate the legal status of draft evaders. They were motivated by the discovery that the US Department of Justice was dropping charges right and left.

I wrote to the lawyers and received a letter in April 1974, on official DOJ letterhead from a United States Attorney, stating that "On February 15, 1973, we dismissed the indictment with the approval of the Department of Justice as there appeared to be no basis in fact for the denial of a CO (Conscientious Objection) classification in light of *United States* vs. *Anderson*, 447 F.2d 1063 (9th Cir. 1971)." Just like that, out of the blue, I was no longer a fugitive from American justice and could cross the border and visit my homeland, family, and friends with impunity. I wasn't even legally a draft dodger anymore, though I've happily accepted that label ever since. And while the DOJ action and letter did not grant me CO status, the admission that I should not have been rejected was sufficient grounds for identifying myself as a CO.

I could now return freely to America, fill my boots with the American zeitgeist. When I told people this, I was asked, again, if I might move "back home."

Are you kidding? I said. Canada is my home.

The other life-altering event of 1974 was my decision, after the therapeutic tutoring project funding at the hospital was not renewed following the defeat of the supportive NDP government by the uninterested Social Credit party, to go on pogey and give writing poetry, short stories, and plays a serious shot for the first time since I was a callow neophyte back in Seattle and San Francisco. As magazine acceptances trickled in and then steadily arrived, along with a five-hundred-dollar (rent for three months) first prize in a poetry competition, I worked up the courage to apply to the summer writing program at The Banff Centre School of Fine Arts, led by Canadian icon W.O. Mitchell.

There, among Canadian writers from Newfoundland to Vancouver Island and a few Americans, I set out, with splendid traveling companions (including Joan Clark and L.R. "Bunny" Wright), on my yearned-for, lifelong journey as a writer: *Homo Scriptor*, subspecies *Canadian*, once-in-a-lifetime migratory due to political climate change.

That foothold on the slopes of Canadian literature and culture at Banff became a base camp when I was invited back as teaching assistant the following year, and joined the resident summer faculty and became head of poetry a year later.

During the Banff workshop, I decided that I wanted to apply to grad school and specialize in Canadian literature. My poetry mentor at Banff, Eli Mandel, was a prof at York, but he strongly recommended Queen's in Kingston, where I could work with poet and critic Tom Marshall and the venerable George Whalley, who had been Michael Ondaatje's mentor there. Eli and Michael were close friends, and he arranged for me to rent the Ondaatjes' summer home in Bellrock, north of Kingston, for the academic year, a handsome old farmhouse with abandoned fields, idyllic stream, and venerable woods, including mature sugar maples.

One winter's day in Bellrock, with a clear blue sky and frigid temperature, we brought out the Ondaatjes' maple sugaring equipment and I felt like the sorcerer's apprentice, hastening over the packed snow with teeming buckets to the boiling trough. That night, while the syrup thickened, the northern lights appeared. The entire sky was filled with white streamers, like shredded cirrus clouds, like a gigantic flock of snow geese, racing across the sky. As the Aurora Borealis performed its high-wire act of electrically charged particles, this kid from Seattle felt as Canadian as one can get.

I felt, however, even more Canadian when I strapped on ice skates, for the second time in my life—the first was on a pond near the Ondaatjes' farm—on the Ottawa canal. As I wobbled along, I saw a lithe man striding swiftly and effortlessly, hatless, wearing a stylish long black coat, hands clasped behind his back. Laboring to keep pace were four burly men in thick black coats and Mounties' fur caps. Guarding Prime Minister Pierre Elliott Trudeau.

There would be a final migration for me, a Canadian one from the familiar landscape of the Pacific Northwest to the Maritime East, with my then partner Valerie. We arrived in the Annapolis Valley in Nova Scotia at the tail end of the back-to-the-land era. We were exuberantly welcomed by a vibrant community of artists and artisans, organic growers, "alternate" health professionals with rock-solid credentials, academics, and devoted non-profit workers. She, a doctor, opened a practice in the tourist-brochure village of Canning, and I found work as a freelance "resource" journalist, specializing in agriculture and forestry.

During the day, freelance journalism was incredibly rewarding, and I loved my beats. But it required long hours and depleted my energy for writing poetry and fiction. I continued to teach in the summer writing program at The Banff Centre, but that left me no time to write. So I applied to Dalhousie's Ph.D. program in English and for a Killam fellowship, with a specialization in Canadian and Commonwealth literature.

In 1982, my first poetry book was published by Pottersfield Press, located at Lawrencetown Beach north of Halifax and owned by Lesley Choyce, another ex-American, who was a prolific author and key figure in the burgeoning renaissance of Atlantic Canadian writing and publishing. And a pioneer surfer on the Lawrencetown waves. I knew the saying that you're not a real Maritimer until your family has lived here for several generations. But Lesley had already become a Nova Scotian institution. And we were part of a long tradition dating back to the refugees from the American Revolution.

As well, I'd become close friends with Greg Cook, a Valley resident, and the Nova Scotian-born and dynamic executive director of the vibrant Nova Scotia Writers' Federation. Greg had a genius for getting people involved. I was soon an eager volunteer and embraced by a highly supportive family of local writers and publishers—a clan, camaraderie, and mutual aid that extended to the other Atlantic provinces. Just as I'd felt welcomed by the farmers and foresters I'd interviewed in the Valley, among these literary and book people I was beginning to feel like a real Nova Scotian and Atlantic Canadian.

My doctoral thesis advisor at Dalhousie was Dr. Andy Wainwright, poet, novelist, and Canadian literature scholar. He was also an excellent athlete and a devout Expos baseball fan. Our literary conversations segued into tennis matches at his club and Friday afternoons with cold beer watching a ballgame in his living room. When I was writing my thesis and had two years of funding left, Andy said that I could do that work anywhere in the world, no doubt assuming I would take the money and run to the Greek islands, England's Lake District, Tuscany, or Paris.

I moved to Prince Edward Island, enticed by a relationship with Libby Oughton, a veteran of CanLit's early days in Toronto, and now publisher of Ragweed Press, the Island's only trade publisher, and its feminist/lesbian imprint, Gynergy Books. I divided my time among writing my thesis, drafting poems, teaching in Banff, working at Ragweed, and finding my place once again in a new landscape and deep-rooted community, this one with an intense island identity.

A regular visitor to Ragweed and bardic presence around Charlottetown was Milton Acorn, who had moved back to PEI from Toronto in 1980. He had worn the title of "the People's Poet of Canada" for a decade, formally bestowed on him, with a medal, by a group of writers including Leonard Cohen and Margaret Atwood. During our first encounter at Ragweed, I told the story of meeting him on my first evening in Canada as a draft dodger and new immigrant. He stared at me sternly, said, "I don't know, you still might be CIA, clever bastards," then broke into a huge smile and shook my hand.

The shift from Nova Scotia became permanent when the University of Prince Edward Island offered me the Canadian Literature position. An American working-class kid from the Pacific Northwest had become this east coast island university's specialist not only in Canadian literature but also in Atlantic Canadian literature, a course pioneered by Bob Campbell, a Cape Bretoner and the person I'd be replacing. When I nervously told Bob that as a come-from-away and relative newcomer I lacked the street cred to teach this course, including the region's history and culture, he said, "On the contrary, you're perfect. A fresh and keen set of eyes." Two years later, I was elected department chair, introduced post-colonial literature courses, and, when revered poet and creative writing professor Frank Ledwell retired in 1995, added creative writing to my UPEI repertoire.

That year, Harry Baglole, founder-director of the Institute of Island Studies, planted a seed in my brain that grew into a biography of Milton Acorn and a PEI Heritage Award. I was geographically a long way from my native place, but I was intimately connected—by serendipity or destiny, take your pick—to that evening long ago in Vancouver with the people's poet from PEI and to the young person who had just left one promised land behind for another.

One more symbolic connection with my earliest Canadian days, Leonard Cohen, included Charlottetown in his final world tour. I was fortunate to secure a ticket for the concert at the Confederation Centre of the Arts in Charlottetown, in front of which Acorn sometimes declaimed his poetry. Acorn's popularity and importance in Canadian culture had waned. Cohen's had flourished. The lineup for tickets down Queen Street was arguably the longest for a cultural event in Island history. The Centre was founded in 1964 "as Canada's National Memorial to the Fathers of Confederation." I, who had grown up just above Lake Washington, named after America's most famous founding father, was now sitting in a Canadian monument, eyes and ears affixed with reverence on a Canadian avatar of sublime imagination, whose novels I had egregiously shelved in American fiction. Only once did he speak during that concert, to say he was traveling with and reading poetry books by the great Canadian and PEI poet Milton Acorn, and that we should buy his books and read him too. I wanted to shout out to Cohen and the audience, not boasting but embracing my fortune, "I met Acorn during my first night as an immigrant on the west coast of Canada and wrote his biography on the east coast." *A Mari usque ad Mare*, From Sea to Sea. Thank you, Leonard, I silently said, for closing the circle of my transformed identity.

As I shared in the audience's veneration of that Canadian genius and legend, I thought back to a common assertion I'd heard and read in Canada in the Seventies and Eighties: that Canadians have no distinct identity. While Americans have a sturdy identity and can tell you what it is, Canadians do not and cannot. Canada, the assertion continued, has distinctive regional identities, but we are amorphous and opaque as a nation. A common sidebar was that Canadians have an inferiority complex, in contrast to Americans' overweening sense of superiority. I countered with the fact that

Americans are constantly arguing about their identity, often rancorously. That the United States, too, is a conglomeration of regional cultures and identities, which have withstood the mythic melting pot, American migrations and mobility, and pan-nationalism. That America's historic and ongoing exceptionalism—Americans' belief in their superiority, their destined greatness—is matched by ageless and intense insecurity based on their fears that the Republic is in decline and faces mortal peril from within and without.

Indeed, I had complained in my earlier Canadian years about so many Canadians' lack of respect for, and disparagement of, Canada's heritage and of its culture in the larger sense, from business to the arts. That has changed remarkably over the decades, and there is now no dearth of appreciation for Canadians' myriad praiseworthy achievements in countless domains. But there is a greater modesty about such accomplishments north of that border.

Similarly, our communal rivalries and fears are expressed with much less volume, heat, and vitriol. We aren't going to hell in a handbasket and don't need another revolution. We need a Truth and Reconciliation Commission. We need a Royal Commission of Inquiry with distinguished Canadians. Modesty and moderation, these were and are reliable traits and differences with many Americans—with many exceptions, of course, and on an ever-sliding scale of variations. I had missed, in my early Canadian years, that passion with which Americans expressed their opinions, and was frustrated at times by Canadian restraint, tactfulness, discretion. I no longer miss American hotheads and I bless Canadian prudence.

As a boy studying American history, I learned about Hessian soldiers, Germans serving as "auxiliaries," mercenary villains, for the British Army during the Revolutionary War. Now, my wife, Lee Ellen Pottie, and I live next door to a grand but decrepit house built in 1796 by Major Dockendorff, a German Hessian officer fighting for the British against the American rebels, who fled to Canada and PEI as a German-British Loyalist. Directly across from our home on Farm Lane is Rocky Point, the site of the first permanent non-Indigenous settlement, Port-la-Joye, founded by the French in 1720 on Île Saint-Jean (Prince Edward Island), and renamed Fort Amherst by the British after the conquest and expulsion of Acadians. Lee Ellen is half-Acadian (Pottie was originally Paté) on her Nova Scotian father's side and keenly aware of this history; she has edited a history of this historic site, washed by the waters of her ocean beside which she grew up. The capital city and its lovely Victoria Park, located in Queens County, are visible in the distance across the water. The county and city were named after Charlotte, wife of King George III, the tyrant monarch my American revolutionary heroes rebelled against. The British villains of my childhood were, for different reasons, also hers.

When I was seventeen and imagining my future life, Canada and Prince Edward Island weren't remotely on the horizon, in my peripheral vision, or on the map in my subconscious. During my first year on PEI, in the early 1980s, I sometimes worried about its insularity and, back then, relative lack of ethnic diversity. This small island is certainly a place where ethnocentrism can thrive. But an island is also a locus, intersection, port-of-call for transnational currents—cultural, economic, technological. A place where tribes and traditions can be honored, but where they may also be transcended, or transmuted through cross-cultural alchemy. Moreover, it is harder on a small island to ignore the ecological reality of the natural environment and human impact. It was no great surprise that the Green Party formed the Opposition, for the first time in Canada, on PEI in the 2019 election. Our largest immigrant groups are now Chinese and South Asian, with many others from Africa, the

Middle East, and Latin America. Our farm and seafood plant work-ers are increasingly from Mexico, Central America, the Philippines, and fewer are descendants of Scots, English, Irish, French. Did the ancestors of one of those Filipinos and my grandfather fire at each other when the Americans betrayed the local rebels?

At a recent gathering of my book club in a seaside home, we talked about climate change and rising seas, mass migration of ref-ugees and roving bands of marauders. The threat to Prince Edward Island, someone said, will be Americans, coming here with their guns, wanting our farmlands and fish. You were a draft dodger and conscientious objector, weren't you, Rich, another said. What would you do if your ex-countrymen stormed ashore?

I would, I said, stand on guard for thee.

10

The Greatest Country on Earth

How circumstantial is the nature of one's birth and place, cultural identity, mythic consciousness. I look at photographs of German cities taken the year I was born, residents loading rubble onto trucks. I read novels set in postwar Britain and France, the rationing, loss and mourning, trauma. China, torn by civil war while still reeling from the ravages of the Japanese invasion. Not to mention Eastern Europe and Russia under a victorious and vicious Stalin. And I think of my father driving to nightclubs in his two-toned coupé, my mother buying enough bread and milk to feed a large Dutch or Polish family for a week.

Americans in the 1950s, spared destruction and suffering on their native soil by virtue of their geopolitical fortune, emerged triumphant and triumphalist as the world's new economic and imperial power. With cornucopias of material wealth spilling across the land, Americans could more easily let the war dissolve in the alembic of mythic imagination, in glossed and glossy entertainment. Americans could get on with the peace-time endeavor of being the Greatest Nation on Earth, of fashioning and celebrating the genius of American democracy, enterprise, culture, and military prowess. There was plenty of trouble in paradise, from segregation to the Cold War, pesticides to poverty, the anxieties captured in Hitchcock's films to the exploitation of Elvis and Marilyn Monroe by their managers. But the radiant glow of greatness dominated, in the spreading suburbs and interstate highways and soaring urban skyscrapers, teeming super-market shelves and new car lots, proliferating college campuses, sports fields, and amusement parks.

My generation has been so often labeled the "Sixties" generation. But our formative years were the 1950s—the 1960s were transformative. Children of the Fifties, Darlene and I moved to San Francisco in early December 1966. Soon after we were settled, Neil Beck, now a Vietnam veteran blessedly home safe and sound, descended from Seattle on very short notice and whisked us away to Disneyland, all-expenses paid, in typical Neil Beck fashion.

At age eight, I had watched on *Walt Disney's Disneyland*—the original incarnation of this television series—footage of Disneyland under construction. Bulldozers leveling fields, excavations for under-ground rides, the realms of Frontierland, Fantasyland, Adventureland, Tomorrowland, and Main Street USA assuming their fabulous forms. Disneyland opened on July 17, 1955.

As an ironic juxtaposition to Disneyland's optimistic embodiment of the American dream, three months later Allen Ginsberg first read, in San Francisco, his visionary, epochal poem "Howl"—a poem and reading about which fellow-writer Michael McClure said, "a human voice and body had been hurled against the harsh wall of America." That year, James Dean in *Rebel Without a Cause* became an icon of a radically different vision of America than that of the Walt Disney Company, following in the footsteps of *The Wild Ones* (1953), starring black-leather-jacketed Marlon Brando and the antiheroes of his Black Rebels Motorcycle Club. Jackie Robinson was playing baseball and otherwise conducting himself with great poise and bril-liance in spite of innumerable death threats, and on December 1, 1955, Rosa Parks refused to give up her seat in the "colored section" of a Montgomery, Alabama bus to a white passenger. Lucille Ball, on the one hand an American sweetheart, on the other transgressed the happy housewife norm in every episode of *I Love Lucy*. Marine biologist and acclaimed nature writer Rachel Carson would soon, in 1957, commence her research into the poisonous chemicals helping to grow America's agricultural bounty and damaging the biosphere, work that would result in *Silent Spring*, which launched the modern ecology movement. And the concerned scientists in charge of *The Bulletin of Atomic Scientists*, who had conceived the Doomsday Clock as a warning about the growing danger of nuclear war, moved the hands closer to midnight. At age eight, I knew about none of this, apart from Jackie Robinson's baseball feats. I was enthralled with Disneyland's beatific and thrilling evocation of America's magical greatness—past and present, near and far, hyper-real and fantastically imagined.

In 1966, my burgeoning critique of American capitalism, racism, and imperialism, of bureaucratic and technological society, of the rapacious downsides of "progress," and of the elements of national mythology which were detrimental to a democratic, egalitarian, conservationist, and just society, had not displaced my childhood romance with *Walt Disney's Disneyland*. I rode south with Darlene and Neil, with no trace of disdain or cynicism, but as gleeful as Mr. Toad on his wild ride.

Inside the gates, standing in the middle of Main Street, I was back in that hallowed time when America was the Greatest Country on Earth and it was a glorious time to be a middle-class, white, male child, especially one endowed by nature and nurture with gifts to succeed in a wide variety of land-of-endless-opportunity ways. America was the world's giant magic kingdom, and at age eight I'd known that as my birthright. I'd also believed it was the birthright of all my friends in my ethnically diverse neighborhood and schools—Black, Jewish, Asian, Filipino, girls and boys. Annette

Funicello, my heartthrob on *The Mickey Mouse Club*, was Italian, a group still facing obnoxious stereotypes. I'd been taught by my elders that my friends and I would, naturally, have to work hard to earn success. America's greatness didn't guarantee that everyone would be a winner. The American formula of opportunity + dedication = success was branded on my brain. I didn't know, of course, how simplistic, how reductionist, that formula was, leaving out the vast array of factors—advantages and impediments—that complicated the formula and cleared or blocked the paths to success.

At that moment in Disneyland, however, I wasn't thinking of Sinclair Lewis' caustically satirical novel *Main Street* about narrow-mindedness and smug complacency. I didn't know that Walt Disney, from the early 1940s on, became a political reactionary, attacking certain labor organizers and film artists as communists. I wasn't listening to my inner conservationist voice about the loss of arable soil and draining of the aquifer in southern California. I was transported back to the secular vision of America as a sparkling clean and halcyon utopia of endless material bounty and comfort, neighborly compatibility, and old-fashioned tastes blended seamlessly with state-of-the-art modernity. It was a vision alive and well in 1966, commercially, politically, and mythically. But it was inaccessible for tens of millions of Americans; many others already were lamenting its disappearing act and longing for its restoration or its idealized version. A growing legion were skeptics and critics, myself included. But not on that day.

I was dazzled and thrilled by Pirates of the Caribbean, one of the "dark" rides, not only by the imaginative experience but also by Disneyland as a marvel of engineering and planning—the efficient use of space and management of crowds on only 166 acres. Above ground, I was fascinated by the lightning speed of maintenance staff appearing out of nowhere with broom and dustpan whenever someone dropped a burger wrapper or cigarette butt. If only the rest of America was this pristine.

Darlene's only response that I remember was her blissful expression when Tinker Bell flew up the wire to the crow's nest of a ship. Darlene needed no Peter Pan, but some part of her wanted magic wings. She identified with the Yugoslav grandmother, living in her childhood home, whom she'd grown up with—influenced, as Darlene said, "by her earthly weight bred in Balkan rock and soil." This helped make Darlene strong and solid, but perhaps too earthbound and dark. One of her alter egos: the airborne, glowing pixie.

Neil was Neil, relishing every experience, every moment, his spirit ever grateful to be alive. "We're here," Neil would say, "to help each other enjoy our time on earth." That was his philosophy, pure and simple, and he lived it. As much as I could discern, that's how he endured his year in Vietnam. Disneyland, for Neil, was neither the American dream nor the facade of an underlying nightmare. It was, simply, a place to have fun, like any carnival, county fair, or holiday parade—most of all, to treat his friends to hours of delight. And his only criteria for friendship were honesty, benevolence, empathy, and decency. His tribe was humanity. He wasn't a reformer or revolutionary. Neil simply made the world a better place every time he interacted with members of his tribe.

After supper, we lined up for Disneyland's famous evening parade. I'm not sure what I expected, but it wasn't "Yankee Doodle" blaring over the loudspeakers, and the lead group—the trio of Revolutionary soldiers known as "The Spirit of '76"—bandaged and limping, playing fife and drums, with the flag of the rebellious colonies carried behind them. That wasn't, however, what stunned and dismayed me. It was the giant heads atop the rebels' bodies— the towering heads of Goofy, Mickey Mouse, and Donald Duck. Here was the iconic procession of my childhood America, with its pageantry brilliantly blending foundational myth, military triumph, and postwar entertainment empire with its technological and artistic magnificence. These potent mythic forces of my upbringing—the American and Hollywood revolutions—collided as negative and positive charges in my brain.

More giant heads on costumed bodies appeared: George Washington, Betsy Ross, Davy Crockett, Abe Lincoln. All around us, the crowd cheered ecstatically. I, though, was suffused with disgust at what seemed a puerile, crass diminishment—worse, a vulgar violation—of my native land's sacred foundations. Those giant heads had shrunk the myth. The Disneyland illusion had fled, like Keats' nightingale, but leaving no glimpse of truth or beauty. My disbelief had ceased to be willingly suspended. What I saw in Crockett's head was an ongoing frontier myth con game, and in Washington's and Lincoln's an exploitative travesty. This was America's commercial genius trivializing its history and festooning the trivial for consumption and profit and patriotism.

Finally, I thought of Homer's *The Iliad*, in which the heroes were multifaceted—tragic and venal, noble and obtuse, grand and grandiose and petty. Disneyland had reduced our heroes to one-dimensional cartoons, without even Mickey's layered humanity, let alone—from another studio realm—Daffy Duck's and Bugs Bunny's satirical complexity and dazzling intelligence.

When I finally looked at Darlene, I saw her soured visage. Much less imbued than me with heroic male legends, she was more bluntly sickened by the jingoism. The Founding Fathers may have been strongly motivated by Enlightenment reasoning, but enlightened logic wasn't sending troops to Vietnam and rallying the citizenry. Emotional chauvinism, not empirical thinking, was fueling the fires of war.

As for Neil, I had a hard time reading his face. He wasn't smiling or cheering, his expression distant. Where was he? Back in

Vietnam, hauling the wreckage of choppers back to base after the wounded and the body bags had been evacuated? He had bought beer for the combat grunts between their patrols and firefights, looked into the eyes of the spirit of '65. His face and smile came alive again as the fireworks bloomed above us, signaling America's glory and the Disney day's end.

I loved fireworks too much to remain rancorous and glowering. And I could not be a spoilsport in the presence of our munificent friend and his revived bonhomie. I tamped down sardonic thoughts about "the rockets' red glare, bombs bursting in air," and left Disneyland with sufficiently grateful contentment, the eight-year-old in me still breathing after an outraged howl.

When I settled permanently in Canada and began working at Duthie Books, Tricky Dick Nixon was the new American president. The murder of Robert F. Kennedy had extinguished the dream of a resurrected Camelot—that fairy tale concocted by Jackie Kennedy, shortly after JFK's death and based on his favorite musical, about his presidency. Now, King Richard the Immoral was on the throne. He and his reactionary regime and supporters seemed anathema to the teeming enhancement of freedom, equality, justice, and communal well-being during the 1960s. But Camelot had relocated north of the forty-ninth parallel, and the leader of my new country's round table was Pierre Elliott Trudeau—part gallant Lancelot, part young magus Merlin, and part sage and commanding Arthur.

Fast-forward a half-century. America, after dazzling much of the world with its enthronement of Barack and Michelle Obama in the White House, had flipped the reactionary switch once more and installed a crossbreed of several other American rootstock varieties: con artist, flamboyant millionaire, limelight hog, anti-intellectual, paranoid and rabble-rousing xenophobe, nativist, and racist. A staggeringly ignorant, dishonest, shameless, venomous, incompetent, and vainglorious hominid now wore the mantle once draped around the shoulders of Jefferson, Lincoln, and the Roosevelts. America's stars were misaligned.

In another continental reversal of fortune and déjà vu all over again, Justin Trudeau was ensconced on the Parliamentary bench as Prime Minister where his father once ruled. Watching Obama give his acceptance speech on the night of his first victory, I felt proud of my native land and its people, at least of the majority who voted for him. Viewing the hideous result of the 2016 presidential election, I felt devastating sorrow for my homeland. And for the thousandth time, and one of the most overwhelming, I was suffused with pride in my adopted country and gratitude for the gift of Canadian citizenship.

During the next four years, I was once again reflecting on the differences between Americans and Canadians, between my two countries, a half-century after my immigration. I was discussing these often with many keenly interested students, friends, and even casual acquaintances on the island's golf courses, who were amazingly riveted by America's psychotic Trumpian episode.

When a Canadian, surprised to learn I am an ex-American, would say, "But you don't seem like an American," I would ask what that means. Loud, obnoxious, arrogant, aggressive, entitled. A great many Americans, I would say, are none of those. And some Canadians are. Thanks to America's antiquated Electoral College, a minority of voters in 2016 installed as president a person for whom all those nefarious boxes and many malevolent more could be checked. Yet only four years later a majority elected as president a man who could easily pass as a stereotypical Canadian.

I thought back to my Uncle Curt and Aunt Fern's summer sojourn by camper from Alberta to Newfoundland and back, after

Curt finished a secondment at the Edmonton plant of Boeing, his lifelong employer after the war. They felt right at home all the way, they said, because "Canadians are just like us, except in Quebec." They had been attuned to the similarities, which were and are abundant. Amiable and appreciative people, they would have been treated kindly and, without their American accents, might have been often mistaken for Canadians.

Curt and Fern had voted for Nixon in 1968. Even then, the Republican Party was moving away from Teddy Roosevelt's progressive policies and Eisenhower's moderation into a malignant extremism that would metastasize rampantly in the Trumpian years. During Trump's reign of bumbling terror, I and my compatriots were so focused on the differences between Canadian society and the culture of America—from gun mania and religious hyperventilation to climate change denial and conspiracy cults—that it was easy to overlook traits and values we have in common, especially with those many Americans whose values could be called "Canadian."

I also know well that my acceptance into Canadian society was facilitated by my white skin and my unobtrusive English dialect which crosses the Pacific Northwest border. One could add my gender, heterosexuality, and Christian background. Still, I believe that my acceptance also flows from the shared benign attributes of Americans and Canadians and of all people, whatever their ancestry and land of origin. This belief is reinforced when I ride the subways of Toronto, the world's second most culturally diverse city, and shop in a Charlottetown supermarket with people of Punjabi, Chinese, Mexican, Syrian, Nigerian, Bengali, Croatian, and Vietnamese heritage. Cultural identity since the onset of the Industrial Revolution or perhaps the European Renaissance has been transforming, variable, volatile, dynamic, and increasingly so—the reactionary nativist movements notwithstanding.

During my first year on Prince Edward Island, I was invited to a PEI Multicultural Council celebration. The host, Jacob Mal, a high school English teacher and principal who arrived with his family in 1967, asked for my ethnic origin.

"Diverse," I said.

"Did you not immigrate from America?" he asked.

"Yes, but that's not an ethnic origin."

Unlike my citizenship clerk ten years before, Jacob said, "Of course it is. Not as old as India, of course, but much older than Pakistan," and wrote "America" beside my name on the list of multicultural celebrants. When it was my turn to introduce myself, I did so as an "American-Canadian," to heartwarming applause.

We can lovingly nurture our devotion to our birthright or adopted place, region, tribe, country, culture. But we must also transcend those narrow attachments and be even more devoted to our superseding tribe of *homo sapiens*, of humanity, and to our sole habitat, the Earth in its entirely—to the wealth of peoples, cultures, homelands, and landscapes we can share and appreciate. This has been made possible, even inexorable, by technological inventions and transnational commerce and industry, as well as the tragedies of war and environmental crisis and resulting migrations. This widening of our devotion results, too, from our growing ecological knowledge: our deepening discovery of the interconnectedness of species, of organisms within habitats, and of habitats themselves. Biology and anthropology have established that we are one tribe, one "race," and the Earth sciences insist that we inhabit one home, one inextricably unified biosphere, one Earth Household in the words of American poet and ecologist Gary Snyder.

We can choose to open ourselves or close ourselves off to the wealth of humanity and habitats, to feast from the cornucopia of experience and existence or deprive ourselves, subsisting on a meager and debilitating diet of human and ecological reality.

Looking around the courtroom during my citizenship ceremony, I saw that white faces were in the minority. I also saw, on every face, the same radiant joy I felt inside, the same lustrous pride in becoming a Canadian citizen. I was conscious that such pride might seem to jar with my antipathy to the jingoistic manifestations of American patriotism. But I made a distinction then, and still do, between Canadian patriotism, even at its most fervent, and American chauvinism and exceptionalism. A distinction which few, if any, Canadians have challenged me on. I know this risks oversimplification. I'm aware of the wide range and complexity of attitudes about one's country in any citizenry. I have my own deep love for America and its virtues, a love tangled in my distress over America's flaws and lamentable behaviors, as I perceive them. Is there a citizen anywhere whose love of country isn't enmeshed with some disappointment or anger about the state of the union? Patriotism, national pride, love of country, tribal attachment—whatever we call it—is a kaleidoscopic phenomenon. Fans at a football or hockey game sing their national anthem as one proud people, then go back to their separate factions and accuse each other of endangering the nation's future, the people's well-being, and the culture's authenticity and worth.

For nearly ten years after awaking, during my last year of high school, to the larger world, I vowed that I was a citizen of Earth, a patriot of humanity. I readily quoted Boswell, who ascribed this to Samuel Johnson: "Patriotism is the last refuge of a scoundrel." I failed to note that Boswell insisted Johnson referred to false patriotism. I was fervently reacting to what we refer to as gung-ho, flag-waving American patriotism—boastful, arrogant, militaristic. As a Canadian immigrant, I could embrace a different kind of national pride: lower-keyed and more modest than Americans' boisterous posturing, and definitely less threatening. Our Snowbirds jets and pilots, our iconic 431 Squadron, would perform their dazzling stunts over CFL football games, at air shows, on the first of July, but they didn't seem like deadly weapons and symbols of neo-imperialistic war. Yet, as a boy, I'd worshipped the Blue Angels and Thunderbirds of the American Navy and Air Force, and imagined myself in one of those cockpits as they twirled and wove over Lake Washington during the Gold Cup Week hydroplane races. Long before the sorties in Southeast Asia and Iraq.

Is there a certain smugness, a sense of superiority, a more subtle arrogance, in this restrained, less toxic Canadian patriotism? Aren't citizens' attitudes toward their country, and the nuanced or strident manifestations in their form of patriotism, shaped entirely by historical forces, and not a reflection of any innate benevolence or malignance as a people?

Canadian patriotism is partly shaped by historical pride in being dissimilar in vital ways from Americans. In fact, a foundational myth is Canada's difference from the United States. Canadians are distinct from Americans, we assume and often say, but infrequently say what those differences are. When we do, they are often expressed in terms of what we are not. We are not as intensely and egocentrically individualistic as Americans. We are a much less violent society and not obsessed, irrationally, with guns. Canada may be racist, but not quite as racist as America—except, we now may add, when it comes to Indigenous peoples. Canada has socioeconomic inequality, but it's less extreme. We are not as hostile as Americans to taxation, and therefore more supportive of government-funded programs.

There are debatable claims: that Canadians are more tolerant, that we are more aware of the great world beyond our shores. The "less racist" claim can readily be challenged by Canadians of numerous descents from Irish to Italian, African to Arab, Chinese and Japanese to Jewish and Jamaican, Hungarian to Honduran, Ugandan to

Ukrainian. And, again, try telling Indigenous people we're less racist, and residential school survivors that we're less violent.

As for national pride, the phrase I heard and used in my early Canadian years was "quiet patriotism," as opposed to the "loud," "excessive," and even "obnoxious" American variety. That quiet Canadian love of country, which I experienced in my earlier years as a Canadian immigrant and citizen, had transformed by the 2010 Vancouver Winter Olympics into a vociferous, ebullient patriotism as passionately demonstrative as any American exhibition of national pride. This transformation was underway years before the Canadian and American hockey teams faced off for the gold medal in Vancouver. Yet, it still seemed to me, the ex-American, as I watched the cheering crowds in Vancouver streets with their maple leafed clothing, to possess less edge, vehemence, defiance than the American variety, with its "Give me liberty or give me death" and "Don't tread on me" resonance. American patriotism so often seemed to embody America's battles with and triumphs over enemies, a quality rooted in the nation's origins. Too, there was and is in Americans' patriotic displays the trumpeting of their nation's alleged primacy in the realm of liberty and opportunity—America's foundational myths: "the greatest country on earth," "the wealthiest and most powerful," the country where freedom and opportunity reign supreme." As a boy, I had belted out the anthem, hand over my heart, gazing in reverence at the Stars and Stripes, with pride in those battles and that liberty.

In 1973, standing in a Canadian courtroom, I felt that quiet but beaming pride in a country that was, in crucial ways, different from the United States. On my citizenship day, I could confidently say that Canada was a more peace-inclined country. That Canada was less molded by the mythology of individualism, and, hence, more cooperative, generous, and compassionate in its health care, social programs, safety nets, and cultural funding. I could assert that Canadians valued and practiced liberty as firmly and admirably as Americans, and that Canada afforded ample opportunity for just as many or even more of its people, but without America's overbearing vanity. I also knew that these differences, these qualities, were the consequence of historical forces and not the result of inner virtues. To think otherwise, as did so many Americans—inspired by their history, from Puritans and Founding Fathers to later military, economic, technological, and cultural triumphs—was specious, harmful, and perilous, as evidenced by the Vietnam War and, later, the war in Iraq.

Such thoughts were floating in my head as the judge mouthed the expected platitudes about citizenship. Floating in a warm lagoon of euphoria, I also recall a fleeting dark form beneath the surface—a shadowy sorrow that I was leaving behind my inheritance of pride in the American experiment with all its defects and merits, shameful and resplendent history. Which I, for a brief moment, myopically thought I was abandoning.

Over the years, I've often thought of my American identity as a slowly receding landscape, gradually replaced by Canadian scenery. Yet there are events, such as the glorious election of Barack Obama and the loathsome triumph of Donald Trump, when the American aspects of my personality come roaring back, in all their Americanesque anguish, hope, outrage, fascination, pride, fear, disgust, and bittersweet humor. In that citizenship courtroom, and that evening when I celebrated over supper with Canadian-born and ex-American friends, I was indifferent to the arbitrary and transient nature of national identity and its symbolic representations. I was deliriously glad there was a border separating the artificial entities known as Canada and the United States, and that the former's extradition treaty with the USA did not include draft dodgers.

Several years ago, I visited the English village of Washington near Newcastle. I was doing research for a novel that features the remarkable Gertrude Lowthian Bell, archaeologist, adventurer, and only British female political officer during the First World War. Working in the Middle East, she had a complex relationship with Lawrence of Arabia and had a key influence on the troubled geopolitical realities still wreaking havoc a century later. Her first home, Dame Margaret Hall, was located next door to the ancestral estate of George Washington's family. By coincidence, I went there on the Fourth of July and joined an annual ceremony of some two hundred locals on the estate's front lawn. As the American flag was raised, I sang, for the first and only time since I immigrated to Canada, my native land's national anthem, and took comical pride in knowing the words by heart, while the villagers sang from a handout.

I was the genuine article at that Fourth of July ceremony. But I was an imposter on Remembrance Day in Charlottetown in 2005, which the Canadian Government had declared the Year of the Veteran.

A friend without a car had asked me to help escort her aged and Canadian Forces veteran father, Peter, increasingly infirm, to the Legion on Pownal Street where veterans and military personnel were gathering. We picked him up at his nursing home; he was wearing his medals on his blazer and a regimental beret.

While helping him into the car and then driving downtown, it occurred to me that my father, were he still alive, would be older than Peter. Until that moment, my mind had persisted in picturing my father in his twenties, athletic and debonair in his stylish virility, confidence, and hopefulness. Now, with Peter beside me, I saw my father as an old, dwindling man, slowly drifting away into a gossamer realm of memory. I remembered how I used to refuse to wear the red poppy, a trifling anti-war gesture, until a friend told me to "Wear one for your father." Suddenly, I longed to have my father alive, beside me, even if he had half-vanished, kindly and fragile, into an ethereal world.

We parked and joined the large and growing throng. Directly in front of the Legion was a chartered bus, and that was where Peter would ride in the parade, along with other veterans too elderly, infirm, or disabled to walk. We guided him up the steps, and I was about to join the civilians who would follow behind the veterans, the cadets, the sailors from the HMCS *Charlottetown* in harbor, the uniformed soldiers and reserves, the military band. But my friend urged me onto the bus with her and Peter, needing my ongoing support.

Seated behind Peter and his daughter, I was sharply aware that I was an outlier on a veterans' bus. Surrounded by men and women who had donned military uniforms in the service of their country. Some who had seen action, that euphemism for the hell storms, the bursting open and fragmenting of bodies and minds, which I had feared and detested and fled four decades earlier. Their motives for joining were no doubt diverse. But all on this bus wore their uniforms with dignified self-esteem, with a compelling aura that said: however else we may not have succeeded during our years on earth, in this service we fulfilled our duty. Our dharma.

When I was a child, "duty" was an honorable word, concept, and purpose. I'm sure that I resented the use of this word, at times, when it was employed as a prod at home or school—when I did not want to get out of bed to serve early morning mass, or stand in a frigid January rain on safety patrol, or accompany my grandmother to her doctor's office when I passionately believed I should be at baseball practice. But I also know that doing my "duty" was something I took pride in, as a Boy Scout, a member of the safety patrol, an altar boy, the grandson the doctor patted on the head with dignifying approval.

In the 1960s, however, with a deeply misguided and reprehensible war going on, I regarded the frequent reference to "duty" as a profound subversion and corruption of that value. Duty took on a new meaning for me: refusal of tainted military service, resistance to war and its machinery, profiteers, zealots, enablers, duped citizens—that was one's duty, my duty. Self-esteem came from not wearing a uniform.

As for the men on this bus, their relationship with duty and uniforms was, no doubt, different from mine. If any of them had felt any ambivalence, it was unlikely, I assumed, to be as deep a fault line in their psyche as mine had been. Theirs were the uniforms of admirable, necessary duty. To what? It didn't matter to me at that moment. I wasn't analyzing the predations and cupidity of nation-states or the uncivil wars of factions. I wasn't critiquing the riling of patriotism and xenophobia to rouse men and women to acts of slaughter and support of wanton destruction for the aggrandizement of the privileged and ruling elite. Absent from my mind was the bloodthirst of tribal rivalry, religious mania, ideological fervor. I was seeing only the venerable faces of people wearing uniforms without apparent irony, angst, or disillusion.

Another veteran boarded and took a seat beside me. A tall, distinguished-looking gentleman, he seemed in excellent shape, and perhaps because he knew that I might wonder why he was on the bus, volunteered that, as one of the oldest veterans, he preferred to ride with people of his vintage, some of whom were dear old friends. He had served in the Korean War. What was my service history, he wanted to know.

I had lived with the identity of a draft dodger, a conscientious objector, a "war resister" as we once sometimes referred to ourselves, for over forty years. For the past two decades, with the Vietnam era receding into the History Channel realm, a contextual footnote for my students to the more intriguing Sixties' paradigms of sexual liberation, civil rights, and drugs and rock n' roll, I have infrequently thought of myself in those terms, at least on my own. I would still be asked, fairly often, when people learned that I had immigrated from the United States, "Why did you come to Canada?" or "Were you a draft dodger?" I would answer, yes, but offer no commentary, no long-winded or even abridged narrative as I would have in the 1970s and 1980s, unless I was asked.

On this Remembrance Day, a veteran was asking me why I was on the veterans' bus. I had white hair and a white goatee, so I must be a veteran, probably with some disability. I explained why I was on the bus, but without mentioning my anti-war past. My omission, I like to believe, was mostly because I felt it was inappropriate to mention my conscientious objection and draft dodging.

Yet, no doubt, there was, and is, a lingering, reticent awkwardness in certain situations, with certain people, about admitting my draft evasion. These situations have been rare in my four decades in Canada, certainly because almost every Canadian with whom I have discussed my decision, including members of the Canadian Forces, has been supportive, but also because I have never doubted or regretted my choice. It was my honorable service. And yet. There has been my reluctance, on those few occasions, as with this veteran, to fess up. As if I had failed to answer some call. As if I had let down some part of my childhood American self, of my historic heritage and family legacy. George Washington and his men freezing in Valley Forge, without me. Lincoln weeping over sending men to the slaughter, but not for me. My father, gazing from his spectral realm, thinking, You could have been there in Nam to warn Frank Bozello, your friend and football teammate, to take cover and not take a bullet on the numbers.

The distinguished veteran and I made small talk for a short while, about the lovely weather, the superb turnout, the virtue of honoring veterans, and then he surprised me by saying, unexpectedly, "It's a shame what's happening in Iraq."

"How do you mean?" I asked, cautiously.

"Afghanistan was a necessity, and the international community gave its support. But Iraq is a terrible mistake. It should have never happened. Some people will have a lot to answer for someday."

Here was a war veteran holding the same opinion as the draft dodger sitting beside him. We fell silent as the bus, at the head of the procession, moved forward.

Unlike those chill, blustery Remembrance Days when a few hundred people huddled and shivered around the cenotaph and the streets were otherwise desolate, the sidewalks were lined with people cheering, smiling, and waving at the veterans on the bus, including senior citizens with their hands folded in prayers of gratitude and blessing. Many people were applauding the august veterans and I suddenly realized that my white-bearded face was one of those visible in the windows, and the spectators' gaze and smiles were falling on me. As the bus crept toward the cenotaph, I felt profoundly chagrined. I wanted to hold a sign up to the window, saying, "Not me. You've got the wrong guy."

The chagrin and mild bout of guilt gave way to a sweet sense of irony, and I was smiling too. For the first time in my life, I was in a Remembrance Day parade, and all those people were honoring, unwittingly, another kind of veteran: a conscientious objector, one of those people who made a tiny contribution toward ending a war that most Canadians opposed. Yes, the Vietnam War lasted for over a dozen years, but the waves of American emigrants to Canada were significant in shifting the moral and political currents and altering the patriotic flow from support to opposition.

At the cenotaph, I stayed on the bus with Peter and his daughter. The veteran beside me disembarked for the ceremony. Speeches done, bugle played, wreaths laid, he returned and sat down beside me, and the bus began moving back toward the legion. As neutrally as possible, I mentioned the conflicts in Iraq and Afghanistan, saying that I appreciated his earlier remark on the Iraq invasion and war. I said that

I'd been reading about an extraordinary British adventurer, scholar, and diplomat, Gertrude Lowthian Bell, who had been responsible, after the end of the First World War, for drawing up the boundaries of Iraq, Jordan, and Syria, one of the legacies of imperialism. I said that she'd had, arguably, much more influence on the subsequent history of the Middle East than Lawrence of Arabia.

"Lawrence of Arabia," said the veteran. "My grandfather knew him. He served with the British forces in Arabia during the war. Yes, it all started back then, for the oil, of course. And that's still what it's about."

Lawrence, another of my mythic warrior influences, albeit entering my psyche at the same time I was applying for conscientious objector status. Mesmerized one evening by the cinematic grandeur and epic drama of *Lawrence of Arabia*, and the next day riveted by the heart-blasting imagery and music of Wilfred Owen's First World War poems. Owen's dead soldier in "Strange Meeting" speaking to the dead enemy soldier who had killed him: "I went hunting wild / After the wildest beauty in the world . . ."

I had chosen, instead, the peaceful beauty of Canada.

Now, I had a vision: a group of conscientious objectors joining the Remembrance Day ceremony, not to protest, and not to be equated in any way with those who served in uniform and, especially, risked their lives and made "the ultimate sacrifice." Rather, to place a wreath at the cenotaph as an act of respect to those whose historical contexts and tribes and psyches and values compelled them to wear their country's uniform and to shoulder arms. As my grandfathers and father had. As I had chosen not to. And to honor those who succumbed, as Owen wrote, to "the pity of war, the pity war distilled."

Acknowledgments

I am exceedingly grateful to Dr. Melissa Carroll, a sagacious reader as well as gifted writer and scholar. A native of Prince Edward Island, she graciously came aboard this memoir when it was still struggling to leave the shoals and riptides. She helped steer it away from the rocks and into the trade winds.

Bonnie Johannes, a local historian and genealogist in Gray's Harbor County, Washington, provided invaluable information about my maternal family. For my paternal ancestors, I am deeply beholden to Ruud J. Lemm, the foremost genealogist of the Lem/Lemm/Lemmens/Lemke "clan," his primary assistant, Gerard Lemmens, and Ruud's masterwork, *Genealogica Lemniana*. While Ruud and Gerard conducted their research from their homes in England, Connie Melton, another Lemm clan genealogist to whom I am much indebted, conducts her work from her home in the American Midwest, where many of our people settled in the nineteenth century.

Lydia Grimm, my chosen sister and a splendid human being, has been wonderfully supportive, and I am thankful for the friendship of Linda Haney, with whom I shared many of this book's stories in the Oregon home of Bob and Nancy Grimm.

Kyle Roy Ward's *In the Shadow of Glory: The Thirteenth Minnesota in the Spanish-American and Philippine-American Wars, 1898-1899* was an excellent source for the section on my paternal grandfather, a veteran of the Spanish–American War.

A substantial part of the first draft was written at the Hawthornden International Writers' Retreat in Scotland, in a castle on the River North Esk built by poet William Drummond in 1603. I am eminently thankful for that fellowship, the Hawthornden staff's support, and the inspiring companionship of my fellow writers. I am most appreciative, too, of a travel grant from The Canada Council for the Arts and a research grant from the University of Prince Edward Island.

My eternal gratitude flows to Lynn Duncan and Kilmeny Jane Denny, publishers of Tidewater Press, for their devoted commitment to this story and for their keenly insightful vision of the kind of book it needed to be. I have the highest regard for their editorial acumen.

Most of all, I have been blessed with the glorious support and advice of my wife, Lee Ellen Pottie, whose expertise as a historian, genealogist, and editor have been invaluable.